TEACHER GUIDE

Elizabeth A. McAllister, Ed. D.

BIBLE PROPHECY FOR KIDS TEACHER GUIDE
Published by Precept Ministries of Reach Out, Inc.
P. O. Box 182218
Chattanooga, TN 37422

ISBN 978-1-888655-48-3

All Scripture quotations, unless otherwise indicated, are taken from the *NEW AMERICAN STANDARD BIBLE®* (NASB)
© Copyright 1960, 1962, 1963, 1968, 1971, 1972, 1973, 1975, 1977, 1995 by the. Used by permission. (www.lockman.org)

Copyright © 2013 Precept Ministries International

All rights reserved. No part of this publication may be reproduced or transmitted in any form or by any means electronic or mechanical, including photocopying and recording, or by any information storage and retrieval system, without the prior written permission of the publisher.

Printed in the United States of America

Precept, Precept Ministries International, Precept Ministries International the Inductive Bible Study People, the Plumb Bob design, Precept Upon Precept, In & Out, Sweeter than Chocolate!, Cookies on the Lower Shelf, Precepts For Life, Precepts From God's Word and Transform Student Ministries are trademarks of Precept Ministries International.

BIBLE PROPHECY for Kids

TEACHER GUIDE
TABLE OF CONTENTS

BIBLE PROPHECY For Kids
TEACHER GUIDE

Introduction

Thank you for selecting this Bible study for your child and/or class. Leading children to read, observe, interpret, and apply the Bible for themselves offers them a bridge from hearsay to real truth. As they learn to be comfortable with the idea that they can read the Bible, they will take the task seriously.

The Discover 4 Yourself series is designed to lead young students through the process of inductive study: question, question, question, search, think, understand, and apply. They will be comfortable with this process only after you prove that the possibility is within their reach.

BIBLE PROPHECY FOR KIDS is a study of the book of Revelation. Students will learn about how God their Father and Jesus their Lord conquer Satan and evil. The first seven chapters give us a glimpse of heaven, God's messages to seven churches in Asia Minor, unusual and scary creatures, God's judgments and His promises to those who know and serve Jesus.

In preparation for leading ***BIBLE PROPHECY FOR KIDS*** please work through each "Day" on your own before consulting the Teacher Guide. Since this is an Inductive Bible Study, your teaching will be more effective if you do the work first and God reveals His truth to you.

Whether you're home schooling a child, teaching a Sunday school class, teaching in a Christian school, or simply using these studies for your child's quiet time or family Bible study, this Teacher Guide will show you how to clearly and carefully lead each child through Inductive Bible study. We offer suggestions to guide you step-by-step. *Instructional Strategies* explains why certain activities are used throughout the book. Choose the activities that best fit your situation.

Home schooling Parents and Family Bible Study

We suggest you do one "Day" per day unless it's too much for your child's reading and/or writing skills. You can work with your child and discuss what you learn together or let him/her work independently, saving discussion times for later.

You may want to join or create a home school group that meets once a week to do these studies. The teacher will assign a week of homework in class. The following week the teacher will lead the students to discuss what they discovered, how to apply it, and to work on any creative elements included in the study or play a game to review what they have learned.

Sunday School Teachers

To use these studies in a weekly Sunday school class we suggest you do one "Day" together with your children each week in class, since you will have children from different backgrounds, even some from families that are not members of or even regularly attend a church.

Each Sunday briefly review the prior Sunday's work to put them in context for the next day of study in their book. After completing a week in the book you may want to have a "Game Time Sunday" to review the material before you move on to the next week. Game time makes learning fun for children and shows you the extent to which they understand what they learned.

You can keep the books at church and have the children take home verses on index cards or pieces of paper to memorize.

Classroom Teachers

Generally, classroom teachers face many different learning abilities within their groups. It is important for you to understand these different learning abilities so that you can meet each child where he or she is so that no one is left behind during the process.

It is important for you to bring in *schemata* (background information) for students to draw on. If you tie studies to something children already know, they will grasp the lessons clearly.

Grasp is also affected by *metacognition*—the ability to monitor understanding of the text. Students must be able to perform several functions to develop metacognitive control over reading and understanding. He or she must be able to:

1. Ask first, "What do I already know about this topic?" then, "Do I have enough information to understand this text?" Answers to these questions will directly influence the use of the inductive method.

2. Identify the purpose for reading each selection.

3. Focus on particular information.

4. Monitor understanding by recalling background knowledge and relating it to the context by asking questions like: "How am I doing?" "Am I keeping the big picture in mind?" "Am I bogged down?" "If so, how do I fix it—reread the passages or ask for help?" (Nothing wrong with the latter.)

5. Evaluate understanding of the context by asking, "What did I learn?" With respect to Inductive Bible Study, "How do I apply this information?"

Instructional Strategies

Writing as a response reinforces learning and so this method is prevalent in these books. Encourage students to share ideas and insights with you and other students.

Reading is the highest intellectual activity of the human experience. More sectors of the brain are active than in other endeavors including mathematics and flying an airplane. It's the most totally interactive processing of information, even when children are reading Mother Goose.

Take time for students to read aloud with a friend. Reading *out loud* and listening promote interactions between the brain's left and right hemispheres and activate little-used pathways. Reading *silently* activates a much smaller part of the brain.

Give students a chance to express themselves at every opportunity. This forces them to retrieve information stored in their *schemata* (background knowledge) for application to new information. What better opportunity is there than to *inductively* look at curriculum and context?

You will notice that you are asked to read some content aloud as students follow along. This frees unsure readers to focus on context rather than decoding strategies. By doing this, you will remove stumbling blocks to understanding; otherwise, reluctant readers will be convinced that inductive study is impossible for them—the last thought you want to instill!

We have included weekly quizzes with memory verses and also multiple-choice questions that will force students to think about what they have learned. Based on how they answer these questions, you will know whether they have grasped the material adequately.

In view of this sparse introduction to learning requirements for success, it's important that you apply strategies that lead students to develop the ability to self-monitor understanding of context each step of the way. These **Teacher Guides** offer suggestions to assure that students, regardless of their abilities, will learn to read the Bible with understanding as you lead them, step-by-step, through the Inductive Study Method.

Discover 4 Yourself Objectives

The Discover 4 Yourself series objectives are not the same as the behavioral objectives of general subject matter. The books contain outstanding biblical subjects of course, but they are written *primarily* to be a tool for young students to learn the Inductive Bible Study Method.

Playing an instrument well requires repetition and application of skills learned. Similarly, effective study is developed by repeated practice and good role modeling of an outstanding study method. Accordingly these **Teacher Guides** contain global objectives for the student *and the teacher.*

We'll start with the teacher.

Discover 4 Yourself Teacher Guide Objectives

- ✓ To help the teacher identify students' metacognitive needs as they read texts.
- ✓ To show the teacher how to model use of the Inductive Study Method so students will be able to apply the techniques independently when studying God's Word.
- ✓ To offer the teacher effective teaching strategies to assure that students succeed when they study the Bible.

Discover 4 Yourself Student Workbook Objectives

- ✓ To learn how to read, observe, and interpret the Bible for themselves.
- ✓ To practice this method independently within an encouraging environment.

Scripture quotations in this book are taken from the New American Standard Bible®, © 1960, 1962, 1963, 1968, 1971, 1972, 1973, 1975, 1977, 1995 by The Lockman Foundation. Used by permission. (www.Lockman.org)

Illustrations by Steve Bjorkman

Cover by Left Coast Design, Portland, Oregon

DISCOVER 4 YOURSELF is a registered trademark of the Hawkins Children's LLC. Harvest House Publishers, Inc., is the exclusive licensee of the federally registered trademark DISCOVER 4 YOURSELF.

BIBLE PROPHECY FOR KIDS

Copyright © 2006 by Precept Ministries International
Published by Harvest House Publishers
Eugene, Oregon 97402
www.harvesthousepublishers.com

ISBN 978-0-7369-1527-4 (pbk.)
ISBN 978-0-7369-3554-8 (eBook)

All rights reserved. No part of this publication may be reproduced, stored in a retrieval system, or transmitted in any form or by any means—electronic, mechanical, digital, photocopy, recording, or any other—except for brief quotations in printed reviews, without the prior permission of the publisher.

Printed in the United States of America

12 13 14 15 16 17 / ML–BG / 16 15 14 13 12 11

(page 3)

1

2 CONTENTS

Unveiling a Mystery—
A Bible Study You Can Do!

Guided Instruction

1 Give each student a copy of ***Bible Prophecy for Kids***.

2 Together, turn to the CONTENTS page and give students a quick overview of the book. Point out the structure of each chapter, noting that there will be a lesson and activities to do each day for five days.

Satan does not want us to know the truth. But God does; He reveals (unveils) to John the mystery of what will take place after Jesus has returned to heaven. Then John describes what he has seen including things that will take place on earth in the future.

Revelation 2-3 include special messages God gave to seven churches in Asia. He tells each church what their people are doing right and doing wrong, gives them warnings and instructions, and then reminds them of His Promises to Overcomers.

In Revelation 3, God finishes the messages to the churches and gives a clear understanding of what it takes to be an OVERCOMER. How do you match up? Have you accepted Jesus Christ? Only He gives the power and faith to overcome trials in your life. That's awesome!

In Revelation 4 and 5, God gives us a glimpse of heaven. You will see what heaven looks like and discover Who is worthy to worship before God's throne.

In Revelation 6 and 7 you will learn about God's "book" that is closed with seven seals. Jesus breaks these seals open. With the opening of each seal, frightening events that bring on pain, suffering, and destruction take place. Only those who do not know Jesus have to be worried about these future events.

3 When you finish your overview, turn to ""Unveiling a Mystery" on page 7 and read it aloud.

Guided Instruction

(page 4)

3

UNVEILING A MYSTERY— A BIBLE STUDY YOU CAN DO!

Hey! Are you ready to unveil a great mystery—one that a lot of grown-ups are afraid to try to uncover? Great! Then climb up in the tree house with Molly, Sam (the great detective beagle), and me. My name is Max. WHAT is this great mystery adventure? We are going to help The Discovery Bible Museum create and try out exciting, interactive, hands-on exhibits for the new Revelation wing in the museum so that kids everywhere will be able to understand the Book of Revelation.

Revelation is a very exciting book in the Bible that a lot of people think is too hard and scary to understand. But we know from 2 Timothy 3:16-17 that "*all* Scripture is inspired by God and profitable for teaching, for reproof, for correction, for training in righteousness; that the man of God may be adequate, equipped for every good work." That includes the Book of Revelation.

God put the Book of Revelation in the Bible because it tells us the rest of His story. Did you know that Revelation is the only book in the Bible that promises a blessing? Pretty cool, huh? You'll also discover WHAT happens in the future and HOW it happens. Revelation reveals WHO is in control. There's even a mysterious, sealed up book! Revelation is an *awesome* book packed with fascinating creatures and exciting events!

You can uncover the mystery of what's going to happen by studying God's Word, the Bible, the source of all truth, and by asking God's Spirit to lead and guide you. You also have this book, which is an inductive

(page 5)

Bible study. That word *inductive* means you go straight to the Bible *yourself* to investigate what the Book of Revelation shows us about Jesus Christ and the things that must soon take place. In inductive Bible study, you discover for yourself what the Bible says and means.

Doesn't that sound like fun? Grab those art supplies and stir up your imagination as we create and experiment with some very cool exhibits to help kids uncover the Bible's biggest mystery!

Guided Instruction

Guided Instruction

WEEK 1

Ask God to be with you during this study. You are beginning to go deeper into God's Mystery and you will need His help to understand it.

4 Read "Revelation 1" and "Uncovering the First Mystery."

4

1

REVELATION 1

It's great to have you back at the tree house! Molly and I are soooo excited about this new mystery adventure! Our Uncle Jake, the archaeologist that we helped dig up truth in the Book of Genesis, works with The Discovery Bible Museum on some of his different adventures. When the museum told him about their new wing, Uncle Jake asked if we could help them create and try out the awesome exhibits.

But before we can help out, we need to do research on the Book of Revelation. Have you ever read the Book of Revelation? Being inductive Bible detectives, we know there is only one way to do our research, and that's to go straight to the main source: the Bible, God's Word. So before we head to the museum to the meet Uncle Jake and Miss Kim, the museum teacher, we need to get started by searching God's Word.

UNCOVERING THE FIRST MYSTERY

Are you ready to begin your research? WHAT is the first thing you need to do? Do you remember? Pray! Way to go!

7

Bible study should always begin with prayer. We need to ask God to help us understand this great mystery of what is going to happen in the future and to lead and direct us by His Holy Spirit. Then we can understand what God says and make sure we handle His Word accurately.

The Book of Revelation reveals how God and Jesus triumph over Satan and evil. Because Satan doesn't want us to know the truth, he will try to discourage us and keep us from studying God's Word. So not only do we need to pray, we also need to make sure we have our armor on so we can stand firm against our enemy now and be prepared for the war against the Lamb (Revelation 17:14). We need to be strong in the Lord and in the strength of His might. Read Ephesians 6:10-17 to help you remember what your armor is.

All right, mighty warriors! Let's pray and put our armor on. Now we are ready to get started. Turn to Revelation 1 on page 141. These are our Observation Worksheets. Observation Worksheets are pages that have the Bible text printed out for you to use as you do your study on the Book of Revelation. Let's read Revelation 1:1-3.

Let's find out WHO gave the Book of Revelation, to WHOM

(page 141)

Chapter 1

1 The Revelation of Jesus Christ, which God gave Him to show
to His bond-servants, the things which must soon take place; and
He sent and communicated *it* by His angel to His bond-servant
John,
2 who testified to the word of God and to the testimony of
Jesus Christ, *even* to all that he saw.
3 Blessed is he who reads and those who hear the words of
the prophecy, and heed the things which are written in it; for
the time is near.

Guided Instruction

5 Read Revelation 1:1-3 to complete the diagram and questions on pages 9 and 10.

Guided Instruction

The Revelation of Jesus Christ which God gave Him to show His bond-servant the things which must soon take place.

WHO gave the revelation? God

TO WHOM did God give the revelation (the unveiling)? Jesus

WHO is going to get the revelation? To WHOM is God going to show something? His bond-servants

Underline in red WHAT God is going to show His bond-servants. the things that must soon take place (Teacher Guide page 13)

(page 8)

Let's read Revelation 1:1-3.

Let's find out WHO gave the Book of Revelation, to WHOM it was given, and WHAT the revelation is. Read the first part of Revelation 1:1 again. Then fill in the blanks of the diagram on the next page and answer the questions to solve this first mystery.

The Revelation of Jesus Christ

which God gave Him

to show His bond-servants

the things which must soon take place.

WHO gave the revelation? God

WHAT does the word *revelation* mean? Do you know? The New Testament, where the Book of Revelation is found, was originally written in Koine Greek. The Greek word for revelation is *apokalupsis,* which is pronounced like this: ap-ok-al'-oop-sis. It means "an unveiling."

Do you remember how Toto in the movie *The Wizard of Oz* pulled back the curtain and unveiled the wizard as a small man standing on a stool instead of the giant, powerful wizard Dorothy and her friends were expecting? Just like the real wizard in the movie was unveiled and they saw him as he really was, God is going to unveil what this Book of Revelation is about.

Looking back at the diagram, to WHOM did God give the revelation (the unveiling)? Jesus

WHO is going to get the revelation? To WHOM is God going to show something?
His bond-servants

WHAT is God revealing? WHAT is God going to show the bond-servants? Go back to the diagram and underline in red WHAT God is going to show His bond-servants.

Wow! God is going to show His bond-servants what is going to happen in the future. Isn't that awesome?

Now look back at Revelation 1:1 on page 141 and get

the complete picture by filling in the details in the diagram below that shows HOW God gave the revelation to His bond-servants.

G o d

↕

gave it (the revelation) to J e s u s

↕

who communicated it by His a n g e l

↕

to His bond-servant J o h n

↕

to show to His B o n d-s e r v a n t s

WHAT is going to be shown?

The t h i n g s which must s o o n t a k e p l a c e.

Way to go! You have uncovered your first mystery. You have discovered WHO gives the revelation, to WHOM He gives it, and HOW He gives it. And you know WHAT the revelation is: You are going to study the things that will take place in the future. You know the revelation is true because WHO is giving it? That's right. It's coming from God.

Let's sketch what we just discovered to show Miss Kim, our

Guided Instruction

HOW did God give the revelation to His bond-servants? G o d

gave it (the revelation) to J e s u s

who communicated it by His a n g e l

to His bond-servant J o h n

to show to His B o n d - s e r v a n t s

WHAT is going to be shown?

The t h i n g s which must s o o n t a k e p l a c e

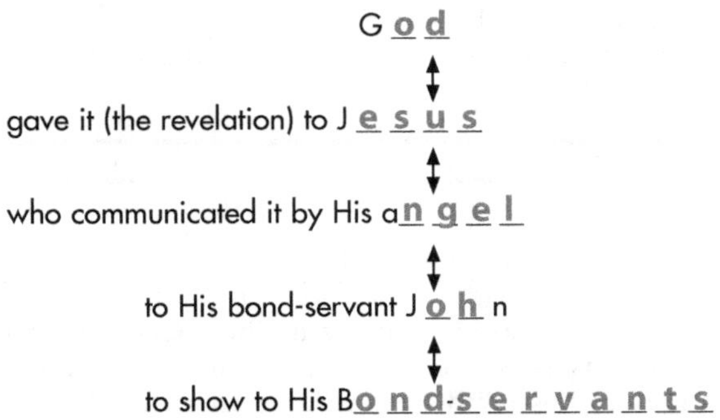

Guided Instruction

6 Draw a picture on page 11 to show how we got the book of Revelation.

(page 10)

it? That's right. It's coming from God.

Let's sketch what we just discovered to show Miss Kim, our museum teacher. Because museums are places of learning, there are classes, workshops, and tours to teach people about what is in the museum and why it's there. The museum teacher is in charge of all the educational programs at the museum, so Miss Kim will be the one who helps us create and experiment with the exhibits at The Discovery Bible Museum.

Draw a picture in the box on the next page to show how we got the Book of Revelation. Make sure your drawing shows

what you discovered in your diagram. Show God giving the revelation to Jesus, Jesus communicating the revelation to His angel, to give to His bond-servant John, to show His bond-servants the things that must soon take place.

You can use symbols if you would like. Draw a triangle to represent God, a cross for Jesus, an angel or wings for the angel, a stick man for John, and several stick people for the bond-servants.

6

Great artwork! Did you know that God has a special blessing for you when you study the Book of Revelation? Let's unveil this week's memory verse to see what God has to say about this blessing. Look at the clouds below. Inside each cloud is a word from this week's verse that has been mixed up. Unscramble each word in the clouds and place it on the correct blank below the clouds.

After you have unscrambled your verse, look at Revelation 1 and find the reference for this verse. Then hide this verse in your heart by saying it aloud three times in a row three times every day.

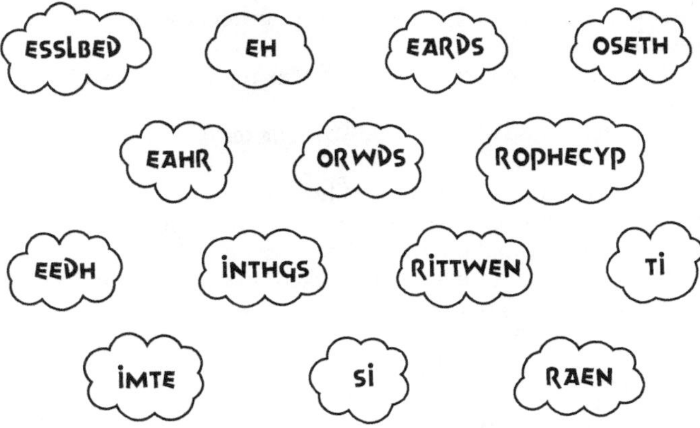

7 __Blessed__ is __he__ who __reads__ and __those__ who __hear__ the __words__ of the __prophecy__, and __heed__ the __things__ which are __written__ in __it__; for the __time__ __is__ __near__.

Revelation 1:__3__

You did it! Tomorrow we will head to the museum to meet Miss Kim and show her our sketches.

Guided Instruction

7 Turn to page 12 and unveil the memory verse. Then copy it to an index card and practice reading it.

Blessed is he who reads and those who hear the words of the prophecy and heed the things which are written in it; for the time is near.

Revelation 1:3

Guided Instruction

Ask God to lead you to a clear understanding of this study.

8 Turn to page 13 and read "The Mystery—How Do You Receive the Blessing?"

8

THE MYSTERY—HOW DO YOU RECEIVE THE BLESSING?

"Hey, guys! Over here!" Uncle Jake called as we walked into the museum. "This is the entrance to the Revelation wing, where we will discover God's plan for the future. Isn't it awesome?"

"Wow!" exclaimed Molly. "This is amazing! Look, Max, there's the mural that shows how John received the Book of Revelation."

"I can't believe how huge it is," Max replied. "I wish I could paint like that!"

"Me, too, buddy," answered Uncle Jake. "Come on over and meet Miss Kim."

"Hi, guys. It's so nice to finally meet you. Your Uncle Jake has told me all about your Bible adventures and all about the amazing Sam," laughed Miss Kim.

Sam, recognizing his name, barked and jumped up to give Miss Kim's face a good licking.

"Whoa, boy! Better get down before Miss Kim bans you from this adventure," Max said as he pulled on Sam's leash. Everyone laughed as the kids handed Miss Kim the sketches they did at the tree house to show how God gave John the Book of Revelation.

"Great job! I love your artwork! We'll put these on our kids' art wall. Do you see the area right over there with the tables and chairs? Kids who visit the museum will be able to sit there and use the art supplies to create their own sketches. Then we'll hang them on this special wall over here. What do you think about that?"

"That is soooo cool!" Max replied.

"Are you excited about what you have learned so far?" Miss Kim asked as she led the kids down the hall.

(page 14)

Kim asked as she led the kids down the hall.

"Yes, it's awesome!" cried Molly. "We know why Revelation was written, and we can't wait to find out what's going to happen in the future."

Miss Kim smiled at Molly as she led Max, Molly, Uncle Jake, and Sam inside one of the resource rooms. "This is one of the rooms kids will work in as they learn about Revelation. Today you will work in here as you continue your research on Revelation 1."

"All right! Let's get started," Max said. "What's the first thing we need to do?"

"Pray," responded Molly.

She's right! Okay, Bible detectives. Don't forget to pray.

Yesterday as you unveiled your memory verse, you saw that someone is going to be blessed. Do you know WHO? Let's find out. Turn to page 141, and read Revelation 1:1-3 again.

Revelation is the only book in the Bible that promises a

(page 141)

Observation Worksheets

REVELATION 1-7

9 **Chapter 1**

1 The Revelation of Jesus Christ, which God gave Him to show
to His bond-servants, <u>the things which must soon take place</u>; and
He sent and communicated *it* by His angel to His bond-servant
John,

2 who testified to the word of God and to the testimony of
Jesus Christ, *even* to all that he saw.

3 Blessed is he who reads and those who hear the words of
the prophecy, and heed the things which are written in it; for
the time is near.

(page 14)

Revelation is the only book in the Bible that promises a special blessing. WHO receives this blessing, and HOW do they receive it? Look at Revelation 1:3. WHO is blessed?

He who ___reads___ and those who ___hear___
___the words of the prophecy___, and ______
___heed the things which are written in it.___

Guided Instruction

9 Turn to page 141 and reread **Revelation 1:1-3. WHO is blessed according to this passage? (Fill in the bottom of page 14.)**

He who <u>reads</u> and those who <u>hear</u>

<u>the words of the prophecy</u>, and

<u>heed the things which are written in it</u>.

Guided Instruction

WHAT do we have to do? **We read it. We hear it. And we h e e d it.**

Discuss what *heeding prophecy* means and the application questions.

Do you know what a prophecy is? A prophecy is when God reveals to us what is going to happen in the future. Do you see why it is so important to study this book of the Bible? But we're not just studying it. WHAT do we have to do?

We read it. We hear it. And we h e e d it.

WHAT does it mean to heed? The word *heed* means we pay close attention to the words and keep watch. It means we don't just read and hear the words. We also pay close attention to what God is saying, and then we do it. "To heed" means to do. Are you doing what God says? ___________

Think about the things you do every day. HOW do they line up with what God says? For an example, do you pay close attention to what you look at on the Internet? Does what you look at measure up to what God says is okay, or do you look at things the world says is okay but would not please God?

Write out what kind of things you look at on the Internet on the lines below and tell if they would please God.

____

____

Do you have time to get on the Internet and talk to your friends, but you don't have time to read the Bible and talk to God?

____

WHAT do you think God thinks about that?

____

WHAT do you need to do? Is there anything you need to change? Write out any changes you need to make on the lines below.

____

____

Great! Now that you have discovered how to receive God's blessing, let's turn back to Revelation 1 on page 141 and see what else we can discover today.

Read Revelation 1:4-8.

(page 141)

10 4 John to the seven churches that are in Asia: Grace to you
and peace, from Him who is and who was and who is to
11 come, and from the seven Spirits who are before His throne,
5 and from Jesus Christ, the faithful witness, the firstborn of
the dead, and the ruler of the kings of the earth. To Him who
loves us and released us from our sins by His blood—
6 and He has made us *to be* a kingdom, priests to His God and
Father—to Him *be* the glory and the dominion forever and ever.
Amen.
7 BEHOLD, HE IS COMING WITH THE CLOUDS, and every eye will

see Him, even those who pierced Him; and all the tribes of the
earth will mourn over Him. So it is to be. Amen.
8 "I am the Alpha and the Omega," says the Lord God, "who is
and who was and who is to come, the Almighty."
9 I, John, ... fellow partaker in the tribulation and

Guided Instruction

10 Turn to page 141 and read Revelation 1:4-8 aloud as students follow along.

11 Reread Revelation 1:4–5 and underline in blue the first three times the word *from* appears.

Guided Instruction

Turn to page 16

To WHOM is John writing? The seven churches

FROM WHOM is John receiving this message? from (verse 4) Him who is and who was and who is to come

WHOM are these words describing?
G o d

12 from (verse 4) The seven spirits before His throne.

from (verse 5a) Jesus Christ

Read Revelation 1:4 and 1:8 and list how God is described in the box.

What I learned about God

(v. 4) He is, was, and is to come.

(v. 8) He is the Alpha and Omega.

He is the Almighty.

(page 16)

Revelation 1:4 To WHOM is John writing?

The seven churches

The letters to the seven churches are not only to the seven churches in Asia but also to the bond-servants.

Read Revelation 1:4-5 again and underline in blue the first three times the word *from* appears in these verses to find out from whom John is receiving this message.

Now, fill in the blanks.

John to the seven churches...Grace to you and peace,

from (verse 4) Him who is and who was and who is to come

WHOM are these words describing? Here's a hint: G o d

from (verse 4) The seven spirits before His throne. (This is the Holy Spirit.)

from (verse 5a) Jesus Christ

Now that we have discovered WHOM this is from, let's see WHAT we can learn about God. Read Revelation 1:4 and Revelation 1:8 and list in the box on the next page HOW God is described in these two verses.

12

WHAT I LEARNED ABOUT GOD

(v. 4) He is, was, and is to come.

(v. 8) He is the Alpha and Omega.

He is the Almighty.

Isn't God amazing? Do you know what the words *alpha* and *omega* mean? The word *alpha*, A, is the first letter in the Greek alphabet and *omega*, Ω, is the last letter in the Greek alphabet. By calling Himself the Alpha and the Omega, God is showing us that He is the first and the last. Wow!

Now let's see what we can discover about Jesus. Read Revelation 1:5 and Revelation 1:7. WHAT are the big things you see about Jesus? List HOW Jesus is described in these two verses in the box below.

13

WHAT I LEARNED ABOUT JESUS

(v. 5) **He is the faithful witness, the firstborn of the dead, the ruler of the kings of the earth.**

(v. 7) **He is coming with the clouds, every eye will see Him, even those who pierced Him; and all tribes of the earth will mourn Him.**

That's a pretty awesome description, isn't it? Did you know that Jesus is coming with the clouds? Just wait. We'll discover more about His coming as we continue our study. It's going to be quite an adventure!

All right! You have uncovered quite a few mysteries today. You have gotten a glimpse of how awesome God and Jesus are, you know Jesus is coming with the clouds and everyone will see Him, and you know how to receive a blessing. As you head out, don't forget to practice saying your memory verse (Revelation 1:3) to remind you of this special blessing.

Guided Instruction

13 Read Revelation 1:5 and 1:7 and list how Jesus is described in the box.

What I learned about Jesus

(v. 5) **He is the faithful witness, the firstborn of the dead, the ruler of the kings of the earth.**

(v. 7) **He is coming with the clouds, every eye will see Him, even those who pierced Him; all tribes of the earth will mourn Him.**

Practice saying the memory verse with a partner.

"Blessed is he who reads and those who hear the words of the prophecy and heed the things which are written in it; for the time is near."

Revelation 1:3

Guided Instruction

God has more mysteries to reveal to us. Ask Him to lead you as you study.

14 Turn to page 18 and read "The Mystery: Where is John?"

15 Turn to page 142 and read Revelation 1:9–11 aloud as students follow along.

14

THE MYSTERY: WHERE IS JOHN?

Hey, guys! It's great to have you back at the museum. You did a fantastic job yesterday as you discovered some awesome things about God and Jesus. Today let's find out WHAT we can discover about John. WHERE is he, WHY is he there, and WHAT is he told to do? There's only one way to find out, and that's to head back to Revelation 1. Don't forget to pray!

Now turn to page 142 and read Revelation 1:9-11. Uncover the mystery of WHERE John is and WHAT he is doing by asking the 5 W's and an H questions. What are the 5 W's and an H? They are the WHO, WHAT, WHERE, WHEN, WHY, and HOW questions.

(page 142)

and who was and who is to come, the Almighty."

15

9 I, John, your brother and fellow partaker in the tribulation and kingdom and perseverance *which are* in Jesus, was on the island called Patmos because of the word of God and the testimony of Jesus.

10 I was in the Spirit on the Lord's day, and I heard behind me a loud voice like *the sound* of a trumpet,

11 saying, "Write in a book what you see, and send *it* to the seven churches: to Ephesus and to Smyrna and to Pergamum and to Thyatira and to Sardis and to Philadelphia and to Laodicea."

(page 18)

16

1. Asking WHO helps you find out:
   WHO wrote this?
   WHOM are we reading about?
   To WHOM was it written?
   WHO said this or did that?

2. WHAT helps you understand:
   WHAT is the author talking about?
   WHAT are the main things that happen?

3. WHERE helps you learn:
   WHERE did something happen?
   WHERE did they go?
   WHERE was this said? When we discover a WHERE, we double underline the WHERE in green.

4. WHEN tells us about time. We mark it with a green clock or a green circle like this: ○.

WHEN tells us:
WHEN did this event happen or WHEN will it happen?
WHEN did the main characters do something? It helps us to follow the order of events.

5. WHY asks questions like:
   WHY did he say that?
   WHY did this happen?
   WHY did they go there?

6. HOW lets you figure out things like:
   HOW is something to be done?
   HOW do people know something happened?

Now ask the 5 W's and an H of Revelation 1:9-11.

Revelation 1:9 WHERE was John?

On the Island of Patmos

Did you know that John was banished to this island? That means he was sent to the island. He was not there of his own free will. Do you know WHY he was banished here? Read Revelation 1:9.

WHY was John on the island of Patmos?

Because of the **word** of **God** and the **testimony** of **Jesus**

Guided Instruction

16 Review the inductive study questions on pages 18-19.

Now answer the 5W and H questions on pages 19-21.

Read Revelation 1:9. WHERE was John?
On the Island of Patmos

WHY was John on the island of Patmos? Because of the word of God and the testimony of Jesus

Guided Instruction

Lead a discussion and have students respond independently to the question on page 20.

Reread Revelation 1:9. **WHAT was John a fellow partaker in?** The tribulation and kingdom and perseverance which are in Jesus

Lead a discussion and answer independently.

testimony is a witness—someone who tells the truth about a person's character, about who he is. John was a witness. He told the truth about Jesus. Because he would not compromise what he believed about Jesus, he was sent away. John was exiled because of his faith in Jesus.

Do you believe the truth about Jesus? If someone told you he or she believed that Jesus died to save us but that He really wasn't God, WHAT would you do? Would you be a witness for Jesus and tell the truth that Jesus was and is God, even if it meant you would be made fun of and left out of your group of friends? Or would you compromise your beliefs by not saying anything or by changing the way you think?

Write out WHAT you would do.

____

____

Look at Revelation 1:9. WHAT was John a fellow partaker in?
The tribulation and kingdom and
perseverance which are in Jesus

WHAT does this mean? John is suffering for what he believes. He is going through tribulations (great distress) and persevering (enduring) in Jesus for his faith. Did you know that according to tradition John was dropped in a pot of hot oil? Even though John was persecuted by being put in a pot of hot oil, he remained steadfast (firm) in Jesus' love.

Do you have faith like John? Are you willing to suffer for knowing Jesus? __________

Read Revelation 1:10. WHAT did John hear, and WHAT did it sound like? A loud voice like the sound of the trumpet

Revelation 1:11 WHAT did the loud voice tell John to do? Write what you see in a book and send it to the seven churches.

Name these seven churches.

1) Ephesus 2) Smyrna
3) Pergamum 4) Thyatira
5) Sardis 6) Philadelphia
7) Laodicea

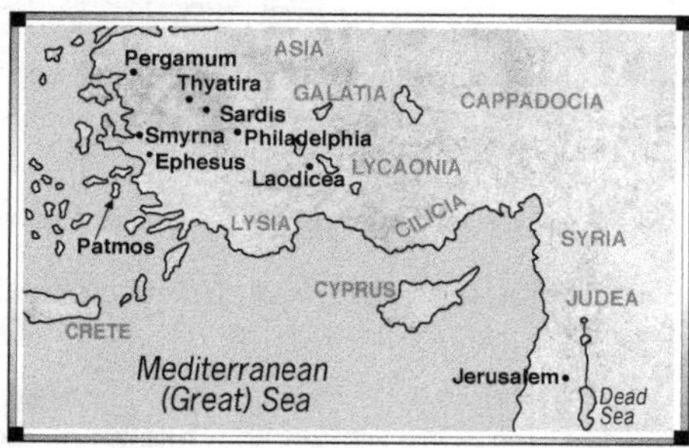

Go back and look at Revelation 1:4. WHERE are these seven churches?

In Asia

Did you know that the Roman province of Asia is located in what we know today as Turkey? Pretty cool, huh?

You did a fantastic job today! Now, before you head out, don't forget to practice saying your memory verse. Tomorrow you will discover more of what John sees in Revelation 1:12-18.

Guided Instruction

Read Revelation 1:10 WHAT did John hear, and WHAT did it sound like? A loud voice like the sound of the trumpet

Revelation 1:11 WHAT did the loud voice tell John to do? Write what you see in a book and send it to the seven churches.

Name these seven churches.

1. Ephesus
2. Smyrna
3. Pergamum
4. Thyatira
5. Sardis
6. Philadelphia
7. Laodicea

Go back and look at Revelation 1:4. WHERE are these seven churches? In Asia

If you have a wall map, locate Turkey. Compare it to the map on page 21.

Guided Instruction

God is with you during this study. Concentrate and see the wonderful mystery unfold.

17 Turn to page 22 and read "The Mystery: One Like a Son of Man."

18 Turn to page 142 and read Revelation 1:12-18 aloud as students follow along.

22 WEEK ONE

17

THE MYSTERY: ONE LIKE A SON OF MAN

Hey, guys, come on in. Are you ready to do some more research? Today we are going to work in the resource room to discover what John sees. Yesterday in Revelation 1:10 we saw that John heard a loud voice that told him to write in a book what he sees. WHOSE voice was it? And WHAT can we learn about Him? Let's find out. Don't forget to pray first. Now turn to page 142 and read Revelation 1:12-18. Now ask the 5 W's and an H.

(page 142)

12 Then I turned to see the voice that was speaking with me.
And having turned I saw seven golden lampstands;
13 and in the middle of the lampstands *I saw* one like a son of man,
clothed in a robe reaching to the feet, and girded across His chest
with a golden sash.
14 His head and His hair were white like white wool, like snow;
and His eyes were like a flame of fire.

Observation Worksheets 143

15 His feet *were* like burnished bronze, when it has been made
to glow in a furnace, and His voice *was* like the sound of many
waters.
16 In His right hand He held seven stars, and out of His mouth
came a sharp two-edged sword; and His face was like the sun
shining in its strength.
17 When I saw Him, I fell at His feet like a dead man. And He
placed His right hand on me, saying, "Do not be afraid; I am the
first and the last,
18 and the living One; and I was dead, and behold, I am alive
forevermore, and I have the keys of death and of Hades.
19 "Therefore write the things which you have seen, and the

(page 22)

Revelation 1:12 WHAT did John see?
Seven golden lampstands

Revelation 1:13 WHOM did John see?
One like the Son of Man

WHERE was He standing?
In the middle of the lampstands

WHAT is He wearing?
A robe reaching to His feet with a golden sash across His chest

Revelation 1:14 WHAT does His hair look like?
White wool

WHAT are His eyes like?
A flame of fire

Revelation 1:15 WHAT do you see about His feet?
They were like burnished bronze.

Unveiling a Mystery 23

WHAT was His voice like?
The sound of many waters

Revelation 1:16 WHAT is in His right hand?
7 stars

WHAT comes out of His mouth?
A sharp two-edged sword

WHAT is His face like?
The sun

Guided Instruction

Answer the questions on pages 22-23.

Revelation 1:12 WHAT did John see? Seven golden lampstands

Revelation 1:13 WHO did John see? One like the Son of Man

WHERE was He standing? In the middle of the lampstands

WHAT was He wearing? A robe reaching to His feet with a golden sash across His chest

Revelation 1:14 WHAT does His hair look like? White wool

WHAT are His eyes like? A flame of fire

Revelation 1:15 WHAT do you see about His feet? They were like burnished bronze.

WHAT was His voice like? The sound of many waters

Revelation 1:16 WHAT is in His right hand? 7 stars

WHAT comes out of His mouth? A sharp two-edged sword

WHAT is His face like? The sun

Guided Instruction

19 Draw a picture of what the son of man looks like in the box on page 23.

Answer the question at the top of page 24 independently.

Practice saying the memory verse with a friend. (Teacher Guide page 23).

(page 23)

Draw a picture of what this son of man looks like in the box below.

19

Tomorrow we will discover just WHO this son of man is. Do you know? Write out WHO you think this is on the line below.

____

Way to go! Now don't forget to practice saying your memory verse so that you will remember that blessed is he who reads, hears, and heeds the words of the prophecy.

(page 24)

20

THE MYSTERY OF SEVEN STARS AND SEVEN LAMPSTANDS

It's great to have you back at the museum! Miss Kim has us all set up to work in the resource room again today as we finish our research on Revelation 1. It has been an awesome week of discovery, and we are just getting started!

Are you ready to discover WHO the son of man is that John saw standing in the middle of the seven golden lampstands? And WHAT are those lampstands? Do you know? We'll find out as we pray and head back to Revelation 1.

Did you pray? Good. Now read Revelation 1:12-20 on page 142.

(page 142)

aodicea."

12 Then I turned to see the voice that was speaking with me.

And having turned I saw seven golden lampstands;

13 and in the middle of the lampstands *I saw* one like a son of man,

clothed in a robe reaching to the feet, and girded across His chest

with a golden sash.

14 His head and His hair were white like white wool, like snow;

and His eyes were like a flame of fire.

Guided Instruction

Lean back in God's arms. Let His Spirit enlighten you by His Word.

20 Turn to page 24 and read "The Mystery of Seven Stars and Seven Lampstands."

21 Turn to page 142 and read Revelation 1:12-20 aloud as students follow along.

Guided Instruction

15 His feet *were* like burnished bronze, when it has been made
to glow in a furnace, and His voice *was* like the sound of many
waters.
16 In His right hand He held seven stars, and out of His mouth
came a sharp two-edged sword; and His face was like the sun
shining in its strength.
17 When I saw Him, I fell at His feet like a dead man. And He
placed His right hand on me, saying, "Do not be afraid; I am the
first and the last,
18 and the living One; and I was dead, and behold, I am alive
forevermore, and I have the keys of death and of Hades.
19 "Therefore write the things which you have seen, and the
things which are, and the things which will take place after
these things.
20 "As for the mystery of the seven stars which you saw in My
right hand, and the seven golden lampstands: the seven stars
are the angels of the seven churches, and the seven lampstands
are the seven churches.

(page 25)

Do you know WHO this son of man is? Here's a clue: Verse 18 tells us He was dead and is alive forevermore. WHO died and rose again to live forever? Jesus

Wow! What an *awesome* description of Jesus! List HOW Jesus is described in verses 17-18 in the box.

WHAT I LEARNED ABOUT JESUS

22 1:7 He is the first and the last.

1:18 He is the living One.

He was dead, but is alive forevermore.

He has the keys of death and of Hades.

Look at Revelation 1:17 to see HOW John reacted when he saw Jesus like this. WHAT did John do?

He fell like a dead man.

Now head back down the hall to see the museum mural of this awesome description of Jesus. Push the button on the wall next to the mural. WHAT do you hear?

Revelation 1:15 WHAT did John say Jesus' voice was like?

Like the sound of many waters

Isn't it amazing that when you push the button you can hear this awesome sound? It sounds like the roar of the waters over Niagara Falls. HOW about the next button? WHAT happens to Jesus' eyes when you push it?

Revelation 1:14 His eyes were like a flame of fire.

Guided Instruction

WHO died and rose again to live forever? Jesus

22 List HOW Jesus is described in Revelation 1:17-18 in the box on page 25.

What I Learned about Jesus

1:7 He is the first and the last.

1:18 He is the living One.

He was dead, but is alive forevermore.

He has the keys of death and of Hades.

Revelation 1:17 HOW did John react? WHAT did he do? He fell like a dead man.

Revelation 1:15 WHAT did John say Jesus' voice was like? Like the sound of many waters.

Revelation 1:14 WHAT were Jesus' eyes like? His eyes were like a flame of fire.

Guided Instruction

23 Read the information at the top of page 26 and answer the questions.

Revelation 1:20 WHAT do the seven stars represent? The angels of the seven churches

WHAT do the seven golden lampstands represent? The seven churches

John was told to write three things

Revelation 1:19 WHAT are the three things?

1. The things which you have seen.

2. The things which are.

3. The things which will take place after these things.

24 Read Revelation 1:2, 11, and 19 aloud and color the words *see* and *saw* blue in each of these verses.

26 WEEK ONE

23 That's pretty amazing isn't it? Now that we know just WHO this son of man is, let's solve another mystery: WHAT do the seven stars represent, and WHAT are the seven lampstands that Jesus is standing in the middle of? Read Revelation 1:20 to uncover this mystery.

WHAT do the seven stars represent?

The angels of the seven churches

WHAT do the seven golden lampstands represent?

The seven churches

In Revelation 1:19, John is told to write three things. WHAT are those three things?

1. The things which you have seen
2. The things which are
3. The things which will take place after these things

Did you know that the Book of Revelation is written and divided into three segments by the three things that John is told to write? Let's uncover how the Book of Revelation is divided.

24 Read Revelation 1:2, 11, and 19. Color the words see and saw blue in each of these verses.

2 who testified to the word of God and to the testimony of Jesus Christ, *even* to all that he saw. (page 141)

11 saying, "Write in a book what you see, and send *it* to the seven churches: to Ephesus and to Smyrna and to Pergamum and to Thyatira and to Sardis and to Philadelphia and to Laodicea." (page 142)

19 "Therefore write the things which you have seen, and the things which are, and the things which will take place after these things. (page 143)

true in each of these verses. (page 26)

WHAT do you think Revelation 1 is about?

The things which you have **seen**

That's what you have been studying this week—the things John saw. Look at the second thing John is told to write.

The things which **are** (Revelation 1:19).

25 Turn to page 143 and read the following verses in Revelation 2–3. Read Revelation 2:1, 2:8, 2:12, 2:18, 3:1, 3:7, and 3:14.

To WHOM is John told to write in these seven verses?

Chapter 2 (page 143)

1 "To the angel of the church in Ephesus write: The One who holds the seven stars in His right hand, the One who walks among the seven golden lampstands, says this:

8 "And to the angel of the church in Smyrna write: (page 144)
The first and the last, who was dead, and has come to life, says this:

12 "And to the angel of the church in Pergamum write: (page 145)
The One who has the sharp two-edged sword says this:

18 "And to the angel of the church in Thyatira write: (page 146)
The Son of God, who has eyes like a flame of fire, and His feet are like burnished bronze, says this:

Chapter 3 (page 147)

1"To the angel of the church in Sardis write: He who has the seven Spirits of God and the seven stars, says this: 'I know your deeds, that you have a name that you are alive, but you are dead.

7 "And to the angel of the church in Philadelphia write: (page 148)
He who is holy, who is true, who has the key of David, who opens and no one will shut, and who shuts and no one opens, says this:

14 "To the angel of the church in Laodicea write: (page 149)
The Amen, the faithful and true Witness, the Beginning of the creation of God, says this:

Guided Instruction

WHAT is Revelation 1 about? **The things which you have seen**

WHAT is the second thing that John is told to write? **The things which are (Revelation 1:19)**

25 Turn to page 143 and read the selected verses to identify the seven churches. Revelation 2:1, 2:8, 2:12, 2:18, 3:1, 3:7, and 3:14.

Guided Instruction

Revelation 1:4 The seven churches of Asia, which are:

Revelation 2:1 E p h e s u s

Revelation 2:8 S m y r n a

Revelation 2:12 P e r g a m u m

Revelation 2:18 T h y a t i r a

Revelation 3:1 S a r d i s

Revelation 3:7 P h i l a d e l p h i a

Revelation 3:14 L a o d i c e a

These are the second thing John is told to write—the things that *are.*

The third part of Revelation begins in Revelation 4.

Revelation 4:1 WHAT are the first three words in this verse? After these things

WHAT things? WHAT did we discover Revelation 2-3 is about? The things which are, which are the seven churches

WHAT do you think Revelation 4-22 will be about? Look at Revelation 1:19 The things which will take place after these things

Unveiling a Mystery 27

Revelation 1:4	The seven churches of Asia, which are:
Revelation 2:1	E p h e s u s
Revelation 2:8	S m y r n a
Revelation 2:12	P e r g a m u m
Revelation 2:18	T h y a t i r a
Revelation 3:1	S a r d i s
Revelation 3:7	P h i l a d e l p h i a
Revelation 3:14	L a o d i c e a

Messages to these seven churches in Asia are the second thing that John is told to write. The things that *are*. These seven churches exist at the time John is given the revelation, and they are very important.

Jesus has some very specific things to say to these seven churches about how the people are living and whether they are true believers. We'll learn more about these seven churches next week.

Now turn to page 151 to uncover the third part of Revelation. Read Revelation 4:1.

Chapter 4 (page 151)

1 After these things I looked, and behold, a door *standing* open in heaven, and the first voice which I had heard, like *the sound* of a trumpet speaking with me, said, "Come up here, and I will show you what must take place after these things."

(page 27)

WHAT are the first three words in this verse?

After these things

After WHAT things? WHAT did we discover Revelation 2–3 is about?

The things which are, which are the seven churches.

So WHAT do you think Revelation 4–22 will be about? Look at Revelation 1:19.

The things which will take place after these things

Revelation 4–22 will be focusing on the things that happen after the seven churches. They are the things that have not happened yet. Isn't it exciting to know you are going to solve the mystery of what is going to happen in the future? But before you do, let's review all the things you have discovered this week in Revelation 1.

HOW is the Book of Revelation divided up?

Revelation 1 is about the things ___John saw___.

Revelation _2_ – _3_ is about the things _which are_,

which are the seven _churches_

Revelation _4_ – _22_ is about the things _which will take place after these thing_

One more time just for practice, review WHO gave the book, HOW they received it, and WHAT it is about.

WHO? _God_ gave the book (the revelation)

to J _e_ _s_ _u_ _s_

who communicated it by His a _n_ _g_ _e_ _l_

to His bond-servant J _o_ _h_ _n_

to show His _b_ _o_ _n_ _d_-_s_ _e_ _r_ _v_ _a_ _n_ _t_ _s_

WHAT?

The _things_ which must _soon_ _take_ _place_

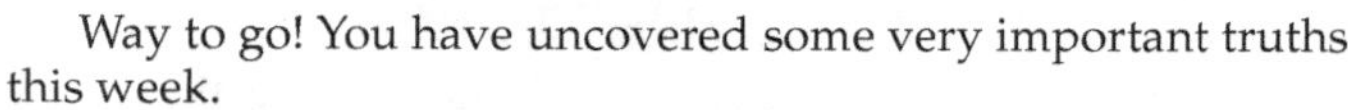

Way to go! You have uncovered some very important truths this week.

Now don't forget to say your memory verse one more time. Why don't you say it to a friend or an adult, and ask if he or she has read the words of the prophecy?

Keep up the good work! See you next week.

Guided Instruction

HOW is the Book of Revelation divided up? **Revelation 1 is about the things _John saw_.**

Revelation _2_ – _3_ is about the things _which are_, which are the seven _churches_.

Revelation _4_ – _22_ is about the things _which will take place after these things_.

Now for review practice:

WHO gave the book? _God_ gave the book (the revelation)

to J _e_ _s_ _u_ _s_

who communicated it by His a _n_ _g_ _e_ _l_

to His bond-servant J _o_ _h_ _n_

to show His _b_ _o_ _n_ _d_ - _s_ _e_ _r_ _v_ _a_ _n_ _t_ _s_

WHAT? The _things_ which must _soon_ _take_ _place_

Practice your memory verse with a friend. (Teacher Guide page 23)

WOW! You have persevered and God is pleased.

If you are a classroom teacher you may want to give your students a quiz on their memory verse. There is also a quiz on Week One on page 154 to check memory and understanding.

If you are a Sunday School teacher this is a great time to review the whole week by playing a game like the *M&M® Draw* on page 164. This is also a great way for classroom teachers and homeschool families to review with students what they learned this week.

Guided Instruction

WEEK 2

God tells the seven churches of Asia things they have to change. Ask Him to show you what you need to change in your life.

26 Turn to page 29 and read "Revelation 2" and "Your First Love."

27 Review the information on key words and pronouns on pages 30-31.

2

REVELATION 2

You're doing a fantastic job researching the Book of Revelation! Just look at what you have uncovered in just one week: You saw HOW John received the Book of Revelation, WHAT the book is about, some pretty awesome things about God and Jesus, and HOW to receive a blessing.

What do you think about the museum so far? Pretty amazing isn't it! Just wait! There is so much more to see and do as you uncover each chapter of Revelation. Are you ready to head back to the resource room and discover the mysteries of Revelation 2?

26

YOUR FIRST LOVE

"Hey, Molly, are you ready to start uncovering the second thing John is told to write about—the things that are?"

"I sure am, Max," Molly responded. "These messages to the churches must be very important. I can't wait to see what God wants us to learn by studying those seven churches in Asia."

29

Guided Instruction

"Me, too! Let's pray so we can get started uncovering clues for Revelation 2."

Now that we've prayed, Bible detectives, let's look for clues in Revelation 2 to discover Jesus' message to the first church. One way you can uncover clues is by looking for key words.

What are *key words?* Key words pop up more than once. They are called key words because they help unlock the meaning of the chapter or book that you are studying and give you clues about what is most important in a passage of Scripture.

- Key words are usually used over and over again.
- Key words are important.
- Key words are used by the writer for a reason.

Once you discover a key word, you need to mark it in a special way, using a special color or symbol, so that you can immediately spot it in the Scripture. This will help you understand what you're studying. Don't forget to mark any pronouns that go with the key words, too! WHAT are pronouns? Check out Max and Molly's research card below.

Pronouns

Pronouns are words that take the place of nouns. A noun is a person, place or thing. A pronoun stands in for a noun! Here's an example: "Molly and Max are excited about their new Bible adventure. They can't wait to uncover the mysteries of Revelation!" The word *they* is a pronoun because it takes the place of Molly and Max's name in the second sentence. It is another word we use to refer to Molly and Max.

Guided Instruction

28 Copy the key word markings shown on page 31 to your bookmark and above the title "Chapter 2" on your Observation Worksheets. Add these markings to your wall chart.

To the angel of the church in (Ephesus, etc.) write (color orange)

Jesus (or any description that refers to Him like The One) (draw a purple cross and color it yellow)

I know (underline in red and color it yellow)

Deeds (draw and color green feet)

Love (draw and color a red heart)

Repent (draw a red arrow and color the word yellow)

He who has an ear, let him hear what the spirit says to the churches (color it blue)

To him who overcomes (or He who overcomes) (color it yellow)

WHERE (double-underline in green words that denote place)

Revelation 2:1 WHO is the first church John is writing to? Ephesus

To discover the main people and events of Revelation 2, you need to mark the following key words on your Observation Worksheets at the back of this book.

You'll also want to make a bookmark for your key words so that you can see them at a glance as you mark them on your Observation Worksheets. Make your key word bookmark by taking an index card and writing the key words we'll show you as well as how you are going to mark them on your Observation Worksheets.

Then turn to page 143. Read Revelation 2:1-7 and mark your key words and key phrases on your Observation Worksheet. A key phrase is like a key word except it is a group of words that are repeated instead of just one word such as "I did it," "I did it," "I did it." The group of words "I did it" is a phrase that is repeated instead of just one word.

Mark the key words and key phrases on your bookmark and your Observation Worksheets. And don't forget to mark the pronouns!

28 To the angel of the church in (Ephesus, etc.) write (color orange)

Jesus (or any description that refers to Jesus like *The One*) (draw a purple cross and color it yellow)

I know (underline in red and color it yellow)

deeds (draw and color green feet)

32 WEEK TWO

love (draw and color a red heart)

repent (draw a red arrow and color the word yellow)

He who has an ear, let him hear what the spirit says to the churches (color it blue)

To him who overcomes (or He who overcomes) (color it yellow)

Don't forget to mark anything that tells you WHERE by double underlining the WHERE in green.

Now, read Revelation 2:1.

Revelation 2:1 WHO is the first church John is writing to?

Ephesus

Before you uncover what John writes to the church in Ephesus, let's get a little background on this ancient city in Asia. Why don't we take our books and walk out into the museum to take a look at the exhibit on the seven churches?

The Roman province of Asia is located today in what we know as Turkey. As we look at the seven models of the churches in Asia (modern-day Turkey), WHAT does the museum's plaque tell us about the city of Ephesus?

(page 143)

Chapter 2

1 "To the angel of the church in Ephesus write: The One who

144 OBSERVATION WORKSHEETS

holds the seven stars in His right hand, the One who walks
among the seven golden lampstands, says this:
2 'I know your deeds and your toil and perseverance, and that
you cannot tolerate evil men, and you put to the test those who
call themselves apostles, and they are not, and you found them
to be false;
3 and you have perseverance and have endured for My name's
sake, and have not grown weary.
4 'But I have *this* against you, that you have left your first love.
5 'Therefore remember from where you have fallen, and repent
and do the deeds you did at first; or else I am coming to you and
will remove your lampstand out of its place—unless you repent.
6 'Yet this you do have, that you hate the deeds of the
Nicolaitans, which I also hate.
7 'He who has an ear, let him hear what the Spirit says to the
churches. To him who overcomes, I will grant to eat of the tree
of life which is in the Paradise of God.'
8 "And to the angel of the church in Smyrna write:

Jesus' Messages to the Churches 31

Watch for these other pronouns when you are marking people:

I	you	he	she
me	yours	him	her
mine	his	hers	
we	it		
our	its		
they	them		

2 you

Guided Instruction

29 Turn to page 143 and read Revelation 2:1–7 aloud as students follow along. If you are teaching in a classroom and have an overhead projector, make a transparency of your Observation Worksheet for a visual aid. You may want to blow it up to poster size and hang it on a wall and then have your students call each key word out loud as you read it and mark it together—you on the transparency and they in their books. If you're skilled at PowerPoint and have time, you can import an Observation Worksheet then select symbols from PP's palette or elsewhere, color them, place them over the words, and even animate them—bring them in one at a time.

Guided Instruction

30 Read the plaque about Ephesus on page 33.

31 Locate Ephesus on the map and double-underline it in green.

Locate Turkey on a modern-day wall map.

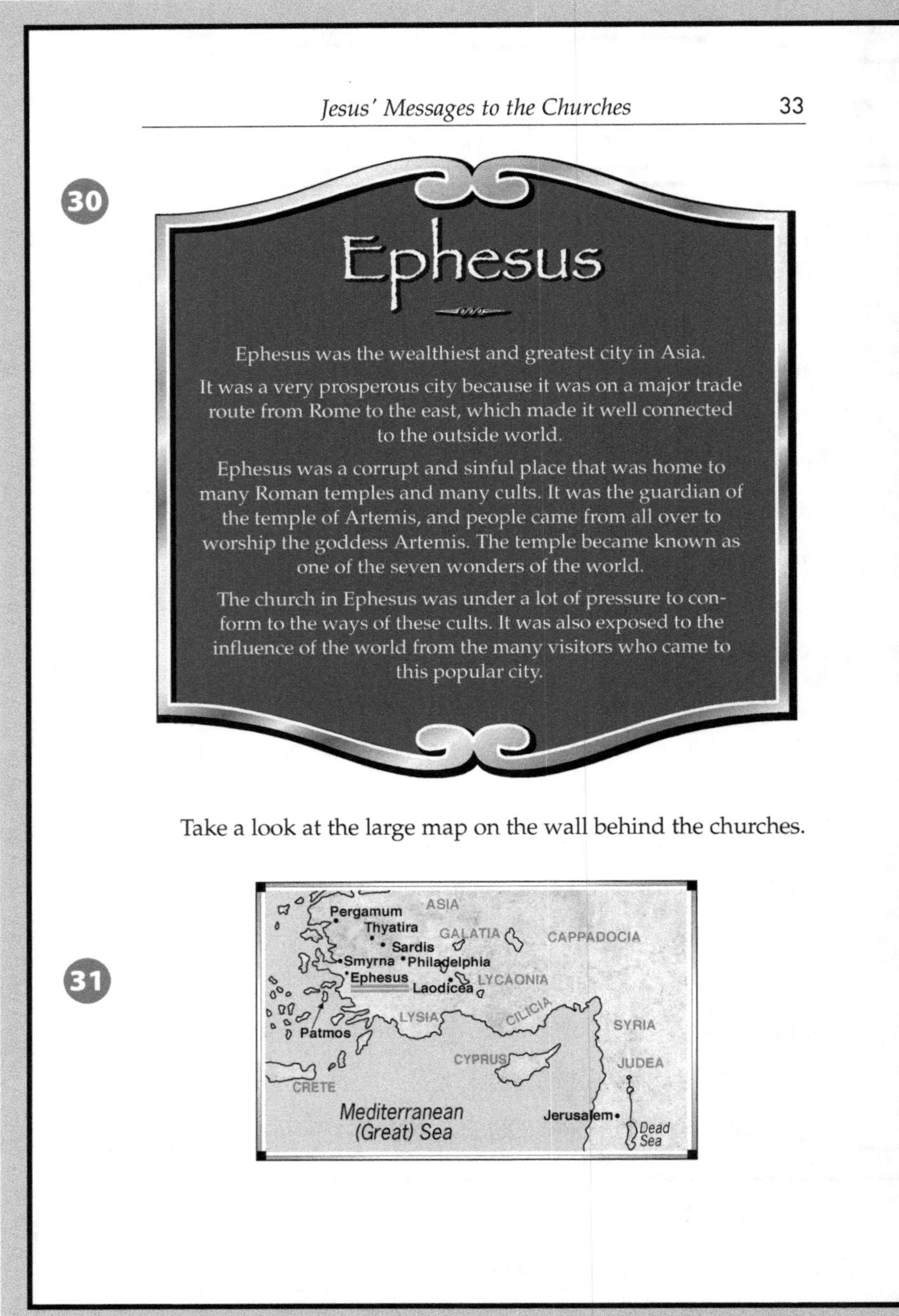

Jesus' Messages to the Churches 33

30

Ephesus

Ephesus was the wealthiest and greatest city in Asia.

It was a very prosperous city because it was on a major trade route from Rome to the east, which made it well connected to the outside world.

Ephesus was a corrupt and sinful place that was home to many Roman temples and many cults. It was the guardian of the temple of Artemis, and people came from all over to worship the goddess Artemis. The temple became known as one of the seven wonders of the world.

The church in Ephesus was under a lot of pressure to conform to the ways of these cults. It was also exposed to the influence of the world from the many visitors who came to this popular city.

Take a look at the large map on the wall behind the churches.

31

32 Do you see Ephesus? Great! Let's find out what we can learn about the church in Ephesus. Read Revelation 2:1-7 on page 143.

WHAT does Jesus say to the church in Ephesus? Find out by filling in the chart on the next page. Start by working on the section called "Description of Jesus."

Next, using these same verses (Revelation 2:1-7), fill in the section of the chart that says "Commendation to the Church." A commendation is when someone praises you for something you did that was good. Look at the good things Jesus says about the church in Ephesus and add those to the chart.

Now look at the section that says "Reproof Given to the Church." To reprove someone is to tell them what they are doing wrong. Fill in the chart to show what the church in Ephesus was doing wrong.

Fill in the section that says "Warnings and Instructions to the Church" by writing what Jesus tells the church at Ephesus

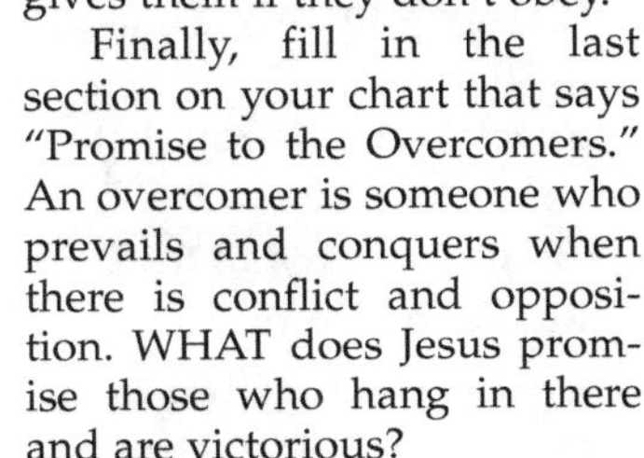

to do and the warning that He gives them if they don't obey.

Finally, fill in the last section on your chart that says "Promise to the Overcomers." An overcomer is someone who prevails and conquers when there is conflict and opposition. WHAT does Jesus promise those who hang in there and are victorious?

Guided Instruction

32 Read the information on page 34.

Read the selected verses to complete the message to the church at Ephesus on page 35.

Guided Instruction

Highlight Commendation to the Church in yellow.

Highlight Reproof Given to the Church in red.

Highlight Warnings and Instructions to the Church in pink

Highlight Promise to the Overcomers in light green.

JESUS' MESSAGES TO THE CHURCHES

Church of Ephesus

Description of Jesus

Revelation 2:1 The One who holds the seven stars in His right hand, the One who walks among the seven golden lampstands.

Commendations to the Church (Praise)

Revelation 2:2 I know your deeds and your toil and perseverance and that you cannot tolerate evil men, and you put to the test those who call themselves apostles, and they are not, and you found them to be false.

Revelation 2:3 You have perseverance and have endured for My name's sake, and have not grown weary.

Revelation 2:6 You hate the deeds of the Nicolaitans, which I also hate.

Reproof given to the Church (What they did wrong)

Revelation 2:4 You have left your first love.

Warnings and Instructions to the Church

Revelation 2:5 Remember from where you have fallen, and repent and do the

Jesus' Messages to the Churches 35

JESUS' MESSAGES TO THE CHURCHES

Church at Ephesus

Description of Jesus

Revelation 2:1 The One who holds the seven stars in His right hand, the One who walks among the seven golden lampstands.

Commendation to the Church (Praise)

Revelation 2:2 I know your deeds and your toil and perseverance, and that you cannot tolerate evil men, and you put to the test those who call themselves apostles, and they are not, and you found them to be false.

Revelation 2:3 You have perseverance and have endured for My name's sake, and have not grown weary.

Revelation 2:6 You hate the deeds of the Nicolaitans, which I also hate.

Reproof Given to the Church (What they did wrong)

Revelation 2:4 You have left your first love.

Warnings and Instructions to the Church

Revelation 2:5 Remember from where you have fallen, and repent and do the deeds you did at first; or else I am coming to you and will remove your lampstand out of its place—unless you repent.

Promise to the Overcomers

Revelation 2:7 To him who overcomes, I will grant to eat of the tree of life which is in the Paradise of God.

33 Wow! What a message! Look at all the good things the church at Ephesus has done: They have endured and hung in there, and they did not allow false teachers in the church.

But look at what Jesus has against them. They left their first love. Jesus is essentially telling them,"I know you love Me, but you are not loving Me the way you did when you first became a Christian. I do not have first place in your heart."

HOW important is it for God to have first place in our hearts? We'll uncover that mystery tomorrow. Look back at the "Promise to the Overcomers" on your chart. He who overcomes, Jesus will grant to eat of the tree of life. Do you know what that means? That means the overcomer will be in the new heaven! HOW do we know that? Revelation 22 shows us what the new heaven will be like. In it, in the middle of the street on either side of the river, is the tree of life bearing twelve kinds of fruit. Isn't that awesome?

Why don't you get a stick from a tree out of your yard and put some different colored gumdrops on it to represent the tree of life in the new heaven to remind you that if you overcome you will be in heaven with Jesus forever!

All right! Now let's solve this week's memory verse.

Look at the maze on the next page. Find the correct path through the church, and write the words you discover on that path on the lines below. Then check your Observation Worksheet to discover the reference of your verse.

Guided Instruction

deeds you did at first; or else I am coming to you and will remove your lampstand out of its place—unless you repent.

Promise to the Overcomers

Revelation 2:7 **To him who overcomes, I will grant to eat of the tree of life which is in the Paradise of God.**

33 Read and discuss the information on page 36.

You may want to make a model of the tree of life in your class.

Guided Instruction

34 Follow the maze on page 37 and write out the memory verse.

But I have this against you, that you have left your first love. Therefore remember from where you have fallen, and repent and do the deeds you did at first; or else I am coming to you and will remove your lampstand out of its place—unless you repent.

Revelation 2:4–5

Jesus' Messages to the Churches 37

34

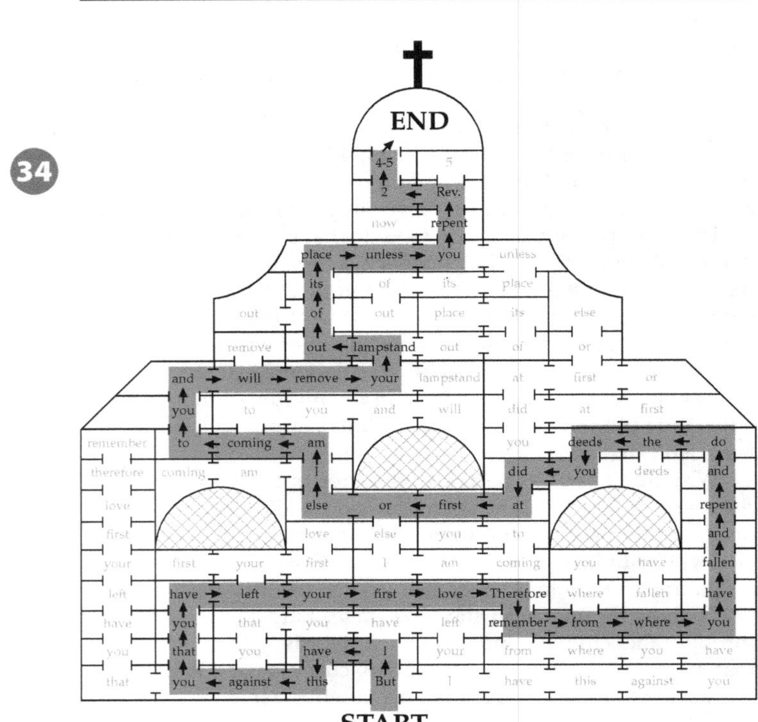

"But I have this against you, that you have left your first love. Therefore remember from where you have fallen, and repent and do the deeds you did at first; or else I am coming to you and will remove your lampstand out of its place—unless you repent."

Revelation 2:4-5

134

Way to go! Don't forget to practice saying your verse aloud three times in a row—morning, noon, and evening today!

38 WEEK TWO

35

HOW IMPORTANT IS LOVE?

Hey! It's great to see you again. Yesterday, as we looked at the first letter John sent to the church in Ephesus, we discovered quite a bit about this church. We saw the church of Ephesus had persevered. That means the people didn't give up even though it was hard and difficult. They endured; they stood firm. And while they had not allowed false teachers in the church, they had lost their first love. They did not love God as they had in the beginning.

HOW important is it for God to have first place in our hearts? Let's find out. Don't forget to pray. Then pull out your sword of the Spirit (the Word of God, your Bible). Look up and read Mark 12:28-31. Answer the 5 W's and an H questions to solve the crossword puzzle.

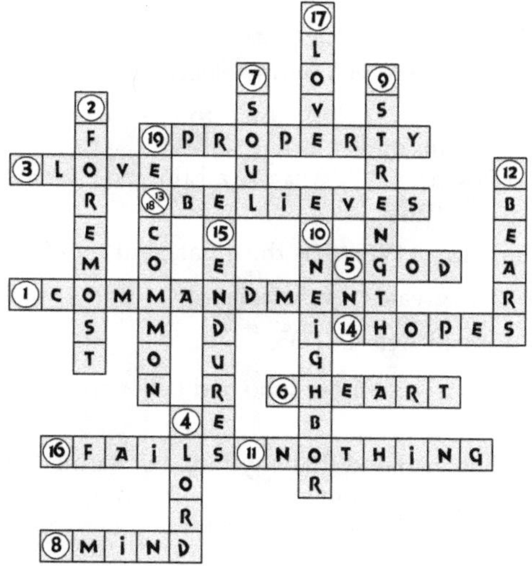

Guided Instruction

The church in Ephesus did not give up. You must not get discouraged, either. Ask God to keep you fixed on His Word.

35 Turn to page 38 and read "How Important is Love?"

Guided Instruction

Read Mark 12:28–31 aloud as students follow along.

36 Answer the questions on page 39 to complete the crossword puzzle.

Mark 12:28 WHAT question does the scribe ask Jesus?

1. (Across) What commandment is the

2. (Down) foremost of all?

Mark 12:29-30 HOW does Jesus answer? WHAT does he say we should do in verse 30?

3. (Across) And you shall love the

4. (Down) Lord your **5. (Across)** God with all your **6. (Across)** heart, and with all your **7. (Down)** soul, and with all your **8. (Across)** mind, and with all your **9. (Down)** strength.

Mark 12:31 WHAT is the second thing He tells them they should do?

10. (Down) You shall love your neighbor as yourself.

Look up and read 1 Corinthians 13:1-13 aloud as students follow along.

1 Corinthians 13:2 WHAT am I if I do not have love?

11. (Across) I am nothing.

1 Corinthians 13:7-8 WHAT do we learn about love? 12. (Down) Love, bears all things, **13. (Across)** believes all things, **14. (Across)** hopes all things, **15. (Down)** endures all things. Love never **16. (Across)** fails.

36

Mark 12:28 WHAT question does the scribe ask Jesus?

1. (Across) What __commandment__ is the
2. (Down) __foremost__ of all?

Mark 12:29-30 HOW does Jesus answer? WHAT does He say we should do in verse 30?

And you shall 3. (Across) __love__ the 4. (Down) __Lord__ your 5. (Across) __God__ with all your 6. (Across) __heart__, and with all your 7. (Down) __soul__, and with all your 8. (Across) __mind__, and with all your 9. (Down) __strength__.

Mark 12:31 WHAT is the second thing He tells them they should do?

10. (Down) You shall love your __neighbor__ as yourself.

Look up and read 1 Corinthians 13:1-13.

1 Corinthians 13:2 WHAT am I if I do not have love?

11. (Across) I am __nothing__

1 Corinthians 13:7-8 WHAT do we learn about love?

12. (Down) Love __bears__ all things, 13. (Across) __believes__ all things, 14. (Across) __hopes__ all things, 15. (Down) __endures__ all things. Love never 16. (Across) __fails__.

1 Corinthians 13:13 WHAT is the greatest of these things?

17. (Down) The greatest of these is __love__

Look up and read Acts 4:31-35.

Acts 4:32 WHAT were those who had believed doing in this verse?

Not one of them claimed that anything belonging to him was his own; but all things were 18. (Down) __common__ 19. (Across) __property__ to them.

Acts 4:34-35 Were there any needy people among these believers?

___ Yes _X_ No

Do you think these people had always taken care of each other and shared what they had, or do you think this happened as a result of believing in Jesus Christ?

___

___

Do you share your things, such as giving away a coat or shoes to someone who has a need? ___

Is this sharing with each other and giving to those in need a way to show God's love? ___

Wow! Jesus tells us that the greatest commandment is to love God with all our hearts, souls, minds, and strength. We also saw that we are to love our neighbors as ourselves.

If you have accepted Jesus Christ as your Savior, God is to be your first love. He is to have first place in your life. We saw from looking at 1 Corinthians 13 that love is the most important thing. Without love we are nothing! That's why we see Jesus warning the church in Ephesus about losing that first love.

HOW did Jesus tell them to fix this problem? Look back at your chart on page 35 at Revelation 2:5.

Jesus tells them to __remember__ from where they have fallen. He wants them to remember how they acted when they first accepted Jesus, when He had first place in their lives.

Then He tells them to __repent__ and do the __deeds__ they did at first.

"To repent" means to change your mind about what you are doing or believing that it is wrong according to God's Word,

Guided Instruction

1 Corinthians 13:13 WHAT is the greatest of these things?

17. (Down) The greatest of these is love.

Look up and read Acts 4:31-35 aloud as students follow along.

Acts 4:32 WHAT were those who had believed doing in this verse?

18. (Down) Not one of them claimed that anything belonging to him was his own; but all things were common

19. (Across) property to them.

Turn to page 40, read the selected verses, elicit discussion, and answer the questions.

Acts 4:34-35 Were there any needy people among these believers?

__ Yes X No

Elicit discussion and have students respond independently

Revelation 2:5 HOW did Jesus tell them to fix the problem?

Jesus tells them to remember from where they have fallen. He wants them to remember how they acted when they first accepted Jesus, when He had first place in their lives.

Then He tells them to repent and to do the deeds they did at first.

Guided Instruction

37 Read and discuss the questions on pages 41-42, then respond independently.

37

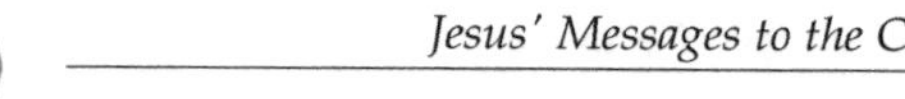

Jesus' Messages to the Churches 41

and to decide to believe and do what God says. "To repent" is to decide to do things God's way.

Jesus is telling the people to do the things they did when they first became believers.

Did you know our actions show what we really believe? First John 3:18 tells us we are not to "love with word or with tongue, but in deed and truth." What we do shows our love.

Jesus warns the people in the church at Ephesus that if they don't do these things, He will remove their lampstand (the church) out of its place. That is pretty serious! How important is it for a church or a group of believers to love God?

____

Now that you have discovered Jesus' warning to the church in Ephesus, examine yourself.

Do you love God with all your heart, soul, mind, and strength? Is He first place in your life or have you put something else, such as friends, being popular, playing sports, or being on the Internet, in His place? Write your answer. Tell where God fits into your life. __________

____

____

____

Do you have a desire to read and study God's Word?

____

How often do you read your Bible?

____

Do you spend time in prayer; do you talk to God every day?

____

Do you care about others? Do you think of them as more important than yourself? Do you put yourself or others first? ______________________________

How do you treat kids at your school? Do you make fun and tease anyone? Do you try to be a friend to a kid who doesn't have a friend? Write out what you do and tell if this shows that you have God's love in you.

____

____

How do you show your love for God?

____

____

____

____

If, after examining yourself, you see you have left your first love, then do what Jesus told the church at Ephesus to do—

r _e_ _m_ _e_ _m_ _b_ _e_ _r_ from where you have fallen,

r _e_ _p_ _e_ _n_ _t_ (confess your sin and change your actions), and d _o_ the d _e_ _e_ _d_ _s_ you did at first!

Remember, he who overcomes, Jesus will grant to eat of the tree of life! Way to go! You've finished Day Two. We are so proud of you!

DAY THREE

Guided Instruction

WHAT does Jesus tell Ephesus to do?

r _e_ _m_ _e_ _m_ _b_ _e_ r from where you have fallen,

r _e_ _p_ _e_ _n_ t and d _o_ the d _e_ _e_ _d_ _s_ you did at first!

Guided Instruction

Ask God to keep your mind focused on His message today.

38 Turn to page 42 and read "Be Faithful—Stand Firm."

Add the new key words to your bookmark, to the margin in your Observation Worksheets beside Revelation 2:8-11, and to your wall chart.

39 Read Revelation 2:8–11 aloud using your Observation Worksheet visual aid as students follow along and call out each key word. Then mark them together as we noted on p. 41.

40 **Satan (devil) (draw a red pitchfork)**

Second death (underline twice in black)

To the angel of the church in Smyrna write (color orange)

Jesus (or any reference to Him) (draw a purple cross and color the word yellow)

I know (underline in red and color it yellow)

He who has an ear, let him hear what the Spirit says to the churches (color it blue)

To him who overcomes (or he who overcomes) (color yellow)

WHERE (double-underline in green words that denote place)

WHEN (draw a green clock over words that denote time)

(page 42)

the tree of life! Way to go! You've finished Day Two. We are so proud of you!

38

BE FAITHFUL—STAND FIRM

"Hold on, Sam! We're in the museum; take it easy!" Max called out as Sam raced down the hallway. Sam had spotted Miss Kim standing by the models of the churches, and he wanted to be the first to greet her with a good face lick!

Jesus' Messages to the Churches 43

Miss Kim looked up in astonishment and smiled as she watched Sam drag Max down the hallway. But her smile started to fade as she realized Sam was making a beeline in her direction. Molly came panting from behind. "Watch out, Miss Kim! Stand firm 'cause here comes Sam!"

Miss Kim braced herself as Sam slid up to her feet and jumped with all his might to lick her face.

"Down, boy," she said. "I missed you, too!

"Come on, cool it, we have to get back to work to find out what Jesus had to say to the second church in Asia," Max said. Sam sighed and then sat down and wagged his tail. He was ready to get to work. How about you? Are you ready to discover what Jesus has to say to the next church?

Don't forget to pray! Now pull out your key word bookmark and add the new key words listed to your index card.

40 Satan (devil) (draw a red pitchfork)

second death (underline twice in black)

Turn to page 144. Read Revelation 2:8-11 and mark your two new key words and the key words listed below on your Observation Worksheet just like they are on your index card. Turn to page 139 if you have lost your card. Don't forget to mark the pronouns!

To the angel of the church in Smyrna write

Jesus (or any description that refers to Jesus)

I know

He who has an ear, let him hear what the spirit says to the churches

To him who overcomes (or He who overcomes)

Don't forget to mark anything that tells you WHERE by double underlining the WHERE in green. And don't forget to mark anything that tells you WHEN by drawing a green clock or green circle like this: ○ .

Revelation 2:8 WHAT church is this message for? _______

39

8 "And to the angel of the church in Smyrna write:
The first and the last, who was dead, and has come to life, says
this:
9 'I know your tribulation and your poverty (but you are

rich), and the blasphemy by those who say they are Jews and
are not, but are a synagogue of Satan.
10 'Do not fear what you are about to suffer. Behold, the
devil is about to cast some of you into prison, so that you
will be tested, and you will have tribulation for ten days. Be
faithful until death, and I will give you the crown of life.
11 'He who has an ear, let him hear what the Spirit says to
the churches. He who overcomes will not be hurt by the
second death.'
12 "And to the angel of the church in Pergamum write:

(page 43)

Revelation 2:8 WHAT church is this message for? Smyrna

Guided Instruction

Reread the selected verses to answer the questions.

Revelation 2:8 WHAT church is this message for? Smyrna

Guided Instruction

41 Read the plaque about Smyrna on page 44 and the information about Polycarp on page 45.

WHAT does the museum's plaque tell us about the city of Smyrna?

41

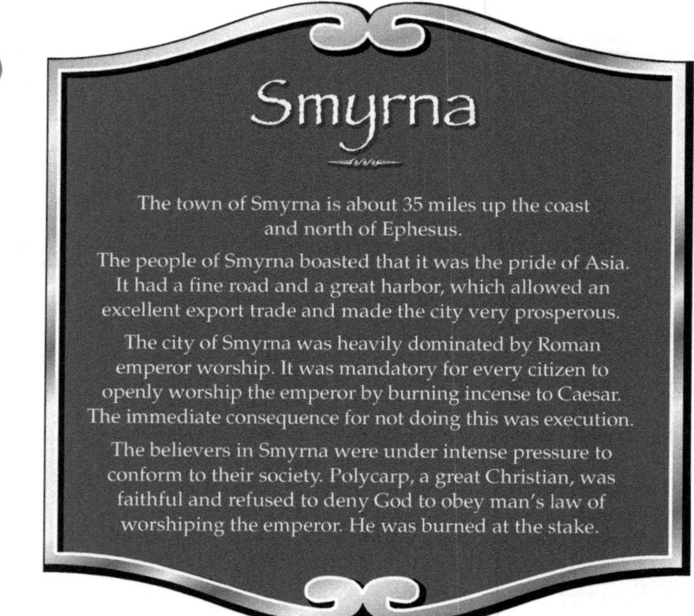

Polycarp was a martyr for his faith. A martyr is someone who chooses to die rather than give up what he or she believes in. It is someone who dies for his or her faith. If you want to learn more about Christians who died for their faith, you can read *Foxe's Christian Martyrs of the World*. Take a look on the next page at what Max and Molly discovered about Polycarp.

Guided Instruction

Polycarp

Polycarpus (also known as Polycarp) was a follower and convert of St. John the Evangelist and served in the ministry of Christ for 60 years.

Polycarp was martyred in his eighty-sixth year.

When Polycarp discovered he was in danger of being killed because he was Christian, he escaped; but a child discovered his hiding place. Then he had a dream of his bed suddenly becoming on fire. Because of these two circumstances, Polycarp thought that it was God's will that he should suffer martyrdom, so he did not try to escape the next time he had a chance.

When Polycarp was taken before the proconsul he was cheerful and serene. He asked for one hour of prayer and was led to the marketplace to be burned alive. Polycarp prayed earnestly to heaven. As the fire and flames grew hot, the executioners had to move away because the heat of the fire was too hot for them to stand near.

Even though the fire was so intense, the fire did not consume Polycarp's body. Polycarp sang praises to God in the middle of the flames while the burning of the wood spread a fragrance around. Astonished at the miracle but determined to put an end to Polycarp's life, the guards stuck spears into his body. There was so much blood that it put out the fire. It took many, many times for them to finally put Polycarp to death, but once he was dead they were finally able to burn his body.[1]

1.John Foxe and other eminent authorities, *Foxe's Christian Martyrs of the World* (Chicago: Moody Press), pp. 55-56.

Guided Instruction

42 Find Smyrna on the map on page 46 and double-underline it in green.

Revelation 2:8-11 Is any reproof (correction) given to the church at Smyrna? No

Wow! Are you amazed at how much Polycarp loved Jesus? Look at how he praised God even when he was being burned alive!

Now, let's find out more about the church at Smyrna.

Take a look at the large map on the wall behind the churches. Can you find the city of Smyrna? Great! Now look back at Revelation 2:8-11 and fill in the chart on the next page to show what Jesus says to the church in Smyrna. The first thing you need to fill in is the section that describes Jesus.

Next, from these same verses, fill in the section of the chart that says "Commendation to the Church." Remember a commendation is when someone praises you for something you did that was good. Look at the good things Jesus says about the church in Smyrna, and add those to your chart.

Look at Revelation 2:8-11. Is there any *reproof* (correction) given to the church at Smyrna?

No

Now, fill in the section that says "Warnings and Instructions to the Church." What is Jesus warning the church at Smyrna about? What should they do?

Fill in the last section on your chart that says "Promise to the Overcomers." WHAT does Jesus promise those who hang in there and are victorious?

43

JESUS' MESSAGES TO THE CHURCHES

Church at Smyrna

Description of Jesus

Revelation 2:8 The __first__ and the __last__, who was __dead__, and has come to __life__.

Commendation to the Church (Praise)

Revelation 2:9 I know your __tribulation__ and your __poverty__ (but you are __rich__), and the __blasphemy__ by those who say they are __Jews__ and are not, but are a __synagogue__ of __Satan__.

Reproof Given to the Church

Does Jesus point out anything they are doing wrong? __No__

Warnings and Instructions to the Church

Revelation 2:10 Do not __fear__ what you are about to __suffer__. Behold, the __devil__ is about to __cast__ some of you into __prison__, so that you will be __tested__, and you will have __tribulation__ for __ten__ days. Be __faithful__ until __death__, and I will give you the __crown__ of __life__.

Promise to the Overcomers

Revelation 2:11 He who __overcomes__ will not be __hurt__ by the __second__ __death__.

Guided Instruction

Read the selected verses to complete the message to the church at Smyrna.

43 On page 47, highlight the headings as you did for the message to Ephesus on page 35.

JESUS' MESSAGE TO THE CHURCHES
Church at Smyrna

Description of Jesus

Revelation 2:8 **The first and the last who was dead, and has come to life.**

Commendations to the Church (Praise) [yellow]

Revelation 2:9 **I know your tribulation and your poverty (but you are rich), and the blasphemy by those who say they are Jews and are not, but are a synagogue of Satan.**

Reproof Given to the Church [red]

Does Jesus point out anything they are doing wrong? **No**

Warnings and Instructions to the Church [pink]

Revelation 2:10 **Do not fear what you are about to suffer. Behold, the devil is about to cast some of you into prison, so that you will be tested, and you will have tribulation for ten days. Be faithful until death, and I will give you the crown of life.**

Promise to the Overcomers [green]

Revelation 2:11 **He who overcomes will not be hurt by the second death.**

Guided Instruction

44 Read the information on page 48, lead a discussion, and answer the questions.

Revelation 2:10-11 WHAT does Jesus promise the people of the church at Smyrna if they remain faithful until death?

I will give you the crown of life.

He who overcomes will not be hurt by the second death.

44

Isn't this awesome? Jesus doesn't have any reproof for the church at Smyrna. Was it a perfect church? Why do you think Jesus didn't have any correction for this church?

____

____

While we saw that Ephesus was a church that lost its first love, Smyrna could be characterized as a suffering church. They have already suffered tribulations and poverty, and now Jesus warns them they are about to be tested with more suffering. Some people will even be cast into prison and lose their lives.

Remember what we read about Polycarp? If people love Jesus so much that they are suffering for His sake, do they need reproving? Jesus doesn't need to correct this church because of the suffering it is going through. When we are willing to suffer and willing to obey, it proves the genuineness of our love for Jesus.

Look back at your chart to the description of Jesus. Why do you think Jesus describes Himself this way to the church of Smyrna? How would this description help those people who are suffering?

____

____

Don't you think it would be a comfort knowing that death didn't have a hold on Jesus if you knew you may be put to death for your faith? Thinking of Jesus as being dead but now alive would give you hope. We do not have to fear death because Jesus conquered it when He died and rose again!

Revelation 2:10-11 WHAT does Jesus promise the people of the church at Smyrna if they remain faithful until death? I will give you **the crown of life**.

He who overcomes **will not be hurt by the second death.**

WHAT does that mean? Look up and read Revelation 20:14. WHAT is the second death?

The lake of fire

If you are an overcomer, you will not be hurt by the lake of fire! The lake of fire is only for those who don't believe in Jesus. Believers in Jesus are not thrown into the lake of fire. They are saved from eternal death. They will live with Jesus forever (Revelation 20:6,13-15)!

Now ask yourself:

Are you willing to be a Polycarp? Do you love Jesus so much that you are willing to suffer and maybe even die for Him? ____________________

Have you ever suffered for your faith by being made fun of because you wouldn't do some of the things other kids do that you know are wrong or for saying you are a Christian? _____

Write what happened. ____________________

Have you seen the movie or read the book *The End of the Spear?* It's about the missionaries who gave their lives to share Christ. Would you be willing to serve God on the mission field if you knew it would cost your life?

____

Would you be willing to witness to someone who took the life of someone you loved? ____________________

Look up and read Matthew 5:10. WHAT are those who have been persecuted for the sake of righteousness? B l e s s e d!

Guided Instruction

Revelation 20:14 WHAT is the second death? The lake of fire

Read the information on page 49 and lead a discussion.

45 Look up and read Matthew 5:10.

WHAT are those who have been persecuted for the sake of righteousness? B l e s s e d!

Guided Instruction

Revelation 2:10 WHAT will we receive when we are persecuted? The crown of life

Discuss information in paragraph. You may want to make a crown of life with the kids in your class.

Practice saying the memory verse to a friend.

Revelation 2:10

Isn't this amazing! We will be blessed when we are persecuted. WHAT will we receive?

The ___crown___ of ___life___.

Make a crown out of some poster board and either draw and color some jewels on it or glue some play jewels from the craft store on it to remind you what the overcomer gets when he or she endures suffering.

Sometimes we are afraid to stand up for what we believe in. We are afraid to say no or to go against the crowd. We don't want to suffer or be hurt so we give in and compromise what we believe.

We need to remember that when we suffer, are made fun of, or left out because of what we believe, it is only a temporary situation, and it will never be more than we are able to handle. We do not need to fear. We need to trust God and do what He says is right.

God is in control of our situation. He knows everything that is happening to us! Sometimes God allows us to go through "the fire" to purify us and test our faith (James 1:2-4). He wants us to be perfect and complete—lacking in nothing!

Jesus reminded the church at Smyrna not to be afraid but to be faithful. We need to remember that. We need to hang in there and overcome so we will be blessed and receive the crown of life!

FOUR

(page 50)

46

THE SHARP, TWO-EDGED SWORD

You made an awesome discovery yesterday as you looked at Jesus' message to the suffering church of Smyrna. WHAT will we uncover today as we look at Jesus' message to the third church? Let's find out. Ask God to open your eyes to His truth, and then pull out your key word bookmark and turn to page 145.

Jesus' Messages to the Churches 51

Read Revelation 2:12-17 and mark the key words on your Observation Worksheet just like they are on your index card. Turn to page 139 if you have lost your card.

Don't forget to mark the pronouns!

To the angel of the church in Pergamum write

Jesus (or any description that refers to Jesus like *The One*)

I know Satan repent

He who has an ear, let him hear what the spirit says to the churches

To him who overcomes (or He who overcomes)

Don't forget to mark anything that tells you WHERE by double underlining the WHERE in green. And don't forget to mark anything that tells you WHEN by drawing a green clock 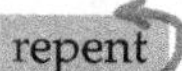 or green circle like this: ◯.

Read Revelation 2:12.

WHAT church is this message for?

Guided Instruction

Ask God to help you persevere as you study His Word today.

46 Turn to page 50 and read "The Sharp, Two-Edged Sword."

47 Turn to page 145 and read Revelation 2:12–17 aloud using your Observation Worksheet visual aid as students follow along and call out each key word. Then mark them together as we noted on p. 41.

To the angel of the church in Pergamum write (color orange)

Jesus (or descriptions like The One) (draw a purple cross and color the word yellow)

I know (underline in red and color it yellow)

Satan, devil (draw a red pitchfork)

Repent (draw a red arrow and color the word yellow)

He who has an ear, let him hear what the spirit says to the churches (color blue)

To him who overcomes (or he who overcomes) (color yellow)

WHERE (double-underline in green words that denote place)

WHEN (draw a green clock over words that denote time)

Guided Instruction

Read Revelation 2:12

WHAT church is this message for?
Pergamum

(page 145)

second death.'

47

12 "And to the angel of the church in Pergamum write:
The One who has the sharp two-edged sword says this:
13 'I know where you dwell, where Satan's throne is; and you
hold fast My name, and did not deny My faith even in the days
of Antipas, My witness, My faithful one, who was killed among
you, where Satan dwells.
14 'But I have a few things against you, because you have there
some who hold the teaching of Balaam, who kept teaching
Balak to put a stumbling block before the sons of Israel, to eat
things sacrificed to idols and to commit *acts of* immorality.
15 'So you also have some who in the same way hold the teaching of the Nicolaitans.

146 OBSERVATION WORKSHEETS

16 'Therefore repent; or else I am coming to you quickly, and I
will make war against them with the sword of My mouth.
17 'He who has an ear, let him hear what the Spirit says to the
churches. To him who overcomes, to him I will give *some* of the
hidden manna, and I will give him a white stone, and a new
name written on the stone which no one knows but he who
receives it.'

(page 51)

WHAT church is this message for? Pergamum

Now take a look at the next museum plaque. WHAT does it teach us about the city of Pergamum?

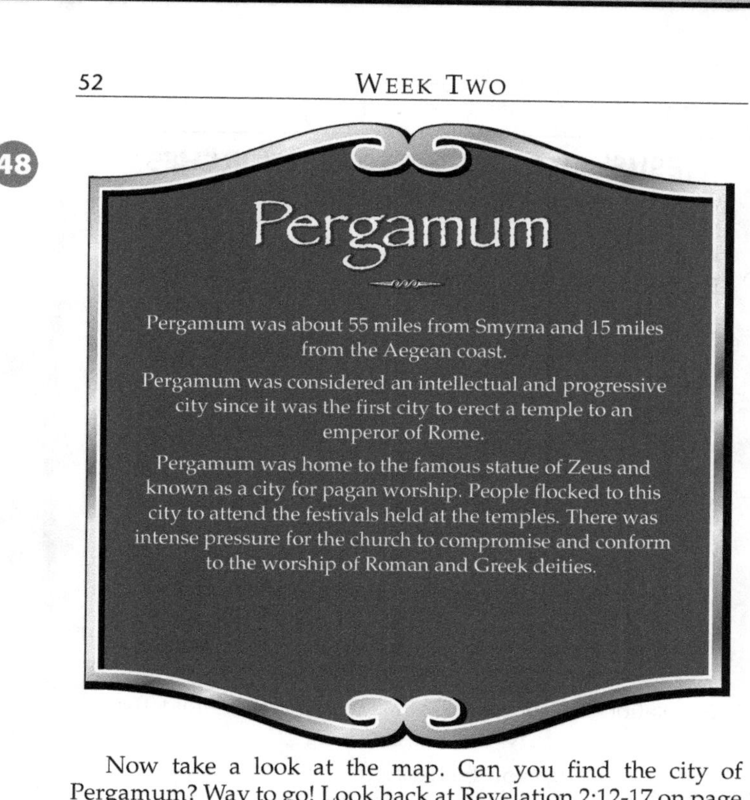

Now take a look at the map. Can you find the city of Pergamum? Way to go! Look back at Revelation 2:12-17 on page 145, and fill in the chart on the next page to show what Jesus says to the church in Pergamum.

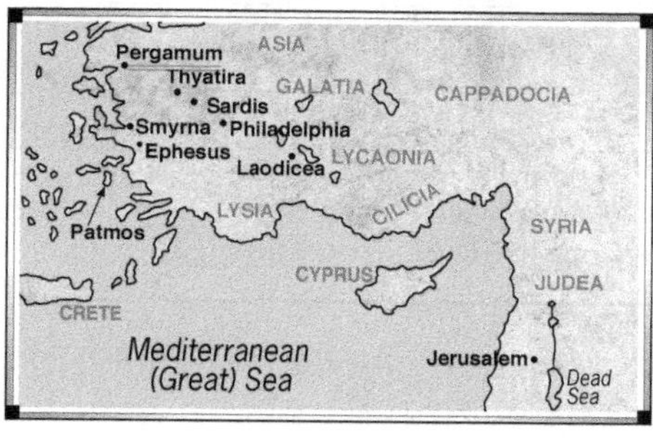

Guided Instruction

48 Read the plaque about Pergamum on page 52.

49 Locate Pergamum on the map and double-underline it in green.

Guided Instruction

50 Read the selected verses to complete the message to the church at Pergamum on page 53.

Highlight the headings as you did in the message to Ephesus on page 35.

JESUS' MESSAGES TO THE CHURCHES
Church at Pergamum

Description of Jesus

Revelation 2:12 **The One who has the sharp two – edged sword.**

Commendation to the Church (Praise) [yellow]

Revelation 2:13 **I know where you dwell, where Satan's throne is; and you held fast My name, and did not deny My faith.**

Reproof Given to the Church [red]

Revelation 2:14 **But I have a few things against you, because you have there some who hold the teachings of Balaam, who kept teaching Balak to put a stumbling block before the sons of Israel, to eat things sacrificed to idols and to commit acts of immorality.**

Revelation 2:15 Some who in the same way hold the teachings of the Nicolaitans.

Warnings and Instructions to the Church [pink]

Revelation 2:16 **Repent; or else I am coming to you quickly, and I will make war against them with the sword of My mouth.**

Promise to the Overcomers [green]

Revelation 2:17 **[He] who overcomes, to him I will give some of the hidden**

Jesus' Messages to the Churches 53

JESUS' MESSAGES TO THE CHURCHES

Church at Pergamum

Description of Jesus

Revelation 2:12 The One who has the sharp two-edged sword

Commendation to the Church (Praise)

Revelation 2:13 I know where you dwell, where Satan's throne is; and you held fast My name, and did not deny My faith.

Reproof Given to the Church (What they did wrong)

Revelation 2:14 But I have a few things against you, because you have there some who hold the teachings of Balaam, who kept teaching Balak to put a stumbling block before the sons of Israel, to eat things sacrificed to idols, and to commit acts of immorality.

Revelation 2:15 Some who in the same way hold the teachings of the Nicolaitans.

Warnings and Instructions to the Church

Revelation 2:16 Repent; or else I am coming to you quickly, and I will make war against them with the sword of My mouth.

Promise to the Overcomers

Revelation 2:17 [He] who overcomes, to him I will give some of the hidden manna, and I will give him a white stone, and a new name written on the stone which no one knows but he who receives it.

 Ephesus had lost their first love; Smyrna was a suffering church. WHAT do we learn about Pergamum? Pergamum had held fast to Jesus' name and did not deny their faith, but they had also allowed wrong teaching in the church. Do you think Jesus is happy about the false teaching? Look back on your chart at Jesus' warning.

WHAT does Jesus tell them to do? R e p e n t. That means to change what they are doing or else WHAT? Jesus will come quickly and make war with them with the sword of His mouth.

HOW is Jesus described on your chart? WHAT could this sword be? Let's find out by going to other passages of Scripture. When we compare Scripture with other Scripture, that's called *cross-referencing*. Always remember that *Scripture never contradicts Scripture.*

Look up and read Ephesians 6:17. WHAT is the sword of the Spirit? The Word of God

Now look up and read Hebrews 4:12.

WHAT do we learn about the Word of God? It is living and active and sharper than any two - edged sword, and piercing as far as the division of soul and spirit, of both joints and marrow, and able to judge the thoughts and intentions of the heart.

Isn't that awesome! God's Word is sharper than any two-edged sword. It is living and active! That's why it is so very important that you learn how to study the Bible for yourself! God tells us in 2 Timothy 2:15, "Be diligent to present yourself approved to God as a workman who does not need to be ashamed, accurately handling the word of truth."

God also tells us in Titus 1:9 that we are to hold fast the faithful word so we will be able to exhort (encourage, preach) in

Guided Instruction

manna, and I will give him a white stone, and a new name written on the stone which no one knows but he who receives it.

51 Read the information on page 54 and respond independently.

WHAT does Jesus tell them to do? Repent

That means to change what they are doing or else WHAT? Jesus will come quickly and make war with them with the sword of His mouth.

Ephesians 6:17 WHAT is the sword of the Spirit? The Word of God

Hebrews 4:12 WHAT do we learn about the Word of God? It is living and active and sharper than any two - edged sword, and piercing as far as the division of soul and spirit, of both joints and marrow, and able to judge the thoughts and intentions of the heart.

Guided Instruction

52 Read and discuss the information on pages 55-56. You may want to pass around some bread for the kids to eat the hidden manna and give them a white stone to show them what the overcomers will receive.

Practice saying the memory verse with a friend.

"But I have this against you, that you have left your first love. Therefore remember from where you have fallen, and repent and do the deeds you did at first; or else I am coming to you and will remove your lampstand out of its place—unless you repent."

Revelation 2:4-5

52

sound doctrine (healthy teaching) and to refute (expose) those who contradict (to speak against), which in this case would be exposing those who speak against the truth.

We have to be diligent to handle God's Word accurately and be very careful not to allow false teachers in the church like they did at Pergamum.

Are you willing to do that? Will you study God's Word so you can know the truth and expose those who aren't teaching the truth? ______________________

Do you think that wrong teaching might be why so many churches are having problems today? ______________
____

Will you measure everything—the movies you watch, the books you read, the friends you hang out with—by God's standard and if it doesn't measure up to what God says, will you continue to do those things? Write out what you will do. ______________________
____
____

All right! Now, WHAT does the overcomer receive this time? This time we see three things: hidden manna, a white stone, and a new name.

In the Old Testament (Exodus 16:31-35), manna was the bread from heaven that God fed the children of Israel in the wilderness, and it was also put into the Ark of the Covenant (or Testimony). In the New Testament, in John 6:31-35, we see Jesus is the bread of life. Overcomers get heavenly bread—the bread of life. They also get a white stone, which was used for voting when someone was tried for a crime by a court. The jurors would cast their vote to acquit the person of the crime by laying down a white stone. Isn't that awesome? Jesus acquitted us of our sins! A white stone was also used as an admission ticket to a banquet. Do you know of a banquet that Christians will attend in heaven? How about the marriage supper of the Lamb (Revelation 19:9)?

56 WEEK TWO

And overcomers receive a new name on the white stone. In Bible times a person's name was very significant because it showed the person's character and attributes. Overcomers receive a new name, one that identifies them with Jesus and shows the new life they have in Him.

Why don't you get a rock and paint it white to remind you that if you overcome, you are completely and totally accepted by Jesus and forgiven of your sins. You belong to Him and have a ticket into heaven!

You have done an awesome job and learned some very important truths today about suffering for what is right and teaching truth. Keep up the good work by practicing your memory verses so the truth will be hidden in your heart! Tomorrow we will discover what God says to the next church.

Guided Instruction

Guided Instruction

This is the final lesson for week two. Ask God to help you focus and understand His message.

53 Turn to page 56 and read "Do You Tolerate Sin?"

54 Turn to page 146 and read Revelation 2:18–29 aloud using your Observation Worksheet visual aid as students follow along and call out each key word. Then mark them together as we noted on p. 41.

To the angel of the church in Thyatira write (color orange)

Jesus (or titles that refer to Him like Son of God) (draw a purple cross and color the word yellow)

I know (underline in red and color yellow)

Deeds (draw and color green feet)

Love (draw and color a red heart)

Repent (draw a red arrow and color it yellow)

Satan (draw a red pitchfork)

He who has an ear, let him hear what the spirit says to the churches (color blue)

To him who overcomes (color yellow)

WHERE (double underline in green words that denote place)

WHEN (draw a green clock over words that denote time)

(page 56)

53

DO YOU TOLERATE SIN?

It's great to have you back at the museum again! Today we are going to find out what Jesus has to say to the next church. Are you surprised by what you have uncovered about these churches? Don't forget to pray! Now let's uncover Jesus' message to the fourth church.

Pull out your key word bookmark and turn to page 146. Read Revelation 2:18-29 and mark the key words listed on your Observation Worksheet just like they are on your index card. Turn to page 139 if you have lost your card.

Don't forget to mark the pronouns!

To the angel of the church in Thyatira write

Jesus (or any description that refers to Jesus, like *Son of God*)

(page 57)

I know deeds love repent

Satan

He who has an ear, let him hear what the spirit says to the churches

To him who overcomes (or He who overcomes)

Don't forget to mark anything that tells you WHERE by double underlining the WHERE in green. And don't forget to mark anything that tells you WHEN by drawing a green clock or green circle like this: ◯.

Read Revelation 2:18.

receives it.'

(page 146)

54

18 "And to the angel of the church in Thyatira write:
The Son of God, who has eyes like a flame of fire, and His
feet are like burnished bronze, says this:
19 'I know your deeds, and your love and faith and service and
perseverance, and that your deeds of late are greater than at
first.
20 'But I have *this* against you, that you tolerate the woman
Jezebel, who calls herself a prophetess, and she teaches and leads
My bond-servants astray so that they commit *acts of* immorality
and eat things sacrificed to idols.
21 'I gave her time to repent, and she does not want to repent of her
immorality.
22 'Behold, I will throw her on a bed *of sickness*, and those who

commit adultery with her into great tribulation, unless they
repent of her deeds.
23 'And I will kill her children with pestilence, and all the
churches will know that I am He who searches the minds and
hearts; and I will give to each one of you according to your
deeds.
24 'But I say to you, the rest who are in Thyatira, who do not
hold this teaching, who have not known the deep things of
Satan, as they call them—I place no other burden on you.
25 'Nevertheless what you have, hold fast until I come.
26 'He who overcomes, and he who keeps My deeds until the
end, TO HIM I WILL GIVE AUTHORITY OVER THE NATIONS;
27 AND HE SHALL RULE THEM WITH A ROD OF IRON, AS THE VESSELS OF
THE POTTER ARE BROKEN TO PIECES, as I also have received *authority*
from My Father;
28 and I will give him the morning star.
29 'He who has an ear, let him hear what the Spirit says to the
churches.'

Guided Instruction

Guided Instruction

Read Revelation 2:18 WHAT church is this message for? Thyatira

55 Read the plaque about Thyatira on page 57.

56 Find Thyatira on the map on page 58 and double-underline it in green.

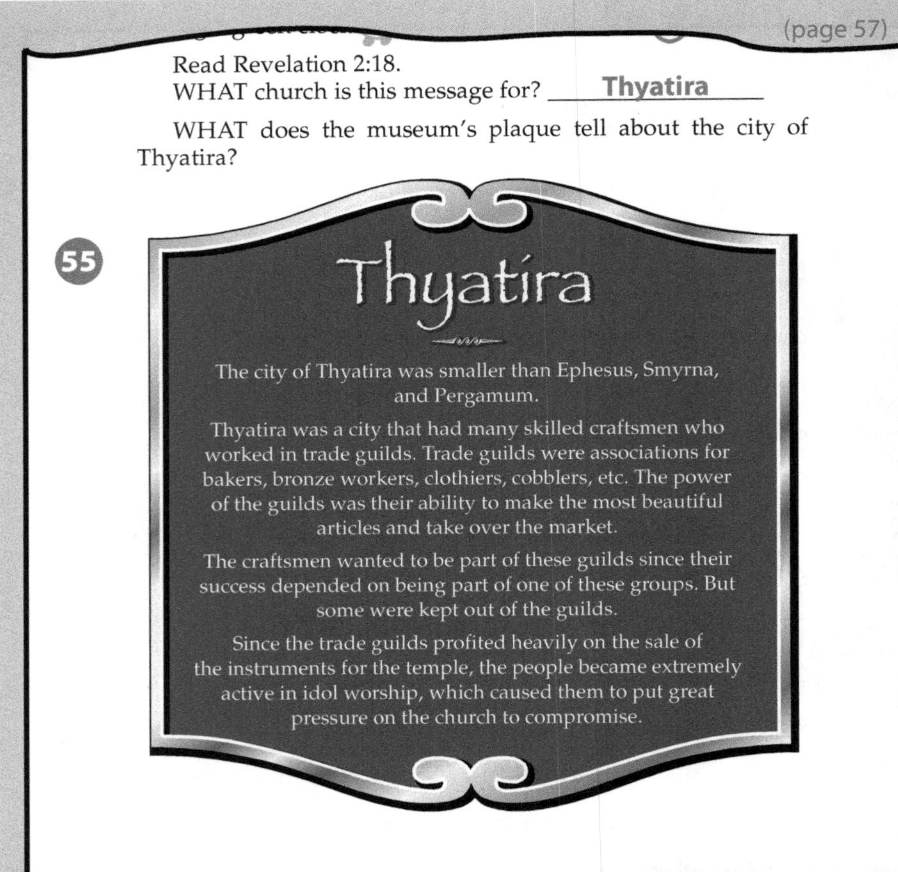

(page 57)

Read Revelation 2:18.
WHAT church is this message for? Thyatira

WHAT does the museum's plaque tell about the city of Thyatira?

55

Take a look at the large map on the wall. Can you find the city of Thyatira? All right! Now look back on page 146 at Revelation 2:18-29 and fill in the chart below to show what Jesus says to the church in Thyatira.

(page 58)

JESUS' MESSAGES TO THE CHURCHES

Church at Thyatira

Description of Jesus

Revelation 2:18 The __Son__ of __God__ who has __eyes__ like a __flame__ of __fire__, and His __feet__ are like __burnished__ __bronze__.

Commendation to the Church (Praise)

Revelation 2:19 I know your __deeds__, and your __love__ and __faith__ and __service__ and __perseverance__, and that your __deeds__ of __late__ are __greater__ than at __first__.

Reproof Given to the Church (What they did wrong)

Revelation 2:20 But I have this against you, that you __tolerate__ the __woman__ __Jezebel__,

who calls herself a __prophetess__, and she __teaches__ and __leads__ My __bond__-__servants__ __astray__, so that they __commit__ __acts__ of __immorality__ and __eat__ things __sacrificed__ to __idols__.

Warnings and Instructions to the Church

Revelation 2:21 I gave her __time__ to __repent__, and she does __not__ __want__ to __repent__ of her __immorality__.

Revelation 2:22 I will __throw__ her on a bed of __sickness__, and those who __commit__ __adultery__ with her into __great__ __tribulation__, __unless__ they __repent__ of her __deeds__.

Revelation 2:23 And I will __kill__ her children with __pestilence__, and all the __churches__ will know that I am He who __searches__ the __minds__ and __minds__ (hearts); and I will __give__ to each one of you according to your __deeds__.

Revelation 2:24-25 The __rest__ who are in Thyatira, who do __not__ hold this __teaching__, who have not known the deep things of __Satan__, as they call them—I place __no__ other __burden__ on __you__. Nevertheless what you have, __hold__ __fast__ __until__ I __come__.

Promise to the Overcomers

Guided Instruction

Read the selected verses to complete the message to the church of Thyatira on pages 58-59.

Highlight the headings as you did for the message to Ephesus on page 35.

JESUS' MESSAGES TO THE CHURCHES
Church at Thyatira

Description of Jesus

Revelation 2:18 **The Son of God who has eyes like a flame of fire, and His feet are like burnished bronze.**

Commendation to the Church (Praise) [yellow]

Revelation 2:19 **I know your deeds, and your love and faith and service and perseverance, and that your deeds of late are greater than at first.**

Reproof Given to the Church [red]

Revelation 2:20 **But I have this against you, that you tolerate the woman Jezebel, who calls herself a prophetess, and she teaches and leads My bond – servants astray, so that they commit acts of immorality and eat things sacrificed to idols.**

Warnings and Instructions to the Church [pink]

Revelation 2:21 **I gave her time to repent, and she does not want to repent of her immorality.**

Revelation 2:22 **I will throw her on a bed of sickness, and those who commit adultery with her into great tribulation, unless they repent of her deeds.**

Revelation 2:23 **And I will kill her children with pestilence, and all the**

Guided Instruction

churches will know that I am He who searches the minds and heart; and I will give to each one of you according to your deeds.

Revelation 2:24–25 The rest who are in Thyatira, who do not hold this teaching, who have not known the deep things of Satan, as they call them—I place no other burden on you Nevertheless what you have, hold fast until I come.

Promise to the Overcomers [green]

Revelation 2:26–28 He who overcomes, and he who keeps My deeds until the end, to him I will give authority over the nations; and he shall rule them with a rod of iron, as vessels of the potter are broken to pieces, as I also have received authority from My Father; and I will give him the morning star.

Read the selected Scripture verses to answer the questions on pages 60-63.

Ephesians 1:4 WHAT did God choose us to be before Him? Holy and blameless

1 Thessalonians 4:3 WHAT are we to abstain from? Sexual immorality

1 Thessalonians 4:4 WHAT are we to know how to do? Possess our own vessel in sanctification (purity) and honor.

1 Thessalonians 4:7 WHAT has God called us for? Sanctification

Romans 12:1 HOW are we to present our bodies? A living and holy sacrifice

(page 59)

Promise to the Overcomers

Revelation 2:26-28 He who overcomes, and he who keeps My deeds until the end, to him I will give authority over the nations; and he shall rule them with a rod of iron, as the vessels of the potter are broken to pieces, as I also have received authority from My Father; and I will give him the morning star.

60 WEEK TWO

Wow! Look at the good things Jesus says to the church in Thyatira. They are loving, serving, persevering, and their deeds are greater now than they were in the beginning. They are a growing church!

So WHAT are they doing wrong? They have allowed an evil woman in the church to teach and lead others into immorality. Immorality is a sin. It means to be intimate with someone you are not married to. They are tolerating sin in the church at Thyatira.

WHAT does God's Word have to say about what we are to be as believers in Jesus and how we are to live? Are we to allow sin in our lives and our church? Let's find out. Look up and read Ephesians 1:4.

WHAT did God choose us to be before Him?

Holy and blameless

Look up and read 1 Thessalonians 4:3-8.

1 Thessalonians 4:3 WHAT are we to abstain from?

Sexual immorality

1 Thessalonians 4:4 WHAT are we to know how to do?

Possess our own vessel in sanctification (purity) and honor.

1 Thessalonians 4:7 WHAT has God called us for?

Sanctification

WHAT does this word "sanctification" mean? The Greek word for sanctification is *hagiasmos*. It is pronounced like this: hag-ee-as-mos´. It means purity, holiness. God has called us to be pure and holy.

Look up Romans 12:1-2.

Romans 12:1 HOW are we to present our bodies?

A living and holy sacrifice

Romans 12:2 WHAT are we not to be?

Conformed to this world

Romans 12:2 HOW are we to be transformed?

By the renewing of our minds

That means we are not to be shaped into the world's mold. We're not to do the things the world says is okay but God tells us in His Word are wrong! We are to be different. We are to line ourselves up with what God's Word says is right.

WHAT does God say about sin in the church? Look up and read 1 Corinthians 5:7-13.

1 Corinthians 5:7 WHAT does Paul tell them to clean out?

Old leaven

Did you know that when the Bible talks about sin it sometimes uses leaven as a picture of sin? So WHAT is Paul really telling them to clean out? Sin

1 Corinthians 5:9 WHO does Paul tell them not to associate with?

Immoral people

1 Corinthians 5:11-13 Does Paul mean all immoral people, or is he talking about those who say they are believers in Jesus but are continuing in sin inside the church?

Those inside the church who say they are believers in Jesus but who continue in sin

Do you see WHY Jesus is upset with the church at Thyatira? They were a loving and growing people who were tolerating sin inside the church when they knew it was wrong and should clean it out.

Now think about your life.

Guided Instruction

Romans 12:2 WHAT are we not to be? Conformed to this world

Romans 12:2 HOW are we to be transformed? By the renewing of our minds

1 Corinthians 5:7 WHAT does Paul tell them to clean out? Old leaven

Did you know that when the Bible talks about sin it sometimes uses leaven as a picture of sin? SO WHAT is Paul really telling them to clean out? Sin

1 Corinthians 5:9: WHO does Paul tell them not to associate with? Immoral people

1 Corinthians 5:10–13 Does Paul mean all immoral people or is he talking about those who say they are believers in Jesus but are continuing in sin inside the church? Those inside the church who say they are believers in Jesus but who continue in sin

Guided Instruction

57 Go over the questions on page 62. Have students respond independently.

57

Have you allowed sin in your life? Are you doing things you know God says is wrong?

____

WHAT are you doing wrong?

____

Is your mind shaped by the world or transformed by God's Word?

____

WHAT kind of friends do you hang out with?

____

Are you tolerating sin by hanging out with friends who say they are believers in Jesus but have a lifestyle of sin?

____

Does the influence and pressure of your friends determine what you wear?

____

WHAT kinds of clothes do you and the kids in your group wear? Do you wear T-shirts with inappropriate messages or clothes that reveal too much?

____

Do you honor God with the way you dress, or do you just want to look cool and popular?

____

WHAT is your language and music like? Do your words and the words in your music glorify God?

____

So WHAT do you do if, after examining your heart, you discover you are like Thyatira, that you have tolerated sin in your life?

Look back at Revelation 2:22. WHAT did Jesus tell them to do?

Repent of her deeds

Go to God and confess what you are doing wrong. Change your mind about what you're doing, and then change your actions. Ask God to forgive you and help you do what He says is right!

First John 1:9 says, "If we confess our sins, He is faithful and righteous to forgive us our sins and to cleanse us from all unrighteousness."

Now look back at your chart. What does Jesus promise the overcomer? Authority over the nations. Wow! What does that mean? Look at Revelation 5:10 and Revelation 20:6. We are going to reign with Christ!

What about the morning star Jesus will give us? Look at Revelation 22:16.

WHO is the bright morning star? J e s u s

When you accept Jesus as your Savior, He comes into your heart and dwells with you. Isn't that awesome? We are given Jesus to be with us always!

58 Why don't you get a piece of cardboard and cut it out into the shape of a star. Cover it with aluminum foil to remind you, as an overcomer, Jesus will give you the morning star! You could also take an empty paper towel tube and make a scepter out of it to remind you that if you overcome you will reign with Christ!

Now don't forget to say your memory verse to a grown-up, to remind you of WHO is to be your first love. God loves you! When you sin, remember and repent. God will cleanse you from all your sins so you will be holy and blameless before Him!

Guided Instruction

Revelation 2:22 WHAT did Jesus tell those who commit adultery with Jezebel to do? Repent **of her** deeds

Revelation 22:16 WHO is the bright morning star? J e s u s

58 Give students the materials to make the Star shown on page 63.

Say the memory verse to a grown-up.

Good job! You have persevered and learned a lot about what God expects of His own children. Thank Him for this privilege.

If you are a classroom teacher you may want to give your students a quiz on their memory verse. There is also a quiz on Week Two on page 155 to check memory and understanding.

If you are a Sunday School teacher this is a great time to review the whole week by playing a game like *The Matching Game* on page 163.

Guided Instruction

WEEK 3

It is such a privilege to delve into the WORD of God. Ask God to lead you to clear understanding.

59 Turn to page 64 and read "Revelation 3" and "The Mystery—Genuine or Fake?"

60 Add the two new key words to your bookmark card and wall chart.

Seven Spirits (draw a purple cloud and color it yellow)

White garments (white robe) (color it yellow)

61 Copy the following key word markings (and the two above) above the heading for Revelation 3 on your Observation Worksheets.

To the angel of the church in Sardis write (color orange)

Jesus (any references to Him) (draw a purple cross and color the word yellow)

I know (underline red and color it yellow)

Repent (draw a red arrow and color the word yellow)

Deeds (draw and color green feet)

He who has an ear, let him hear what the spirit says to the churches (color blue)

To him who overcomes (color yellow)

3

59

REVELATION 3

This week as we begin our research on Revelation 3, we will finish up Jesus' last three messages to the churches in Asia. We'll also answer the question "Are you an overcomer?" Jesus has some pretty awesome promises for those who overcome (persevere and conquer), and we need to find out just what it takes to be an overcomer.

Are you ready to continue this great adventure? Okay! Grab your "sword of truth," warrior of God, and head back to the museum.

THE MYSTERY—GENUINE OR FAKE?

Welcome back to the resource room. Shhhhh! We don't want to wake Sam. You know how he loves messing up the craft supplies in the cabinets. Today we need to start our research by observing Revelation 3:1-6 and marking our key words. Don't forget to pray!

64

Are You an Overcomer? 65

Pull out your key word bookmark and add the two new key words to your index card.

60

seven Spirits (draw a purple cloud and color it yellow)

white garments (white robe) (color it yellow)

Turn to page 147. Read Revelation 3:1-6 and mark your new key words and the key words listed below on your Observation Worksheet just like they are on your index card. Turn to page 139 if you have lost your card.

Don't forget to mark the pronouns!

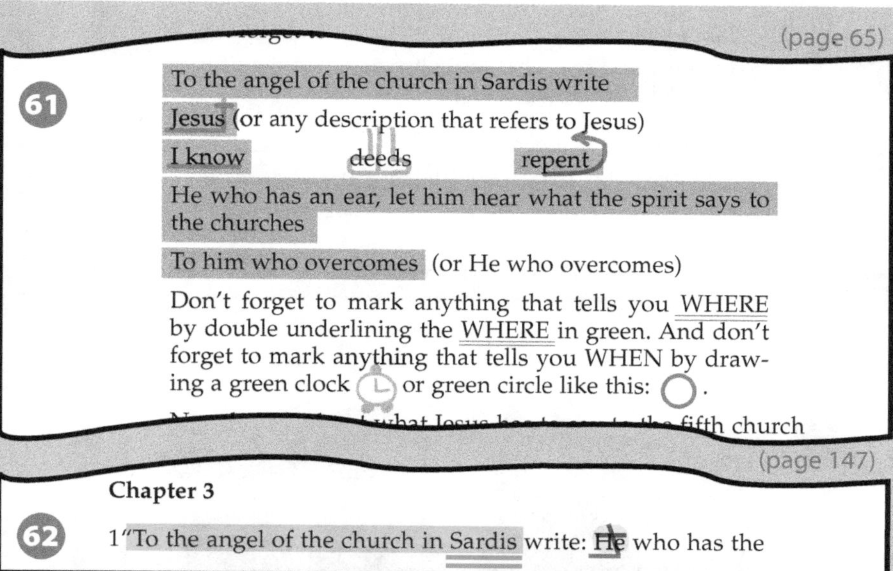

(page 65)

61

To the angel of the church in Sardis write

Jesus (or any description that refers to Jesus)

I know deeds repent

He who has an ear, let him hear what the spirit says to the churches

To him who overcomes (or He who overcomes)

Don't forget to mark anything that tells you WHERE by double underlining the WHERE in green. And don't forget to mark anything that tells you WHEN by drawing a green clock or green circle like this: ◯.

(page 147)

Chapter 3

62

1 "To the angel of the church in Sardis write: He who has the

63

148 OBSERVATION WORKSHEETS

seven Spirits of God and the seven stars, says this: 'I know
your deeds, that you have a name that you are alive, but you
are dead.
2 'Wake up, and strengthen the things that remain, which were
about to die; for I have not found your deeds completed in the
sight of My God.
3 'So remember what you have received and heard; and keep
it, and repent. Therefore if you do not wake up, I will come like a
thief, and you will not know at what hour I will come to you.
4 'But you have a few people in Sardis who have not soiled
their garments; and they will walk with Me in white, for they are
worthy.
5 'He who overcomes will thus be clothed in white garments;
and I will not erase his name from the book of life, and I will
confess his name before My Father and before His angels.
6 'He who has an ear, let him hear what the Spirit says to the
churches.'
7 "And to the angel of the church in Philadelphia write:

Guided Instruction

WHERE (double-underline in green words that denote place)

WHEN (draw a green clock over words that denote time)

62 Turn to page 147 and read Revelation 3:1–6 aloud using your Observation Worksheet visual aid as students follow along and call out each key word. Then mark them together as we noted on p. 41.

63 Now read again Revelation 3:1

Guided Instruction

WHAT church is this message for?
Sardis

64 Read the plaque on page 66 about Sardis.

65 Find Sardis on the map and double-underline it in green.

(page 65)

Now let's find out what Jesus has to say to the fifth church in Asia. Read Revelation 3:1.

WHAT church is this message for? Sardis

Looking at the museum's plaque, WHAT does it tell us about this city?

64

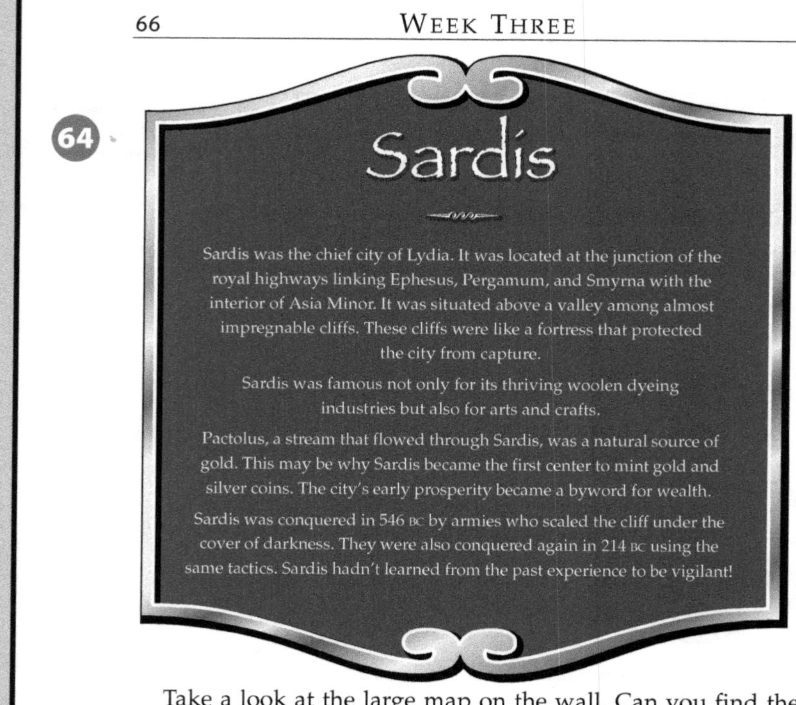

Take a look at the large map on the wall. Can you find the city of Sardis? Good work! Look back on page 147 at Revelation 3:1-6, and fill in the chart on the next page to show what Jesus says to the church in Sardis.

65

66

JESUS' MESSAGES TO THE CHURCHES

Church at Sardis

Description of Jesus

Revelation 3:1 He who has the __seven__ __Spirits__ of God and the __seven__ __stars__.

Commendation to the Church (Praise)

Revelation 3:4 But you have a __few__ __people__ in Sardis who have not __soiled__ their __garments__; and they will __walk__ with Me in __white__, for they are __worthy__.

Reproof Given to the Church (What they did wrong)

Revelation 3:1 I know your __deeds__, that you have a __name__ that you are __alive__, but you are __dead__.

Revelation 3:2 I have not found your __deeds__ __completed__ in the sight of My God.

Warnings and Instructions to the Church

Revelation 3:2 __Wake__ __up__, and __strengthen__ the things that __remain__, which were about to __die__.

Revelation 3:3 So __remember__ what you have __received__ and __heard__; and __keep__ it, and __repent__. Therefore if you do not __wake__ __up__, I will come like a __thief__, and you will not know at what __hour__ I will __come__ to you.

Promise to the Overcomers

Revelation 3:5 He who overcomes will thus be __clothed__ in __white__ __garments__; and I will not __erase__ his __name__ from the __book__ of __life__, and I will __confess__ his __name__ before My Father and before His angels.

Guided Instruction

66 Read the selected verses to complete the message to the church of Sardis.

JESUS' MESSAGES TO THE CHURCHES
Church at Sardis

Description of Jesus

Revelation 3:1 **He who has the seven Spirits of God and the seven stars.**

Commendation to the Church [yellow]

Revelation 3:4 **But you have a few people in Sardis who have not soiled their garments; and they will walk with Me in white, for they are worthy.**

Reproof Given to the Church [red]

Revelation 3:1 **I know your deeds, that you have a name that you are alive, but you are dead.**

Revelation 3:2 **I have not found your deeds completed in the sight of My God.**

Warnings and Instructions to the Church [pink]

Revelation 3:2 **Wake up, and strengthen the things that remain, which were about to die.**

Revelation 3:3 **So remember what you have received and heard; and keep it, and repent. Therefore if you do not wake up I will come like a thief, and you will not know at what hour I will come to you.**

Promise to the Overcomers [green]

Revelation 3:5 **He who overcomes will thus be clothed in white garments; and I will not erase his name from the book of life, and I will confess his name before My Father and before His angels.**

Guided Instruction

67 Read, discuss, and respond to the questions on page 68.

WHAT was the good thing that these few people had done? They had not soiled their garments.

WHAT do you think this means? They had not indulged in immorality; they remained pure.

68 Look up and read Revelation 19:7-8 to answer the questions.

HOW does the bride make herself ready? She is clothed in fine linen, bright and clean.

WHAT is the fine linen? It is the righteous acts of the s a i n t s

69 Discuss the rest of the information on page 68.

67 Did you notice that only a few people in the church at Sardis received praise from Jesus?

WHAT was the good thing that these few people had done?
They had not soiled their garments.

Write WHAT you think this means.
They had not indulged in immorality; they remained pure.

White symbolizes purity. Soiled means to stain or defile. These few people that had not soiled (stained) their garments were pure. They were not living a lifestyle of sin. They were following Jesus. They were true, godly believers in the church.

68 Look up Revelation 19:7-8.

HOW does the bride make herself ready?
She is clothed in fine linen, bright and clean.

WHAT is the fine linen?
It is the righteous acts of the s a i n t s.

So ask yourself: When I get dressed up, I look good on the outside, but what do I look like on the inside?

____

69 If you have a relationship with Jesus then there will be some purity in your life. WHAT did we learn about the church at Sardis—WHAT was wrong with this church? Jesus said they had a reputation of being alive, but they were dead.

The church looked like a good, solid church. It was well regarded in the city and neighborhood. But while it looked alive, it was really dead! The church at Sardis had a religion but not a relationship with Jesus Christ. With the exception of a few people, they were a church in name only. Their deeds were not completed.

70 Look up and read Titus 1:16

WHAT did these people profess?

To know God

Titus 1:16 WHAT did their deeds do?

Denied God

Titus 1:16 HOW are these people described?

Detestable, disobedient, and worthless

71
- So from what you have uncovered, do you think everyone who goes to church is a true believer in Jesus Christ?

  ____

- WHAT is your reputation like? Do you have a reputation of a true believer who walks and has a relationship with God? Or are you a believer in name only—you go to church but you don't spend time with God or do the things God tells you to do in His Word?

  Write out WHAT your reputation says about you and whether it is really true or not.

  ____

  ____

  ____

Remember, you may be able to fool other people, but you cannot fool God. Jesus told the people at the church at Sardis, "I know your deeds..."

72 Jesus knows our hearts. He sees us for what we are, not what we may pretend to be. Read 1 Samuel 16:7: "...for God

Guided Instruction

70 Look up and read Titus 1:16

WHAT did these people profess? To know God

WHAT did their deeds do? Denied God

HOW are these people described? Detestable, disobedient, and worthless

71 Discuss the questions that follow and respond in writing.

72 Read 1 Samuel 16:7.

"...for God sees not as man sees, for man looks at the outward appearance, but the Lord looks at the heart."

Guided Instruction

73 Return to Revelation 3 to answer the next two questions.

Revelation 3:2 WHAT did Jesus say?
Wake up and strengthen the things that remain.

Revelation 3:3 R e m e m b e r what you have received and heard; and keep it, and repent.

74 Read and discuss the rest of the information on page 70.

sees not as man sees, for man looks at the outward appearance, but the LORD looks at the heart."

HOW could the people at the Sardis church fix their problem? Could it be fixed?

73 Revelation 3:2 WHAT did Jesus say?

Wake up and strengthen the things that remain.

Revelation 3:3 R e m e m b e r what you have received and heard; and keep it, and repent.

74 Those R's must be really important because Jesus uses them over and over again! Remember and repent. Jesus wants us to turn to Him and change our ways. He is a God of second chances. The reason He warns us is because He loves us and wants us to return to Him.

WHAT will happen if the church doesn't wake up? Jesus will come like a thief. That's when it will be too late to change.

Remember: God is a God of love and forgiveness, but He is also a righteous God. Because of His righteousness, He must judge sin.

As we wrap up our research today, think about what you have learned. Ask yourself, Do I really believe or am I a Christian in name only? Do I have religion or a relationship with Jesus?

All right! You did great! What does the overcomer receive? He or she is clothed in white garments—that means the overcomer's sin will be covered by Christ's righteousness. Wow! And the overcomer's name will not be erased from the book of life. Did you know that only people whose names are not written in the book of life are thrown into the lake of fire (Revelation 20:15)? If we overcome, we do not need to fear because our names will be written in the book of life and we will live forever with Jesus.

75 Why don't you get some construction paper and notebook paper and make a book? On the front write "The Book of Life," and inside write your name to remind yourself that if you are an overcomer, your name will not be erased from the book!

Before we wake Sam and take him outside for a treat, let's uncover your new memory verse this week by looking at the Bible below. Cross out every third letter inside the Bible, and write the letters that are left (the ones that aren't crossed out) on the blanks underneath the Bible.

76

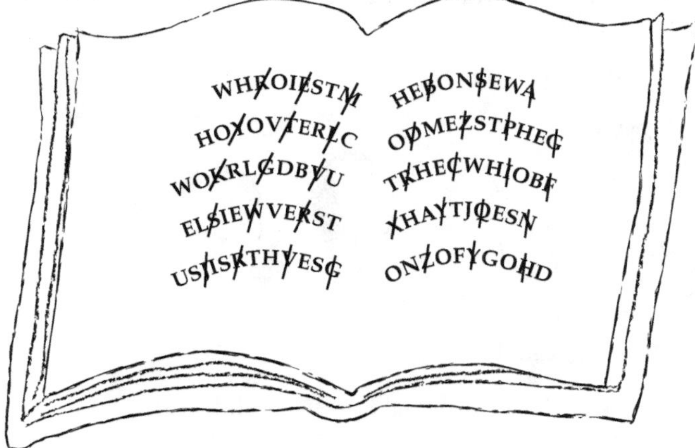

77 Who is the one who overcomes the world, but he who believes that Jesus is the Son of God?

1 John 5: 5

Great work! Now look up and read 1 John 5 in your Bible until you find the reference for this verse. Fill in the reference.

Don't forget to practice saying this verse three times in a row, three times every day this week!

Guided Instruction

75 Provide materials for students to make a book as instructed on page 71.

76 Find the memory verse by crossing out every third letter in the Bible shown on page 71.

77 Write the verse on the lines below and copy it to an index card.

Who is the one who overcomes the world but he who believes that Jesus is the Son of God?

1 John 5:5

Practice saying the memory verse three times, three times daily.

Guided Instruction

Ask God to clarify His message for you today.

78 Turn to page 72 and read "The Mystery—A Little Power."

(page 72)

78

THE MYSTERY—A LITTLE POWER

"Hey, Molly, isn't it cool that we get to see all the things Jesus has to say about the seven churches in Asia?" Max asked as he and Molly looked at the different models of the churches in the museum.

"It sure is. I am so amazed at how much I've learned. Look at how these models are designed to show what the churches were really like. I didn't notice it until we started doing our research. Isn't it awesome?"

"Just wait," Miss Kim said as she walked up. "After you finish your study on all seven churches, you and Max get to pick one church and design a model of it to show that church's strengths and weaknesses."

"That sounds like fun," Max replied. "Will all the kids who

visit the museum get a chance to create their own models of a church?"

"They sure will. After they finish they can either leave it here for our kids' display or they can take it home to remind them of what they've learned about Jesus and that specific church."

"I can't wait," Molly said. "Why don't we pray so we can uncover Jesus' message to the sixth church?"

Let's go, Bible detectives. Pray. Then turn to page 148. Pull out your key word bookmark and add the new key word listed to your index card.

those who dwell on the earth (color it green)

Read Revelation 3:7-13 and mark your new key word and the key words listed below on your Observation Worksheet just like they are on your index card. Turn to page 139 if you have lost your card.

Don't forget to mark the pronouns!

(page 73)

Don't forget to mark the pronouns!

79 To the angel of the church in Philadelphia write

Jesus (or any description that refers to Jesus)

I know deeds love Satan

He who has an ear, let him hear what the spirit says to the churches

To him who overcomes (or He who overcomes)

Don't forget to mark anything that tells you WHERE by double underlining the WHERE in green. And don't forget to mark anything that tells you WHEN by drawing a green clock or green circle like this: ◯.

Read Revelation 3:7.

WHAT church is this message for?

Philadelphia

Look at the museum's plaque on the next page to see WHAT it tells us about the city of Philadelphia.

(page 148)

churches.'

7 "And to the angel of the church in Philadelphia write:
80 He who is holy, who is true, who has the key of David,
who opens and no one will shut, and who shuts and no one
opens, says this:

8 'I know your deeds. Behold, I have put before you an open
door which no one can shut, because you have a little power,
and have kept My word, and have not denied My name.
9 'Behold, I will cause *those* of the synagogue of Satan, who
say that they are Jews and are not, but lie—I will make them
come and bow down at your feet, and *make them* know that I
have loved you.
10 'Because you have kept the word of My perseverance, I
also will keep you from the hour of testing, that *hour* which
is about to come upon the whole world, to test those who
dwell on the earth.

Guided Instruction

79 Add the new key word on page 73 to your bookmark, wall chart, and the margin beside Revelation 3:7 in the Observation Worksheets.

those who dwell on the earth (color it green)

To the angel of the church in Philadelphia write (color orange)

Jesus (and all references to Him) (draw a purple cross and color the word yellow)

I know (underline in red and color it yellow)

Deeds (draw and color green feet)

Love (draw and color a red heart)

Satan (draw a red pitchfork)

He who has an ear, let him hear what the spirit says to the churches (color blue)

To him who overcomes (color yellow)

WHERE (double-underline in green words that denote place)

WHEN (draw a green clock over words that denote time)

Read Revelation 3:7 WHAT church is this message for? Philadelphia

80 Turn to page 148 and read Revelation 3:7-13 aloud using your Observation Worksheet visual aid as students follow along and call out each key word. Then mark them together as we noted on p. 41.

Guided Instruction

81 Read the plaque on page 74 and find Philadelphia on the map. Double-underline it in green.

82 Turn to page 148 and reread Revelation 3:7–13 to complete the message to the church at Philadelphia.

(page 149)

dwell on the earth.

11 I am coming quickly; hold fast what you have, so that no one will take your crown.

12 'He who overcomes, I will make him a pillar in the temple of My God, and he will not go out from it anymore; and I will write on him the name of My God, and the name of the city of My God, the new Jerusalem, which comes down out of heaven from My God, and My new name.

13 'He who has an ear, let him hear what the Spirit says to the churches.'

14 "To the angel of the church in Laodicea write:

81

Philadelphia

Philadelphia was situated about 28 miles southeast of Sardis. It is believed that the founder of this city may have named it Philadelphia to show his love for his brother since the word "Philadelphia" in the Greek means brotherly love.

This district was an area of grapevine growing and wine production. It was a center for the worship of Dionysus, the god of wine and fertility. Religious festivals were a very big part of Philadelphia's culture.

Philadelphia was subject to many natural disasters. It was also called a city of earthquakes. Philadelphia was destroyed in the great earthquake of AD 17. Because of the natural disasters in this city, the church was familiar with unstable conditions.

82 Take a look at the large map. Can you find the city of Philadelphia? Good work! Now look back on page 148 at Revelation 3:7-13 and fill in the chart on the next page to show what Jesus says to the church in Philadelphia.

As you continue to fill out your chart, is anything missing?

WHAT section on your chart is blank? Reproof

JESUS' MESSAGES TO THE CHURCHES

Church at Philadelphia

Description of Jesus

Revelation 3:7 He who is holy, who is true, who has the key of David, who opens and no one will shut, and who shuts and no one opens.

Commendation to the Church (Praise)

Revelation 3:8 I know your deeds. Behold, I have put before you an open door which no one can shut, because you have a little power, and have kept My word, and have not denied My name.

Revelation 3:9 I will make them come and bow down at your feet, and make them know that I have loved you.

Reproof Given to the Church

Warnings and Instructions to the Church

Revelation 3:10 I also will keep you from the hour of testing, that hour which is about to come upon the whole world, to test those who dwell on the earth.

Revelation 3:11 I am coming quickly; hold fast what you have so that no one will take your crown.

Promise to the Overcomers

Revelation 3:12 He who overcomes, I will make him a pillar in the temple of My God, and he will not go out from it anymore; and I will write on him the name of My God, and the name of the city of My God, the new Jerusalem, which comes down out of heaven from My God, and My new name.

Guided Instruction

WHAT section on your chart is blank?
Reproof

JESUS' MESSAGES TO THE CHURCHES
Church at Philadelphia

Description of Jesus
Revelation 3:7 He who is holy, who is true, who has the key of David, who opens and no one will shut, and who shuts and no one opens.

Commendations to the Church [yellow]
Revelation 3:8 I know your deeds. Behold, I have put before you an open door which no one can shut, because you have a little power, and have kept My word, and have not denied My name.

Revelation 3:9 I will make them come and bow down at your feet, and make them know that I have loved you.

Reproof Given to the Church [red]

Warnings and Instructions to the Church [pink]
Revelation 3:10 I also will keep you from the hour of testing, that hour which is about to come upon the whole world, to test those who dwell on the earth.

Revelation 3:11 I am coming quickly; hold fast what you have so that no one will take your crown.

Promise to Overcomers [green]
Revelation 3:12 He who overcomes, I will make him a pillar in the temple of My God, and he will not go out from it anymore; and I will write on him the name of My God, and the name of the city of My God, the new Jerusalem, which comes down out of heaven from My God, and My new name.

Guided Instruction

83 Read and discuss the information on page 76. Let students respond independently.

84 Look up the selected Scripture verses to answer the questions on page 77.

Acts 1:8 HOW do we receive power? From the Holy Spirit

Acts 1:8 WHAT are we to do with this power? Be His witnesses

Ephesians 3:16 HOW is God going to strengthen us? With power through His Spirit in the inner man.

2 Corinthians 12:9

WHAT is sufficient for us? His Grace

HOW is God's power perfected? In our weakness

WHAT is dwelling in us? The power of Christ

(page 76)

83 Wow! Isn't that awesome? Another church that Jesus doesn't correct. Philadelphia is a faithful church. Jesus says the people there have kept His Word and not denied His name. He will make those of the synagogue of Satan bow down to them and know that He loves believers.

Wouldn't you want to be part of this Philadelphia church? They have an open door no one can shut. And they have power. WHAT is an open door—do you know? An open door is the opportunities that God gives us to serve Him and do things for Him, to tell others what we believe about Jesus.

WHAT are the opportunities that God has given you? HOW do you serve Him?

____

____

____

The name Christian means "little Christ." Is there any way you deny Christ's name in the way you live or the things that you do? ____ If you answered yes, tell what you do and how you can change.

____

____

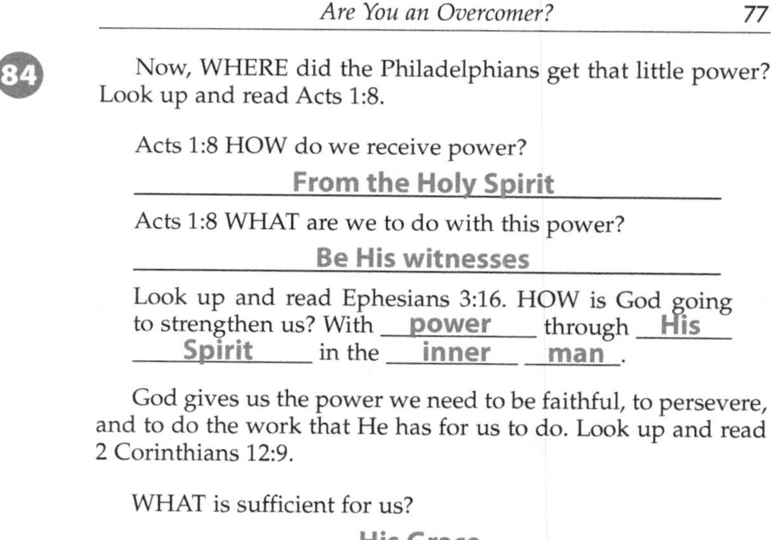

Are You an Overcomer? 77

84 Now, WHERE did the Philadelphians get that little power? Look up and read Acts 1:8.

Acts 1:8 HOW do we receive power?

From the Holy Spirit

Acts 1:8 WHAT are we to do with this power?

Be His witnesses

Look up and read Ephesians 3:16. HOW is God going to strengthen us? With power through His Spirit in the inner man.

God gives us the power we need to be faithful, to persevere, and to do the work that He has for us to do. Look up and read 2 Corinthians 12:9.

WHAT is sufficient for us?

His Grace

HOW is God's power perfected?

In our weakness

So even when we are weak we have WHAT dwelling in us?

The power of Christ

Or do

85 • Are you using the power God has given you? Or do you give up, thinking it is just too hard and you can't do it? ____________________________

Remember, you can't do it—but God can!

- Is there an open door God wants you to walk through? Will you obey? ____________________________
- Is there someone at school that you know who doesn't have a relationship with Jesus Christ? What's that person's name? _________. You need to tell him or her about Jesus. Could you invite your friend to church or to a Bible study? _________

78 WEEK THREE

As we close today, think about the faithfulness of the people at the Philadelphia church. God opens doors that no one can shut. You need to keep His Word by doing all He asks you to do. Even though testing may come, God has the power to see you through it. Hold fast and keep your eyes on Him!

If you overcome, Jesus will make you a pillar in the temple of God, and He will write the name of God, the name of the new Jerusalem, and His new name. You will have access to the city of God, the new Jerusalem. Your new name will identify you with Christ and will allow you entrance to the city of God. You will see God's face!

Why don't you take an empty paper towel tube and paint it to look like a pillar to remind you that if you hold fast and overcome you will enter the new Jerusalem.

Now don't forget to practice your memory verse. Way to go!

Guided Instruction

85 Discuss the remaining questions and respond independently.

86 Do the activity on page 78.

Guided Instruction

Isn't it great that God shares His thoughts with us? Ask Him to make you aware of things in your life you need to change.

87 Turn to page 78 and read "Are You Hot, Cold, or Lukewarm?"

88 Turn to page 149 and read Revelation 3:14-22 aloud using your Observation Worksheet visual aid as students follow along and call out each key word. Then mark them together as we noted on p. 41.

To the angel of the church in Laodicea write (color orange)

Jesus (draw a purple cross and color the word yellow)

I know (underline in red and color yellow)

Deeds (draw and color green feet)

Love (draw a red heart)

Repent (draw a red arrow and color the word yellow)

white garments (color yellow)

He who has an ear, let him hear what the spirit says to the churches (color blue)

To him who overcomes (color brown)

WHERE (double-underline in green words that denote place)

WHEN (draw a green clock over words that denote time)

(page 78)

87 **ARE YOU HOT, COLD, OR LUKEWARM?**

"Hey, guys!" Uncle Jake called out as he headed toward Max, Molly, and Miss Kim. "What's up?"

"Uncle Jake!" cried Max. "You made it back!"

"Sure did. I couldn't wait to get here and see how you like the museum so far. I know Miss Kim is getting you to do your research before you see the exhibits so that what you see won't spoil your joy of discovery."

"We love it!" Molly told Uncle Jake. "We've been working really hard on the seven churches. I never knew how important these letters are and how they pertained to us until we started taking them apart to see what Jesus said to each church."

"That's why I'm so proud of you and Max for being willing to go slow and really study God's Word. God loves us and wants us to be just like Jesus! Miss Kim told me you're going to be making a model of one of the churches. Have you started yet?"

Are You an Overcomer? 79

"Not yet," replied Max. "We have one more church to investigate before we can choose our church."

"Then I came at just the right time," Uncle Jake answered. "Making a model of one of the churches sounds like fun."

"But first," Molly said and smiled, "we have to get to work. Let's pray so we can understand Revelation 3 and Jesus' message to the seventh church. Miss Kim said this is a very important message for the church today."

Let's get started, Bible detectives. Pull out your key word bookmark and turn to page 149. Read Revelation 3:14-22 and mark the key words listed on your Observation Worksheet just like they are on your index card. Turn to page 139 if you have lost your card.

88 Don't forget to mark the pronouns!

To the angel of the church in Laodicea write

Jesus (or any description that refers to Jesus, like *The Amen*)

I know deeds love repent

white garments

He who has an ear, let him hear what the spirit says to the churches

To him who overcomes (or He who overcomes)

Don't forget to mark anything that tells you WHERE by double underlining the WHERE in green.

Turn to page 149. Read Revelation 3:14.

(page 149)

the churches.'

88

14 "To the angel of the church in Laodicea write:

150 OBSERVATION WORKSHEETS

The Amen, the faithful and true Witness, the Beginning of
the creation of God, says this:
15 'I know your deeds, that you are neither cold nor hot; I wish
that you were cold or hot.
16 'So because you are lukewarm, and neither hot nor cold, I
will spit you out of My mouth.
17 'Because you say, "I am rich, and have become wealthy,
and have need of nothing," and you do not know that you are
wretched and miserable and poor and blind and naked,
18 I advise you to buy from Me gold refined by fire so that
you may become rich, and white garments so that you may
clothe yourself, and *that* the shame of your nakedness will not
be revealed; and eye salve to anoint your eyes so that you may
see.
19 'Those whom I love, I reprove and discipline; therefore be
zealous and repent.
20 'Behold, I stand at the door and knock; if anyone hears My voice
and opens the door, I will come in to him and will dine with him,
and he with Me.
21 'He who overcomes, I will grant to him to sit down with Me

Observation Worksheets 151

on My throne, as I also overcame and sat down with My Father
on His throne.
22 'He who has an ear, let him hear what the Spirit says to the
churches.'"

Guided Instruction

Guided Instruction

WHAT church is this message to?
Laodicea

89 Read the plaque about Laodicea on page 80.

90 Find Laodicea on the map and double-underline it in green.

(page 79)

WHAT church is this message for?
Laodicea

Look at the museum's plaque to see WHAT it tells us about the city of Laodicea. Watch very closely as you read about this city. Look for how it goes with what Jesus tells them.

89

Laodicea

Laodicea was the chief city of the wealthy province of Phrygia. It was situated on the major east–west trade route.

The city had a large number of banks and was widely known not only for its vast wealth but also for clothes and carpets.

Laodicea was home to a medical school, which produced an eye salve.

For all its wealth and prominence, Laodicea lacked one vital resource: water. Water was piped in from hot springs much farther south and arrived lukewarm after traveling the distance in stone pipes.

Laodicea was destroyed in AD 60 by a devastating earthquake. It was reconstructed from the people's vast wealth.

Take a look at the large map on the wall. Can you find the city of Laodicea? All right! Now look back on page 149 at Revelation 3:14-22 and fill in the chart on the next page to show what Jesus says to the church in Laodicea.

90

ASIA
Pergamum
Thyatira
GALATIA
CAPPADOCIA
Sardis
Smyrna
Philadelphia
Ephesus
LYCAONIA
Laodicea
LYSIA
CILICIA
Patmos
SYRIA
CYPRUS
JUDEA
CRETE
Mediterranean (Great) Sea
Jerusalem
Dead Sea

As you continue to fill out your chart is anything missing? WHAT section on your chart is blank?

Commendation to the Church

91

JESUS' MESSAGES TO THE CHURCHES

Church at Laodicea

Description of Jesus

Revelation 3:14 The Amen, the faithful and true Witness, the beginning of the creation of God.

Commendation to the Church (Praise)

Reproof Given to the Church (What they did wrong)

Revelation 3:15 I know your deeds, that you are neither cold nor hot; I wish that you were cold or hot.

Revelation 3:16 Because you are lukewarm, and neither hot nor cold, I will spit you out of My mouth.

Revelation 3:17 You do not know that you are wretched and miserable and poor and blind and naked.

Warnings and Instructions to the Church

Revelation 3:18 I advise you to buy from Me gold refined by fire so that you may become rich, and white garments so that you may clothe yourself, and that the shame of your nakedness will not be revealed; and eye salve to anoint your eyes so that you may see.

Guided Instruction

Look at the chart on page 81. WHAT section is blank? Commendation to the Church

91 Read the selected verses to complete the chart on page 81.

JESUS' MESSAGES TO THE CHURCHES
Church at Laodicea

Description of Jesus

Revelation 3:14 The Amen, the faithful and true Witness, the beginning of the creation of God.

Commendation to the Church (Praise) [yellow]

None.

Reproof Given to the Church [red]

Revelation 3:15 I know your deeds, that you are neither cold nor hot; I wish that you were cold or hot.

Revelation 3:16 Because you are lukewarm, and neither hot nor cold, I will spit you out of My mouth.

Revelation 3:17 You do not know that you are wretched and miserable and poor and blind and naked.

Warnings and Instructions to the Church [pink]

Revelation 3:18 I advise you to buy from Me gold refined by fire so that you may become rich, and white garments so that you may clothe yourself, and that the shame of your nakedness will not be revealed; and eye salve to anoint your eyes so that you may see.

Guided Instruction

Revelation 3:19 Those whom I love, I reprove and discipline; Therefore be zealous and repent.

Revelation 3:20 Behold, I stand at the door and knock; if anyone hears My voice and opens the door, I will come in to him and will dine with him, and he with Me.

Promise to Overcomers [green]

Revelation 3:21 He who overcomes, I will grant to him to sit down with Me on My throne, as I also overcame and sat down with My Father on His throne.

Look up the selected verses to answer the questions on pages 82-84.

Revelation 3:15 WHAT did Jesus tell them their problem was? They were neither cold nor hot.

Revelation 3:16 They are lukewarm.

Read and discuss the information on page 82. Have students answer independently.

Revelation 3:19 Those whom I __love__, I __reprove__ and __discipline__; therefore be __zealous__ and __repent__.

Revelation 3:20 Behold, I stand at the __door__ and __knock__; if anyone __hears__ My voice and __opens__ the __door__, I will __come__ in to him and will __dine__ with him, and he with Me.

Promise to the Overcomers

Revelation 3:21 He who overcomes, I will grant to him to __sit__ down with Me on My __throne__, as I also __overcame__ and sat down with My __Father__ on His __throne__.

Isn't it sad? Jesus doesn't have any praise for the church at Laodicea.

Revelation 3:15 WHAT did Jesus tell them their problem was? __They were neither cold nor hot.__

Revelation 3:16 They are __lukewarm__

What Jesus is essentially saying to them is "I would rather you be hot—on fire—for Me, to be surrendered, totally committed, to love, obey, and be wholehearted in your devotion. Or be cold, to oppose Me. But do not be lukewarm—neutral, half-hearted, and complacent about being a Christian."

WHAT would it look like to be "hot" for Jesus?

___

Think about your friends. Are they hot, lukewarm, or cold?

___

And WHAT about you? WHERE do you fit? ___

___

When we are lukewarm we are blind to our true condition. The church at Laodicea is deceived into thinking they are something they aren't. They have religion but no relationship with Jesus Christ.

Revelation 3:16 WHAT is Jesus going to do with them?

Spit them out of His mouth

That word "spit" in the Greek is *emeo,* pronounced em-eh´-o, and it means to vomit. Jesus wants to vomit this church out of His mouth. That doesn't sound very good, does it? Remember what you learned about the water when it reached Laodicea? It was lukewarm. Lukewarm water makes you want to vomit when you drink it.

Did you notice how this very wealthy city thought they were rich but Jesus tells them they are poor?

WHY do you think He tells them they are poor?

____

Look up and read Colossians 2:2.

WHERE does our wealth come from?

The full assurance of the mystery of God—Christ

Look up and read 1 Timothy 6:17.

WHAT does Paul tell Timothy to instruct those who are rich not to do? **Not to be conceited**

WHAT does he tell them to fix their hope on?

God

WHAT does the apostle Paul tell us God will do?

He will richly supply us with all things to enjoy.

Because Laodicea was wealthy, the people thought they had it all together. But they had put their hope in material things

Guided Instruction

Revelation 3:16 WHAT is Jesus going to do with them? **Spit them out of His mouth**

WHY does Jesus tell them they are poor? ***Answer independently after discussion.***

Colossians 2:2

WHERE does our wealth come from? **The full assurance of the mystery of God—Christ**

1 Timothy 6:17

WHAT does Paul tell Timothy to instruct those who are rich not to do? **Not to be conceited**

WHAT does he tell them to fix their hope on? **God**

WHAT does the apostle Paul tell us God will do? **He will richly supply us with all things to enjoy.**

Guided Instruction

Revelation 3:18-19

WHAT does Jesus tell them to do? Buy gold refined by fire, white garments to clothe yourself, and eye salve to anoint your eyes so you can see. Be zealous and repent.

Revelation 3:20

WHERE is Jesus? Standing at the door of our hearts

Lead a discussion and answer the questions independently.

rather than the God of all hope. They were blind. Was there any hope for this church?

Yes! That's why Jesus sends this letter—to give them a chance to change. Jesus tells them, "Those whom I love, I reprove and discipline."

Revelation 3:18-19 WHAT does Jesus tell them to do?

Buy gold refined by fire, white garments to clothe yourself, and eye salve to anoint your eyes so you can see. Be zealous and repent.

Revelation 3:20 WHERE is Jesus?

Standing at the door of our hearts

Isn't that awesome? Jesus is waiting for the people to open the door and let Him come in. Amazing! The Ruler of the universe loves them so much He wants them to sit down on His throne with Him!

- HOW about you? Do you have a relationship with Jesus? Have you opened the door and invited Him into your life? Describe it.

  ____

  ____

- Are you willing to be hot? Are you willing to surrender your life totally to Him? Will you make a decision to put Him first in everything?

  ____

Remember: If you are lukewarm, He will vomit you out of His mouth!

If you haven't invited Jesus into your life and you want to, the first thing you need to do is believe that Jesus is our Savior, that He is God's Son, that He is God, and that He lived a perfect

Are You an Overcomer? 85

life without sin, and that He died on a cross to pay for our sins. Then He was buried, and God raised Him from the dead.

92 You also have to know you are a sinner and be willing to confess your sins to God and turn away from them. You have to be willing to turn your entire life over to God to follow Jesus.

You can pray a prayer like this:

Thank You, God, for loving me and sending Your Son Jesus Christ to die for my sins. I am sorry for the things I have done wrong. I am repenting—changing my mind about my sins. Sin is wrong. I don't want to do things my way any more. I want to receive Jesus Christ as my Savior. Now I turn my entire life over to You. Amen.

If you prayed this prayer then you are part of God's family! You are God's child, and Jesus and the Holy Spirit will come to live in you (John 14:23). You now have God's power!

So why don't you go back to the prayer just mentioned and write out today's date—the month, day, and year—next to the "amen" to remind you of the day God saved you from your sins.

Now that you have become part of God's family, you will want to share this great news by telling others (confessing with your mouth) that you believe in Jesus Christ and are now a child of God.

Way to go! We are so very proud of you! You are an overcomer, and Jesus invites you to sit down with Him on His throne. Awesome! You are going to rule with Christ! Draw a picture of you ruling with Jesus on His throne to remind you of this promise!

Guided Instruction

92 Lead students through the prayer on page 85.

93 Draw a picture of you ruling with Jesus.

Say your memory verse to a friend (Teacher Guide page 83).

Guided Instruction

Ask God to instill His instruction in your heart.

94 Turn to page 86 and read "The Seven Churches."

95 Match each church with the description below.

1. Ephesus	e. endured, didn't allow false teachers but lost their first love
2. Smyrna	c. suffering church—no reproof
3. Pergamum	f. held fast to Jesus' name, did not deny their faith but allowed wrong teaching in the church
4. Thyatira	g. growing church, loving, serving, persevering but tolerated sin in the church (the evil woman)
5. Sardis	b. reputation for being alive but actually dead, had religion but no relationship, a few believers didn't soil their garments
6. Philadelphia	d. faithful church—little power—open door for gospel, no reproof
7. Laodicea	a. lukewarm—vomit out of mouth—no praise

86 WEEK THREE

94

THE SEVEN CHURCHES

Hey, it's great to have you back at the museum! As we head over to the resource room today, we are going to see how much we remember about the seven churches. Remember that these messages aren't just for the seven churches in Asia; they're also for the church today. God put these messages in His Word so that we can apply them to our lives and live the way He wants us to live.

Don't forget to pray.

Match each church below with the correct description of that church in the column next to it.

95

1. e Ephesus
2. c Smyrna
3. f Pergamum
4. g Thyatira
5. b Sardis
6. d Philadelphia
7. a Laodicea

a. Lukewarm—vomit out of mouth—no praise
b. Reputation for being alive but actually dead, had religion but no relationship, a few believers didn't soil their garments
c. suffering church—no reproof
d. faithful church—little power—open door for gospel, no reproof
e. endured, didn't allow false teachers but lost their first love
f. held fast to Jesus' name, did not deny their faith but allowed wrong teaching in the church
g. growing church, loving, serving, persevering but tolerated sin in the church (the evil woman)

96 All right! Now ask yourself: Are the things Jesus praised the churches for seen in my life? Am I willing to suffer for Jesus? Do I need correction? Is there anything in my life I need to change? Do any of Jesus' warnings apply to me? Then go to God and ask Him to forgive you wherever you have fallen short and to help you change the things that need to be changed.

Remember the lessons you have learned from these churches: to stand firm in trials, to remain on fire for Jesus, to love Jesus and others, to teach the truth, to walk through His open door using the opportunities He has given you, to share the gospel, to keep growing in your relationship with Jesus, and to be faithful to Him!

And don't forget to practice your memory verse.

Tomorrow we will find out more about being an overcomer!

Let's have some fun now that we have completed the seven churches. Max, Molly, and Uncle Jake are each going to work on designing their models of the seven churches. You can make a model, too! Just follow the instructions below.

97

JUST FOR FUN

You'll need some construction paper, scissors, glue, markers, colored pencils or crayons, and a small shoebox.

Take the lid off the shoebox and cover it by gluing construction paper on it. Turn the shoebox upside down so that the bottom of the shoebox is facing up. Make a roof for your church with one to two pieces of construction paper, depending on how long your shoebox is. If you need two pieces of paper, glue them together first. Then fold your construction paper in half and fold under about ½" to glue the roof to the flat bottom of the shoebox.

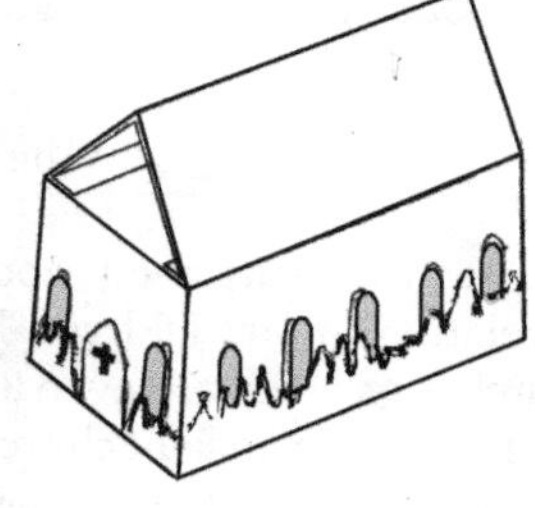

Next, draw or cut out a door on one end of the box. Put windows on both sides of the box.

Now decorate your church by showing the characteristic of the church you've chosen. For example, if you are making the church at Laodicea you could draw a picture of Jesus standing outside the front door and knocking. Use markers, colored pencils, or crayons, and whatever else you want. Be creative and have fun!

Guided Instruction

96 Read and discuss the rest of the information.

97 Supply materials for students to make the model on page 87.

Guided Instruction

Ask God to enter your heart and mind today. He will make His Word clear to you.

98 Turn to page 88 and read "What Does It Take To Be An Overcomer?"

99 Read the selected verses to answer the questions on pages 89-90.

1 John 5:4

WHAT overcomes the world? Whatever is born of God

WHAT is the victory that has overcome the world? Our faith

1 John 5:5

WHO is the one who overcomes the world? He who believes that Jesus is the Son of God

Lead a discussion about the meaning of becoming an overcomer. Respond to the questions independently.

(page 88)

98

WHAT DOES IT TAKE TO BE AN OVERCOMER?

"Hey, Max, I really like your church," Molly said as she looked over Max's model. "It is so cool the way you put the flames around the bottom of the church to show the fire of persecution going on at the church of Smyrna."

"I like yours, too, Molly, especially the way you've drawn Jesus with a heart on His chest, reminding us that He is to be our first love."

"Hey, you two, what about mine?" Uncle Jake smiled. "How do you like the water surrounding the church at Laodicea with Jesus standing at the door and knocking, waiting to be invited in."

"It's awesome, Uncle Jake. This has been so much fun," Max replied. "We'll have to bring mom and dad by so they can see our handiwork."

Miss Kim walked up to admire their churches. "These look great! Let's put them in our display area. Then we have one more very important thing to research before we wrap up Jesus' messages to the churches."

Now that the kids have set up their churches and cleaned up the area, let's pray so we can get to work.

Are You an Overcomer? 89

Are you surprised about all you have discovered in Revelation so far? Did you know that each one of these seven churches received all seven letters? Jesus not only had a message for these seven ancient churches, but these messages are also for the church today! Remember Revelation promises us a blessing if we read, hear, and heed the words of the prophecy.

Let's find out what it takes to be an overcomer, to be able to conquer and prevail.

First let's do a cross-reference to find out what we can learn about overcomers.

99 Look up and read 1 John 5:4-5.

1 John 5:4 WHAT overcomes the world?

Whatever is born of God

WHAT is the victory that has overcome the world?

Our faith

1 John 5:5 WHO is the one who overcomes the world?

He who believes that Jesus is the Son of God

(page 89)

So, from looking at these verses, is every believer (someone who has accepted Jesus Christ as his or her Savior) an overcomer?

____

Can you be a genuine Christian and not be an overcomer? ________ WHY or WHY not?______________

____

100 Look up and read 1 John 3:7-10.

1 John 3:7 WHAT is the one who practices righteousness?

He is righteous.

1 John 3:8 WHAT is the one who practices sin?

He is of the devil.

1 John 3:9 WHAT do you see about the one who is born of God?

He does not practice sin.

1 John 3:10 HOW is it obvious we are children of God?

We practice righteousness and love our brother.

101 Look up and read Titus 1:16.

WHAT do they profess to know?

God

WHAT do their deeds do?

They deny God.

While we are saved by faith in Jesus Christ (Ephesians 2:8), what we do (our deeds) shows what we really believe. Yes, believers in Jesus still sin, but a child of God cannot continue in (practice) sin, doing the same sin over and over again. If we are genuine believers in Jesus Christ, then there should be a change in us. The things we do should show we believe in Him.

Jesus has overcome this world, and when we accept Him we are born of God and become overcomers. We receive His power to overcome anything big or small—being left out of a group of friends, standing up for what we believe in, being called names, practicing sin such as gossiping, stealing, or cussing.

Jesus gives us the power to overcome hurt, suffering, and hardships, as well as the giving up of our lives if we should be called to stand for Him. Those who truly belong to Jesus are overcomers. They overcome the world because of their faith!

Remember Jesus is coming soon and His reward is with Him (Revelation 22:12)!

Now let's review all the things Jesus promises the overcomers. In the following chart fill in the blanks and draw a picture of what the overcomer receives to help you remember Jesus' promises. You can look back in your book if you need to.

Guided Instruction

100 Look up and read 1 John 3:7-10

1 John 3:7 WHAT is the one who practices righteousness? He is righteous.

1 John 3:8 WHAT is the one who practices sin? He is of the devil.

1 John 3:9 WHAT do you see about the one who is born of God? He does not practice sin.

1 John 3:10

HOW is it obvious we are children of God? We practice righteousness and love our brother.

101 Look up and read Titus 1:16

Titus 1:16 WHAT do they profess to know? God

WHAT do their deeds do? They deny God.

Guided Instruction

102 Complete the chart on page 91 and draw a picture of what the overcomer receives to help you remember Jesus' promises.

Ephesus Eat of the tree of life

Smyrna Will not be hurt by the second death

Pergamum Hidden manna, white stone, and a new name

Thyatira Authority over the nations. I will give him the morning star.

Sardis Clothed in white garments, will not erase his name from the book of life

Philadelphia I will make him a pillar in the temple, the name of My God, the name of the new Jerusalem, and My new name

Laodicea Sit down with Jesus on His throne

Practice saying the memory verse with a friend.

Great job! You have persevered and seen God's judging of the churches. What an awesome privilege!

If you are a classroom teacher you may want to give your students a quiz on their memory verse. There is also a quiz on Week Three on page 156 to check memory and understanding.

If you are a Sunday School teacher this is a great time to review the whole week by playing a game like *The Drawing Game* on page 162.

Are You an Overcomer? 91

Promises to the Overcomers

Ephesus	Smyrna
Eat of the tree of life	Will not be hurt by the second death
Pergamum	**Thyatira**
Hidden manna, white stone, and a new name	Authority over the nations. I will give him the morning star
Sardis	**Philadelphia**
Clothed in white garments, will not erase his name from the book of life.	I will make him a pillar in the temple, the name of My God, the name of the new Jerusalem, and My new name.
Laodicea	
Sit down with Jesus on His throne	

Great artwork! Hang on tight because next week you are going to get a glimpse into heaven. That is going to be so cool! Don't forget to say your memory verse to a grown-up this week.

4

REVELATION 4–5

It's great to have you back at the museum! Last week you made some amazing discoveries about the seven churches and being an overcomer. Are you ready to uncover the next mystery in Revelation?

This week you are going to get a glimpse into heaven to reveal WHAT is in heaven and WHO is worthy. Doesn't that sound like fun? Let's head back to the resource room so we can find out WHAT John sees next.

103

WHO IS WORTHY?

"Hey, Molly!" Max called out. "Look at Sam."

"How did he end up with those little pom-pom balls on his nose?" Molly asked as she tried hard not to burst into laughter at Sam's new look.

Max tried to answer as Sam started shaking his head and sneezing. "Someone must have spilled a little glue next to some of the craft supplies. Sam was obviously sniffing for clues inside the cabinet and ended up like this."

92

Guided Instruction

WEEK 4

God is taking you deeper into His mysteries. Ask Him to give you clarity and focus.

103 Turn to page 92 and read "Revelation 4-5" and "Who is Worthy?"

Guided Instruction

104 Add the new key word markings shown on page 93 to your bookmark and wall chart and above the title Revelation 4 on page 151.

God (draw a purple triangle and color it yellow)

I looked (I saw) (color it blue)

Throne (draw and color a blue throne)

Worthy (color it purple)

Worship (circle in purple and color it blue)

Add these key words to the margin.

Seven Spirits of God (or Spirit) (draw a purple cloud and color it yellow)

White garment (white robes) (color it yellow)

WHERE (double-underline in green words that denote place)

WHEN (draw a green clock over words that denote time)

Just as Max finished his sentence, Uncle Jake and Miss Kim walked in and stopped in their tracks when they saw Sam running around the room trying to shake off his added whiskers.

"Oh, no," cried Miss Kim. "What happened to Sam?"

Max grinned as he tried to catch Sam. "He's been sniffing out clues that happened to have a little glue on them. Come on, Sam. Come here, boy. Let's get you cleaned up so we can uncover our next mystery."

Now that Sam has calmed down and gotten rid of his pom-poms, let's pray so we can get started uncovering the clues for Revelation 4. Let's mark our key words. Pull out your key word bookmark and add the new key words to your index card.

104 God (draw a purple triangle and color it yellow)

I looked (I saw) (color it blue)

throne (draw and color a blue throne)

worthy (color it purple)

worship (circle in purple and color blue)

Turn to page 151 and read Revelation 4. Mark your new key words and the key words listed below on your Observation Worksheet just like they are on your index card. Turn to page 139 if you have lost your card.

seven Spirits of God (or Spirit) white garments (white robes)

Don't forget to mark the pronouns!

Mark anything that tells you WHERE by double-underlining the WHERE in green. And don't forget to mark anything that tells you WHEN by drawing a green clock or draw a green ◯. Keep your eyes open. There is a very important time phrase in this chapter. Did you find it?

(page 151)

Chapter 4

 1 After these things I looked, and behold, a door *standing* open
in heaven, and the first voice which I had heard, like *the sound*
of a trumpet speaking with me, said, "Come up here, and I will
show you what must take place after these things."
2 Immediately I was in the Spirit; and behold, a throne was
standing in heaven, and One sitting on the throne.
3 And He who was sitting *was* like a jasper stone and a
sardius in appearance; and *there was* a rainbow around the
throne, like an emerald in appearance.
4 Around the throne *were* twenty-four thrones; and upon
the thrones *I saw* twenty-four elders sitting, clothed in white
garments, and golden crowns on their heads.
5 Out from the throne come flashes of lightning and sounds
and peals of thunder. And *there were* seven lamps of fire

152 OBSERVATION WORKSHEETS

burning before the throne, which are the seven Spirits of
God;
6 and before the throne *there was something* like a sea of
glass, like crystal; and in the center and around the throne,
four living creatures full of eyes in front and behind.
7 The first creature *was* like a lion, and the second creature
like a calf, and the third creature had a face like that of a
man, and the fourth creature *was* like a flying eagle.
8 And the four living creatures, each one of them having six
wings, are full of eyes around and within; and day and night
they do not cease to say,
"HOLY, HOLY, HOLY *is* THE LORD GOD, THE ALMIGHTY, WHO WAS AND
WHO IS AND WHO IS TO COME."
9 And when the living creatures give glory and honor and

Guided Instruction

105 Read all of Revelation 4 aloud using your Observation Worksheet visual aid as students follow along and call out each key word. Then mark them together as we noted on p. 41.

Guided Instruction

(page 153)

9 And when the living creatures give glory and honor and
thanks to Him who sits on the throne, to Him who lives
forever and ever,
10 the twenty-four elders will fall down before Him who sits
on the throne, and will worship Him who lives forever and
ever, and will cast their crowns before the throne, saying,
11 "Worthy are You, our Lord and our God, to receive glory and

honor and power; for You created all things, and because of
Your will they existed, and were created."

106 All right! Now let's discover our memory verse this week by looking at the crowns the 24 elders have cast before the throne. On each crown there is a number and a letter. Under the drawing below are blanks for this week's verse with a number under each blank. Find the letter that matches the number in the crowns and write that letter on the blank to solve your memory verse this week.

W o r t h y   a r e   y o u   o u r
2 22 10 24 12 14   5 10 19   14 22 15   22 15 10

L o r d   a n d   o u r   G o d,   t o
17 22 10 23   5 20 23   22 15 10   1 22 23   24 22

r e c e i v e   g l o r y   a n d
10 19 3 19 9 21 19   1 17 22 10 14   5 20 23

h o n o r   a n d   p o w e r;
12 22 20 22 10   5 20 23   4 22 2 19 10

f o r   y o u   c r e a t e d   a l l
8 22 10   14 22 15   3 10 19 5 24 19 23   5 17 17

t h i n g s   a n d   b e c a u s e
24 12 9 20 1 16   5 20 23   18 19 3 5 15 16 19

o f   y o u r   w i l l   t h e y
22 8   14 22 15 10   2 9 17 17   24 12 19 14

e x i s t e d,   a n d   w e r e
19 7 9 16 24 19 23   5 20 23   2 19 10 19

c r e a t e d.
3 10 19 5 24 19 23

Revelation 4:11

Now read Revelation 4 and locate the correct verse number. Way to go! You did it! Now practice saying this verse to the One who sits on the throne.

DAY TWO

Guided Instruction

106 Match the numbers in the crowns on page 94 to the letters and solve the memory verse.

Worthy are you our Lord and our God, to receive glory and honor and power; for you created all things and because of your will they existed, and were created.

Revelation 4:11

Practice saying this memory verse three times, three times a day.

Guided Instruction

Ask God to clear your mind and help you understand His message today.

107 Turn to page 95 and read the selected verses to answer the questions on pages 95-96.

Revelation 4:1 WHEN is this happening? After these things

Revelation 4:1 WHAT does John see? A door standing open

WHAT does the voice say? Come up here.

Revelation 4:2 WHERE is John? WHERE is this taking place? In the Spirit; in heaven

Revelation 4:3 WHAT was the One sitting on the throne like? A jasper stone and a sardis

Revelation 4:3-4 WHAT was around the throne? A rainbow and 24 thrones

Revelation 4:5 WHAT came out from the throne? Flashes of lightning and sounds and peels of thunder

WHAT was before the throne? Seven lamps of fire

WHAT are these seven lamps of fire? The seven Spirits of God

Revelation 4:6 WHAT else was before the throne? Something like a sea of glass and four living creatures

Revelation 4:6-8 Describe the four living creatures. First creature like a lion

(page 95)

107

FALL DOWN AND WORSHIP

You did great yesterday as you uncovered clues by marking the key words in Revelation 4. Did you notice that your new memory verse solved the mystery of WHO is worthy?

Today let's continue to work on our mystery. Don't forget to pray! Turn to page 151. Let's get the facts of Revelation 4 by asking the 5 W's and an H.

Revelation 4:1 WHEN is this happening? (Did you find this very important time phrase? Did you put a clock over it?)

After these things

Revelation 4:1 WHAT does John see?

A door standing open

WHAT does the voice say?

Come up here.

Revelation 4:2 WHERE is John? WHERE is this taking place?

In the Spirit; in heaven

Revelation 4:3 WHAT was the One sitting on the throne like?

A jasper stone and a sardis

Revelation 4:3-4 WHAT was around the throne?

A rainbow and 24 thrones

Revelation 4:5 WHAT came out from the throne?

Flashes of lightning and sounds and peels of thunder

96 WEEK FOUR

WHAT was before the throne?

Seven lamps of fire

WHAT are these seven lamps of fire?

The seven Spirits of God

Revelation 4:6 WHAT else was before the throne?

Something like a sea of glass and four living creatures

Revelation 4:6-8 Describe the four living creatures.

First creature like a lion

Second creature like a calf

Third creature had a face like a man

Fourth creature like a flying eagle

are full

Fourth creature like a ______ ______ (page 96)

Each creature had six wings and are full of eyes around and within.

Revelation 4:8 WHAT do the four living creatures say?

"Holy, holy, holy is the Lord God Almighty, who was, and who is, and who is to come."

Revelation 4:10 WHAT did the 24 elders do?

They fell down, worshiped, and cast their crowns before the throne

Draw what you have just seen in Revelation 4:2-11 in the box on the next page. Make sure you show what heaven is like, as well as the people, creatures, and the main event.

Revelation 4:11 WHAT did the 24 elders say? Write this out for practice since this is your memory verse.

"Worthy are You, our Lord, our God, to receive glory and honor and power; for You created all things, and because of Your will they existed, and were created."

The Mystery in Heaven 97

108

109 Did you notice that worship is the priority in heaven? WHAT does it mean to worship God? Do you know? Worship means to bow before God. It is to lay flat before God because you recognize He is God and He is to be respected. To respect someone is to hold him or her in high regard, to honor that person. To worship God is to acknowledge God's worth, to honor God as God.

Guided Instruction

Second creature like a calf

Third creature had a face like a man

Fourth creature like a flying eagle.

Each creature has six wings and are full of eyes around and within.

Revelation 4:8 WHAT do the four living creatures say? "Holy, holy, holy is the Lord God Almighty, who was, and who is, and who is to come."

Revelation 4:10 WHAT did the 24 elders do? They fell down, worshiped, and cast their crowns before the throne

108 Draw a picture of Revelation 4:2-11 in the box on page 97.

Revelation 4:11

WHAT did the 24 elders say? "Worthy are You, our Lord, our God, to receive glory and honor and power; for You created all things, and because of Your will they existed, and were created."

109 Elicit discussion about the personal questions on pages 97 and 98. Have students respond independently.

Guided Instruction

(page 97)

Now think about what is happening on earth today. In general, is worshiping God a priority for those who live on the earth?________________________________

WHAT is people's general attitude toward God? Is their attitude one of indifference, not really caring about God, or does their attitude show honor? Do they acknowledge WHO God is and bow before Him to give Him glory?

____

WHAT is your attitude toward God? Do you put Him first? Do you talk about Him to show how important He

is to you? HOW do you feel when other people talk badly about Him? ________________________________

____

Look at Revelation 4:11. WHAT makes God worthy of worship?

____

God is the One who created all things. The reason we exist is for His will, *not* for our pleasure. The scene in heaven shows us what our lives are to be about. We are to live to do the things that please God, not the things that please us. The way we live should bring honor, glory, and blessing to Him.

Are you doing things to bless and honor God, or do you do the things that break His heart? ________________

____

Name one thing you can change in your life that will help you live for God and His honor rather than yours.

____

____

All right! You have just gotten a small glimpse into heaven. What an amazing place! Now before you head out, practice your memory verse to remind yourself of the One who is worthy!

DAY THREE

(page 98)

110 UNCOVERING CLUES: A SEALED BOOK

"Hey, guys, how did you like your glimpse into heaven yesterday?" Miss Kim asked Max and Molly.

"It was so cool," Molly replied.

"Well, are you ready to enter into the museum's room that shows this scene in heaven?"

"We sure are!" Max and Molly both exclaimed. Sam barked his agreement.

"All right then. Let's head down the hallway, past the models of the seven churches. Look for a room on the right that has the word 'Heaven' painted over the doorway. Max, when you're ready, you can open the door that leads to our scene of heaven."

"Wow!" Max and Molly said again as they went through the door and looked in awe at the scene before them. "This is amazing! Look at the throne and the transparent glow on it!" Max cried out.

"Press the first button on the wall, Molly," Miss Kim instructed.

As Molly pushed the button, a beautiful rainbow glittered like a brilliant emerald and surrounded the throne.

"That's fantastic!" Molly laughed.

"Now," Miss Kim replied, "did you notice how many thrones are around God's throne?"

"Twenty-four," Max called out. "And look, there's a gold crown on each throne for the elders to cast before God's throne."

"Right," answered Miss Kim. "When you finish your study

Guided Instruction

God is going to reveal more wonders about His heaven. Ask Him to keep you focused so you can understand His message.

110 Turn to page 98 and read "Uncovering Clues: A Sealed Book."

Guided Instruction

this week, I have a special presentation for you guys right here in heaven. Then once the museum actually opens, there will be special times each day that kids can come into this room and watch the scene from heaven unfold before their eyes. The rest of the time, when there isn't a presentation, they can come in and do things like make the rainbow appear on their own. What do you think about that?"

"That is so wonderful," Max replied. "But what do the rest of these buttons on the panel do?"

"Go ahead and push the next one, Max," Miss Kim said, "and find out." As Max pushed the next button, he and Molly almost jumped out of their skin, while Sam ran around the room barking as peals of thunder boomed overhead and bright flashes of lightning from strobe lights flashed around the throne!

"Whoa!" Max gasped. "I wasn't expecting that. It nearly scared me to death."

"I'll do the next one," Molly said, as she gently pushed the button. Immediately a fiery orange and golden glow came out of each of the seven lamps before the throne. "Cool!" Molly said while clapping her hands. "It's the seven Spirits of God."

Max pushed the next button, and a curtain behind the throne moved to one side to reveal replicas of the four living creatures. Four voices reciting the words of Revelation 4:8 came from the

The Mystery in Heaven 101

speakers around the room. After they were finished, 24 voices spoke the words of Revelation 4:11.

"I can't believe this!" Max told Miss Kim. "It's like we're really there!"

"I know," Miss Kim smiled. "If you think this is awesome, just think what the real heaven is like. Now we'd better leave heaven and head back to our resource room so you can find out what is happening in Revelation 5. We'll come back after we finish our research and watch our special heaven presentation."

"We can't wait!" Max stated. "Now let's pray so we can find out what happens next!"

Now that we've prayed, pull out your key word bookmark (the index card that you made) and add the new key words listed:

angel (draw blue wings or a blue angel and color it yellow)
book (draw a brown scroll)
seals (color it orange)

Now turn to page 153. Read Revelation 5:1-5, and mark your key words (the new ones just listed and the ones below) on your Observation Worksheets, just like they are on your index card. If you have lost your index card, you can look on page 139 to see how you can mark these words:

111 God I looked (or I saw) throne worthy overcome
Jesus (or any description that refers to Jesus, like *the Lion, the Lamb)*

Don't forget to mark the pronouns!

Great work! Now let's find out what is happening in heaven. Read Revelation 5:1-5 on page 153 and answer the 5 W's and an H questions.

(page 153)

Chapter 5

112 1 I saw in the right hand of Him who sat on the throne a
book written inside and on the back, sealed up with seven
seals.
2 And I saw a strong angel proclaiming with a loud voice,
"Who is worthy to open the book and to break its seals?"
3 And no one in heaven or on the earth or under the earth
was able to open the book or to look into it.

Guided Instruction

111 Copy the new key words on page 101 to your bookmark and wall chart and above the title of Revelation 5 on page 153.

Angel (draw blue wings or a blue angel and color yellow)

Book (draw a brown scroll)

Seals (color it orange)

Add the following key words to those on page 153.

God (draw a purple triangle and color it yellow)

I looked (I saw) (color it blue)

Throne (draw and color a blue throne)

Worthy (color it purple)

Overcome (color it yellow)

Jesus (draw a purple cross and color it yellow)

112 Read Revelation 5:1-5 aloud using your Observation Worksheet visual aid as students follow along and call out each key word. Then mark them together as we noted on p. 41.

Guided Instruction

113 Read the selected verses to answer the questions on pages 101-102.

Revelation 5:1 WHAT did John see in the hand of Him who sat on the throne? A book

HOW is it described? It was written inside and on the back, and sealed with seven seals.

Revelation 5:2 **WHAT did the angel proclaim?** "Who is worthy to open the book?"

Revelation 5:3-4 **WHY was John weeping?** No one was found worthy.

Revelation 5:5

WHO did the elders say was worthy to open the book and its seven seals? The lion from the tribe of Judah; the root of David

WHY was He worthy? He overcame.

Practice saying the memory verse with a partner (Teacher Guide page 107).

(page 153)

4 Then I *began* to weep greatly because no one was found
worthy to open the book or to look into it;
5 and one of the elders said to me, "Stop weeping; behold,
the Lion that is from the tribe of Judah, the Root of David,
has overcome so as to open the book and its seven seals."
6 And I saw between the throne (with the four living crea-

(page 101)

Revelation 5:1 WHAT did John see in the hand of Him who sat on the throne?

A book

102 WEEK FOUR

HOW is it described?

It was written inside and on the back, and sealed with seven seals.

Did you know in Bible times there were no books like we have today? Instead their books were rolled-up paper called scrolls, made of either papyrus or vellum. Did you know that seals were used to close up a scroll? Whenever someone wanted to send a message, he would take hot wax and drop it on the rolled-up scroll. Then he would take his signet ring and press it into the hot wax to form a mark and flatten the wax to keep the scroll closed. People did this to make sure the message would only be opened and read by the person to whom it was being sent.

Revelation 5:2 WHAT did the angel proclaim?

"Who is worthy to open the book?"

Revelation 5:3-4 WHY was John weeping?

No one was found worthy.

Revelation 5:5 WHO did the elders say was worthy to open the book and its seven seals?

The lion from the tribe of Judah; the root of David

WHY was He worthy?

He overcame.

You have discovered something very important today. You know that God has a sealed book that is written on the inside and on the back, and that Jesus, who is the Lion from the tribe of Judah, has overcome and can open the book. Tomorrow we will find out more about what John saw and the opening of this very important book.

Now practice saying your memory verse to remind yourself of just how awesome God is!

114

WHO CAN OPEN THE BOOK?

Wow! Wasn't the museum's room in heaven awesome? We can't wait to finish our research this week so we can see the museum's presentation. But before we go back into the heaven room, we need to find out more about God, Jesus, and the sealed-up book.

Let's uncover some more clues. Pray and then turn to page 153. Pull out your key word bookmark and add the new key word listed below to your index card:

prayers (draw a purple and color it pink)

115

Now read Revelation 5:6-10 and mark your new key word and the following key words on your Observation Worksheets, just like they are on your index card. Turn to page 139 if you have lost your card.

God Jesus (Lamb) seven Spirits of God
I saw throne worthy book
seals

Don't forget to mark the pronouns!

(page 153)

116

6 And I saw between the throne (with the four living creatures) and the elders a Lamb standing, as if slain, having seven horns and seven eyes, which are the seven Spirits of God, sent out into all the earth.

(page 154)

7 And He came and took the book out of the right hand of Him who sat on the throne.

8 When He had taken the book, the four living creatures and the twenty-four elders fell down before the Lamb, each one holding a harp and golden bowls full of incense, which are the prayers of the saints.

Guided Instruction

Ask God to keep you focused on His Word. He has a special message for you today.

114 Turn to page 103 and read "Who Can Open the Book?"

115 Copy the new key words on page 103 to your bookmark and wall chart.

Prayers (draw a purple bowl and color it pink)

Add "prayers" and these key words to the margin of your Observation Worksheets for Revelation 5:6-10.

God (draw a purple triangle and color it yellow)

Jesus (Lamb) (draw a purple cross and color the word yellow)

Seven Spirits of God (draw a cloud around Spirits)

I saw (color it blue)

Throne (draw a throne and color it blue)

Worthy (color it purple)

Book (draw a brown scroll)

Seals (color it orange)

116 Read Revelation 5:6–10 aloud using your Observation Worksheet visual aid as students follow along and call out each key word. Then mark them together as we noted on p. 41.

Guided Instruction

117 Read the selected verses to answer the questions on pages 103-105.

Revelation 5:6

WHAT did John see between the throne with the four living creatures and the elders? A Lamb

WHAT are the seven horns and seven eyes on the Lamb? The Seven Spirits of God

Revelation 5:7

WHAT did the Lamb do? He took the book.

Revelation 5:8

WHAT did the four living creatures and the 24 elders do? They fell down before the Lamb holding the golden bowls

WHAT is in the golden bowls? Incense, the prayers of the saints

(page 154)

9 And they sang a new song, saying, "Worthy are You to take the book and to break its seals; for You were slain, and purchased for God with Your blood *men* from every tribe and tongue and people and nation.

10 "You have made them *to be* a kingdom and priests to our God; and they will reign upon the earth."

(page 103)

You did great! Now read Revelation 5:6-10 and ask the 5 W's and an H.

Revelation 5:6 WHAT did John see between the throne with the four living creatures and the elders?

A Lamb

WHAT are the seven horns and seven eyes on the Lamb?

The Seven Spirits of God

104 WEEK FOUR

Revelation 5:7 WHAT did the Lamb do?

He took the book.

Revelation 5:8 WHAT did the four living creatures and the 24 elders do?

They fell down before the Lamb holding the golden bowls.

WHAT is in the golden bowls?

Incense, the prayers of the saints

Do you think that prayer is important since it is in these bowls in heaven? ____________

(page 104)

...ows in heaven? ____

Draw a picture of what John sees in Revelation 5:6-8 in the box below.

118

Revelation 5:9 WHY was the Lamb worthy to break its seals?

He was slain and purchased for God with His blood men of every tribe, tongue, people, and nation.

Revelation 5:10 WHAT are those who have been

purchased by Jesus' blood (those who are Christians) made to be?

A kingdom and priests for God

WHAT will they do?

Reign upon the earth

Isn't this awesome? God has made us a kingdom and priests to rule and reign on the earth. Stop and think about it. You are going to be a ruler. You are going to rule on the earth! Isn't that amazing?

119 Do you remember WHAT God told Adam and Eve to do back in Genesis 1:28 after He created them? Look up and read Genesis 1:27-28.

WHAT did God tell Adam and Eve to do?

Be fruitful and multiply, and fill the earth, and subdue it; and rule over the fish of the sea and over the birds of the sky and over every living thing that moves on the earth.

...ted the...

Guided Instruction

118 Draw a picture of Revelation 5:6-8 in the box.

Revelation 5:9

WHY was the Lamb worthy to break the seals? He was slain and purchased for God with His blood men of every tribe, tongue, people, and nation

Revelation 5:10

WHAT are those who have been purchased by Jesus' blood? A kingdom and priests for God

WHAT will they do? Reign upon the earth

119 Read the selected verses in Genesis to answer the rest of the questions on page 105.

Genesis 1:27-28

WHAT did God tell Adam and Eve to do? Be fruitful and multiply, and fill the earth, and subdue it; and rule over the fish of the sea and the birds of the sky and over every living thing that moves on the earth.

Guided Instruction

Genesis 3:3-6
WHAT did Adam and Eve do? They ate fruit from the tree of the knowledge of good and evil.

Genesis 3:24
WHAT happened to man? They were driven out of the Garden of Eden.

120 Read the information on pages 105-107 and elicit discussion.

(page 105)

120 Adam and Eve were to rule over the earth. God created the earth to belong to mankind, but something happened to change that. Do you remember WHAT happened? Look up and read Genesis 3:3-6.

Genesis 3:6 WHAT did Adam and Eve do?

They ate fruit from the tree of the knowledge of good and evil.

Read Genesis 3:24 WHAT happened to man?

They were driven out of the Garden of Eden.

When Adam and Eve disobeyed God and ate the fruit in Genesis 3, sin entered the world. To sin is to disobey God. It is

106 WEEK FOUR

to know the right thing to do and not do it (James 4:17). To sin is to not believe what God says.

Once Adam sinned, sin was passed from one generation to the next generation. It was like sin was in our genes, in our DNA. The Bible says in Romans 5:12, "Therefore, just as through one man sin entered into the world, and death through sin, and so death spread to all men, because all sinned." When Adam sinned, he passed his sin on to everyone born after him. Because of sin, mankind lost his right to rule over the earth.

Can you believe that Jesus would leave heaven to save us from our sins? Jesus came to earth as a human being, but He was born without Adam's "sin" genes because He was born of a virgin mother and His father was God! Jesus became a human being so He could redeem us (buy us back) from Satan with His precious blood! Man lost his right to rule the earth to Satan in the garden of Eden, but Jesus, as a man without sin, died on a cross to pay for our sins. Then He rose from the dead—defeating sin, death, and Satan—to give us back our right to rule and reign with Him on earth.

WHAT kind of animal is used to describe Jesus in Revelation 5:6-12? Do you wonder why Jesus is called a lamb? It's because the blood of a lamb was used during one of the plagues God sent when Pharaoh would not let God's people leave Egypt.

God told the children of Israel to kill a lamb, take its blood, and put it on the doorposts of their houses. Then when the angel of death came to kill all of the firstborn in Egypt, he would pass over the houses that had the blood of the lamb on the doorposts (Exodus 12:1-13). This "Passover" is a picture of what Jesus would do for us when He died for our sins!

Did you know that Jesus was crucified on the very day of Passover, when all the Passover lambs were being killed for the Passover feast? Jesus is the perfect Lamb without blemish who was slain so we could have eternal life. That's why we see Jesus as the slain Lamb in Revelation 5. Because Jesus paid for our sins with His blood, He is the only One worthy to open the book and break its seals.

One day very soon, the Lamb of God will take the book and break its seals so we can get back the right to rule that Adam and Eve lost when they disobeyed God and believed Satan. Isn't it exciting to know that one day, if you belong to Jesus, you will rule and reign on earth? Unbelievable!

As you head out today, don't forget to practice saying your memory verse.

Guided Instruction

Guided Instruction

Ask God to be with you as you complete the reading of Revelation 5.

121 Turn to page 107 and read "Worship the Lamb."

122 Turn to page 154 and read Revelation 5:11–14 aloud using your Observation Worksheet visual aid as students follow along and call out each key word. Then mark them together as we noted on p. 41.

God (draw a purple triangle and color it yellow)

Jesus (draw a purple cross and color it yellow)

I looked (color it blue)

Angel (draw blue angel wings and color them yellow)

Throne (draw a throne and color it blue)

Worthy (color it purple)

Worshiped (circle in purple and color blue)

WHEN (draw a green clock over words that denote time)

Read the selected verses to answer the questions.

(page 107)

121

WORSHIP THE LAMB

"Good morning, Miss Kim!" Max called out as he and Molly entered the resource room.

"Good morning, guys. Are you ready to wrap up Revelation 5 today?"

"We sure are!" Molly replied. "All we can talk about is how once we're finished we will get to see the presentation in the heaven room."

"I hope you like it! Why don't we pray so you can get to work? Yesterday you uncovered some pretty amazing things

108 WEEK FOUR

about the Lamb being worthy to open the book. Today you will discover more about the Lamb and worship," Miss Kim said.

"That sounds awesome!" Max answered. "I'll pray."

Okay, Bible detectives, get to work. Find out what is happening in heaven. Read Revelation 5:11-14 on page 154 and mark the following key words that are on your bookmark:

122

God	Jesus (Lamb)	I looked	angel
throne	worthy	worshiped	

Don't forget the pronouns, and don't forget to mark anything that tells you WHEN with a green clock or a green ◯.

Now turn back to Revelation 5:11-14 on page 154 and answer the 5 W's and an H.

(page 154)

...and they will reign upon the earth.

11 Then I looked, and I heard the voice of many angels around the throne and the living creatures and the elders; and the number of them was myriads of myriads, and thousands of thousands,

12 saying with a loud voice, "Worthy is the Lamb that was slain to receive power and riches and wisdom and might and honor and glory and blessing."

13 And every created thing which is in heaven and on the earth and under the earth and on the sea, and all things in

them, I heard saying, "To Him who sits on the throne, and to the Lamb, *be* blessing and honor and glory and dominion forever and ever."

14 And the four living creatures kept saying, "Amen." And the elders fell down and worshiped.

(page 108)

Revelation 5:11-12 WHAT did John hear?

The voices of many angels, living creatures, and elders

Revelation 5:14 WHAT is another word for praising God? What are the elders doing in verse 14?

Amen!

Isn't this awesome? Once again we see worship in heaven to God and the Lamb.

Revelation 5:13 WHAT will God and the Lamb have forever?

Blessing and honor and glory and dominion

Dominion means "power and strength." This shows us that God and Jesus' power and strength will be forever. God will take His great power and begin to reign visibly with His Son! Don't forget: If you are a child of God—a believer in relationship with Jesus—then you are going to get to rule with Him! Isn't that amazing?

Guided Instruction

Revelation 5:11-12 WHAT did John hear? The voices of many angels, living creatures, and elders

Revelation 5:14 WHAT is another word for praising God? Amen!

Revelation 5:13 WHAT will God and the Lamb have forever? Blessing and honor and glory and dominion

Read the rest of the information and elicit discussion.

Guided Instruction

123 Write your own prayer of praise on page 109.

If you are a classroom teacher you may want to give your students a quiz on their memory verse. There is also a quiz on Week Four on page 157 to check memory and understanding.

If you are a Sunday School teacher this is a great time to review the whole week by playing a game like the *Drawing Game* on page 162 or *M&M® Draw* on page 164. This is also a great way for classroom teachers and homeschool families to review with students what they learned this week.

Have you noticed that everyone who sees God and the Lamb as they really are can't help but call out, "Worthy, worthy, worthy" in worship? Can you imagine what it will be like when we finally see God face-to-face?

Why don't you write a prayer of praise on the lines below to worship God and Jesus, to thank them for WHO they are and WHAT they have done for you?

Are you ready to live in a way that brings honor and blessing to God and His Son? Remember, one day you will rule and reign with Jesus. Live as an overcomer until He comes!

Way to go! We are so proud of you for doing this study! Keep up the good work. Don't forget to practice saying your memory verse today. Say it to God and Jesus, who are worthy to be worshiped and praised!

5

THE BREAKING OF THE SEALS

124 **REVELATION 6–7**

It's great to have you back at the museum! How did you like your glimpse into heaven? Wasn't it amazing! So far we have unveiled some awesome discoveries. In Revelation 1 we discovered that God gave the Book of Revelation to His bond-servants through John so that we would know what was going to happen in the future.

In Revelation 2–3 we uncovered Jesus' messages to the churches and how to apply those messages to our lives.

Then in Revelation 4–5 we got a glimpse into heaven and the worship before the throne. We saw Jesus as He prepares to take the book (the scroll) from God's hand and break its seven seals.

WHAT is so important about this sealed-up book? Wait until you find out! If you didn't know God, the future would be flat-out scary. As these seals are broken, you will discover events that frighten a lot of people because the seals bring about a lot of pain and destruction. You need to remember that if you belong to Jesus, you have nothing to fear. You can relax because Jesus has already rescued you. Your future is secure in Him.

Are you ready to watch the Lamb? Then let's head back to watch the scene in heaven unfold!

Guided Instruction

WEEK 5

This is the last week to study *Bible Prophecy for Kids*. God will reveal mysteries that bring the end times into view. Ask Him to fill you with awe as you delve into His Word.

124 Turn to pages 110-111 and read "Revelation 6–7" and "COME!"

Guided Instruction

125 Copy the key word markings on page 112 to your bookmark and above the title for Revelation 6.

God (draw a purple triangle and color it yellow)

Jesus (Lamb) (draw a purple cross and color it yellow)

I looked (I saw) (color it blue)

seals (color it orange)

WHEN (draw a green clock over words that denote time)

COME!

"Wow!" Max exclaimed as he, Molly, Uncle Jake, and Miss Kim walked out of the heaven room. "That was soooo awesome! I got chill bumps, and my skin tingled as the 24 elders got up from the throne, laid down their crowns, and fell down in worship. That was some presentation."

"Especially the four living creatures," Molly joined in. "Those were some pretty amazing costumes. I was a little scared as they came out from behind the curtain to worship God. I thought the room was fantastic when we visited it the first time with all the special effects, but having real people come in and play the parts was unbelievable!"

"I'm glad it had that effect on you." Miss Kim smiled. "That's what we hope everyone will experience as they watch our special show. There is no way we can actually show what it would really be like in heaven, but we hope to at least give people an idea what it might be."

"My favorite part," Max told Miss Kim, "was when John was weeping and, as the elder tells him to stop because the Lion of Judah has overcome, we see Jesus as the slain Lamb walk in and take the book out of God's hand. That was so cool!"

Molly asked Miss Kim, "Will we get to see what happens when the Lamb breaks the seals?"

"We are working on a special video presentation to play on a big screen in the next room, but you can't go in until you discover for yourself what happens when the Lamb breaks the seals."

"All right!" squealed Molly. "Let's get back to work on our research. Race you to the resource room, Max."

"You're on," Max replied as he took off running.

Let's pray before we see what happens in Revelation 6. Okay, now turn to page 155. Read Revelation 6:1-8 and mark the following key words from your bookmark on your Observation Worksheet:

125  God  Jesus (Lamb) 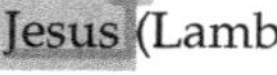 I looked (I saw) 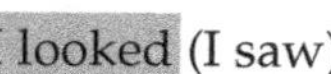 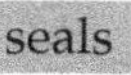 seals

Don't forget to mark the pronouns! And remember to mark anything that tells you WHEN with a green clock or a green ◯.

Great work! Before we wrap up our research for today, you

(page 155)

Chapter 6

126

1 Then I saw when the Lamb broke one of the seven seals,
and I heard one of the four living creatures saying as with a
voice of thunder, "Come."
2 I looked, and behold, a white horse, and he who sat on it had a
bow; and a crown was given to him, and he went out conquering
and to conquer.
3 When He broke the second seal, I heard the second living
creature saying, "Come."
4 And another, a red horse, went out; and to him who sat on it,
it was granted to take peace from the earth, and that *men* would
slay one another; and a great sword was given to him.
5 When He broke the third seal, I heard the third living
creature saying, "Come." I looked, and behold, a black horse;
and he who sat on it had a pair of scales in his hand.

6 And I heard *something* like a voice in the center of the four
living creatures saying, "A quart of wheat for a denarius, and
three quarts of barley for a denarius; and do not damage the oil
and the wine."
7 When the Lamb broke the fourth seal, I heard the voice of the
fourth living creature saying, "Come."
8 I looked, and behold, an ashen horse; and he who sat on
it had the name Death; and Hades was following with him.
Authority was given to them over a fourth of the earth, to kill
with sword and with famine and with pestilence and by the
wild beasts of the earth.
9 When the Lamb broke the fifth seal, I saw underneath the

Guided Instruction

126 Turn to page 155 and read Revelation 6:1–8 aloud using your Observation Worksheet visual aid as students follow along and call out each key word. Then mark them together as we noted on p. 41.

Give students time to reread these verses and apply key words markings.

Guided Instruction

127 Look at the word puzzle on page 112. Write the solution for the memory verse on the lines below.

For the Lamb in the center of the throne will be their shepherd, and will guide them to springs of the water of life; and God will wipe ~~away~~ every tear from their eyes.

—Revelation 7:17

Practice saying the memory verse three times, three times a day.

(page 112)

Great work! Before we wrap up our research for today, you need to uncover this week's memory verse by looking at the rebus. A rebus is a word puzzle that mixes pictures and words. When you combine the pictures and the letters by adding or subtracting letters, you will end up with a new word.

Write the solution on the lines underneath the puzzle. Then look at Revelation 7 on page 157 to discover the verse reference.

127 4-U THE -P+B -P THE

+ER -F THE THR+1

WILL -E THEIR -E+HERD,

-H WILL GUIDE THEM 2-W

SP+ +S -F THE W+ -H+ER

-F LIFE ; -H -L

WILL W+ -P EVERY

FROM THEIR .

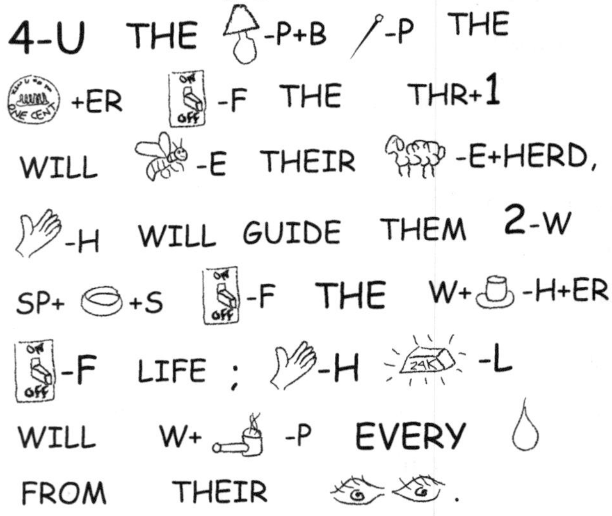

For the Lamb in the center of the throne will be their shepherd, and will guide them to springs of the water of life; and God will wipe ~~away~~ every tear from their eyes.

Revelation 7:17

Don't forget to practice saying this verse three times today!

The Breaking of the Seals 113

128 **THE MYSTERY OF THE FIRST FOUR SEALS**

You did a wonderful job yesterday as you marked key words to reveal what happens in heaven as the Lamb (Jesus) takes the book. Today you are going to solve the mystery of the first four seals as you ask the 5 W's and an H questions. Don't forget to pray, and then turn to page 155. Read Revelation 6:1-8 to reveal WHAT happens when the Lamb breaks the seals.

(page 155)

Chapter 6

129 1 Then I saw when the Lamb broke one of the seven seals,
and I heard one of the four living creatures saying as with a
voice of thunder, "Come."
2 I looked, and behold, a white horse, and he who sat on it had a
bow; and a crown was given to him, and he went out conquering
and to conquer.
3 When He broke the second seal, I heard the second living
creature saying, "Come."
4 And another, a red horse, went out; and to him who sat on it,
it was granted to take peace from the earth, and that *men* would
slay one another; and a great sword was given to him.
5 When He broke the third seal, I heard the third living
creature saying, "Come." I looked, and behold, a black horse;
and he who sat on it had a pair of scales in his hand.

Guided Instruction

Ask God to give you clear understanding as He opens the seals.

128 Turn to page 113 and read "The Mystery of the First Four Seals."

129 Turn to page 155 and read Revelation 6:1-8 to answer the questions on pages 113-116.

Guided Instruction

Revelation 6:1 **WHAT did John see?** **The Lamb broke one of the seven seals.**

WHEN the first seal was broken, WHAT did one of the four living creatures say? WHAT did its voice sound like? **Come! With a voice of thunder**

Revelation 6:2 **WHAT did John see when the first seal was broken?** **A white horse**

WHAT do we see about the rider of this horse? **He had a bow; and a crown was given to him.**

WHAT did he go out to do? **To conquer**

Lead a discussion and answer the next three questions.

156 OBSERVATION WORKSHEETS

6 And I heard *something* like a voice in the center of the four
living creatures saying, "A quart of wheat for a denarius, and
three quarts of barley for a denarius; and do not damage the oil
and the wine."
7 When the Lamb broke the fourth seal, I heard the voice of the
fourth living creature saying, "Come."
8 I looked, and behold, an ashen horse; and he who sat on
it had the name Death; and Hades was following with him.
Authority was given to them over a fourth of the earth, to kill
with sword and with famine and with pestilence and by the
wild beasts of the earth.
9 When the Lamb broke the fifth seal, I saw underneath the

(page 113)

Revelation 6:1 WHAT did John see?

The **Lamb** broke one of the **seven** **seals**.

WHEN the first seal was broken, WHAT did one of the four living creatures say? What did its voice sound like?

Come! With a voice of **thunder**

Revelation 6:2 WHAT did John see when the first seal was broken?

A **white** **horse**

WHAT do we see about the rider of this horse?

He had a **bow**; and a **crown** was given to him.

WHAT did he go out to do?

To **To conquer**

Did you notice anything unusual about the rider of this horse?

He has a bow, but does he have any arrows to shoot?

____

We see he is wearing a crown, and that he goes out to conquer—but he is conquering without a weapon. This could mean that he conquers using peace and diplomacy rather than by using military strength.

WHO do you think this rider of the white horse might be? Do you know of anyone in the end times WHO will bring about peace first in order to conquer? Have you ever studied the Book of Daniel?

____

WHO do you think this rider could be?

____

Revelation 6:3-4 WHAT did John see when the second seal was broken?

A __red__ horse went out.

WHAT was granted to its rider?

To __take__ __peace__ from the __earth__

WHAT was given to this rider?

A __great__ __sword__

If this rider is granted the power to take peace from the earth, does that mean there has to be peace in order for it to be taken away? Yes, you can't take away something you don't have. Since the second rider takes away peace, does it make sense that the first rider on the white horse was the one to *bring* peace?

When we don't have peace, what do we usually have? WHAT is the opposite of peace and is fought with weapons? __W__ __a__ __r__

Is this what the second rider could be bringing? __Yes__

Guided Instruction

Revelation 6:3–4 **WHAT did John see when the second seal was broken?** A red horse went out.

WHAT was granted to its rider? To take peace from the earth

WHAT was given to this rider? A great sword

WHAT is the opposite of peace and fought with weapons? W a r

Is this what the second rider will bring? Yes

Guided Instruction

Revelation 6:5 **WHAT did John see when the Lamb broke the third seal?** A black horse

WHAT did the rider have in his hand? A pair of scales

Revelation 6:6 **WHAT did the voice say?** "A quart of wheat for a denarius, and three quarts of barley for a denarius; and do not damage the oil and the wine."

Discuss the reason for the scales.

WHAT do you think this rider might bring that has to do with a shortage of food? F a m i n e

Revelation 6:7-8 **WHAT did John see when the fourth seal was broken?** An ashen horse

WHAT name did the rider have? Death

WHAT was following after the rider? Hades

WHAT was given to them? "Authority was given to them over a fourth of the earth, to kill with sword and with famine and with pestilence and by the wild beasts of the earth."

Revelation 6:5 WHAT did John see when the Lamb broke the third seal?

A __black__ horse

WHAT did the rider have in his hand?

A pair of __scales__

Revelation 6:6 WHAT did the voice say?

"A quart of __wheat__ for a __denarius__, and three quarts of __barley__ for a denarius; and do not damage the __oil__ and the __wine__."

WHAT do we see in this rider's hand? A pair of scales, which would be used to weigh and measure food. Did you know that a denarius is a day's wage? That means you'd have to work all day to buy a quart of wheat! Food must be scarce to be so expensive. WHAT do you think this rider might bring that has to do with a shortage of food? F _a_ m _i_ _n_ e

Do you know that after war there is often lack of food?

Revelation 6:7-8 WHAT did John see when the fourth seal was broken?

An __ashen__ horse

WHAT name did the rider have?

__Death__

WHAT was following after the rider?

__Hades__

WHAT was given to them?

"__Authority__ was given to them over a __fourth__ of the __earth__, to __kill__ with __sword__ and with __famine__ and with __pestilence__ and by the wild __beasts__ of the earth."

116 WEEK FIVE

WHAT does the fourth rider bring? Famine

We see that this rider is given the authority to kill a fourth of the people on earth. WHERE will these that are killed go? Do you know? WHAT is following death?

To Hades

This seems to show that the fourth of the people of the earth who are killed are not saved and will go to Hades, where the lake of fire is. How awful!

Did you notice something very important in this verse? How about the fact that this rider is *given* authority to kill? This means the rider is not the one in control. God allows the rider to kill. God is in control.

Now go back and find all the words from each of the blanks (starting at the beginning of "Day Two" in this week) and circle them in the word search below.

130

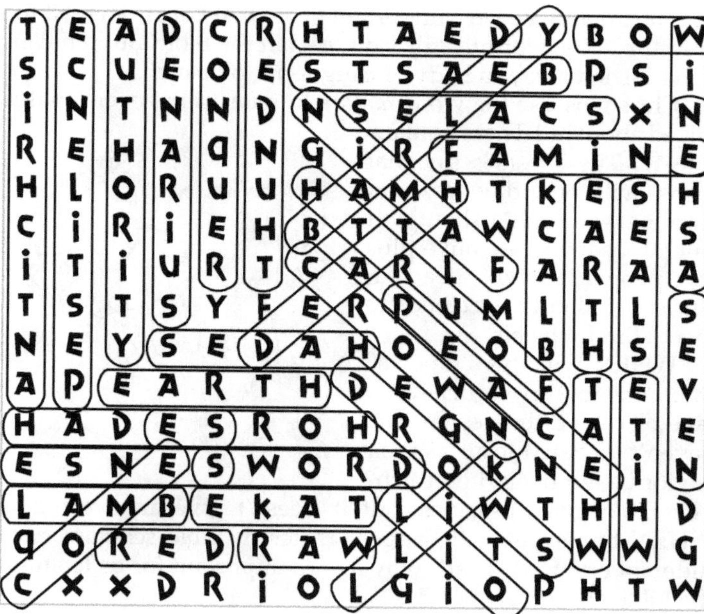

Guided Instruction

WHAT does the fourth rider bring? Famine

Where will these that are killed go? To Hades

130 Go back and find all of the words in the blanks. Circle them in the word search on page 116.

Guided Instruction

131 Read and discuss the rest of the information on pages 117-118.

131

Great work! Did you notice that while the Lamb is breaking the seals in heaven, the events that unfold are happening on the earth? WHO is in control over all these horrible events? God! The things we have uncovered today are very scary to some people, but we have to remember that God is the One in control. He alone has all authority and power in His hand!

Did you know that the breaking of these seals is the beginning of God's judgment on the earth? Yes, God is a God of salvation. He is loving, forgiving, and merciful. But He is also a holy God who must judge sin. These judgments that are coming are to put an end to sin.

One question you may be asking is "If I am a Christian, will I be on the earth when these judgments come?" You have probably heard about a very important event that Christians call the "rapture." The word *rapture* isn't used in the Bible, but it means to be carried away in body or caught up to heaven.

Christians use the word *rapture* to refer to the event that is talked about in 1 Thessalonians 4:16-17. These verses say that Jesus will one day descend from heaven with a shout and catch those who are alive plus the people already dead in Christ together in the clouds to meet Him in the air.

WHEN will this "rapture" (the catching-up of believers) take place and the people who haven't accepted Jesus as their Savior be left behind on earth? The Bible gives us clues, but it doesn't give an exact time WHEN this event will happen. Different Bible scholars have different opinions. That's why it is so important for us to study the Bible for ourselves!

Don't worry over WHEN the rapture will happen. Just know that if you are a believer in Jesus Christ, your future in heaven is secure. Revelation 3:10 tells us that we will be kept from the hour of testing that is about to come upon the whole world. So set your heart, faithful and valiant warrior, on living for Him!

One day very soon the trumpet will sound, Jesus will descend from heaven with a shout, and you will meet Him in the air to live with Him forever! Don't be afraid of the horrible events to come. God is telling us in His Word what will happen so we can be prepared for the future. That way we can share what we know with other people. Put your trust in Jesus!

Now that you have uncovered some very important truths, how would you like to make one of the awesome horses in Revelation 6? Did you know that people call the riders of these horses the four riders of the apocalypse? There are four horses for the four riders of the apocalypse. Pretty cool, huh? Especially since the Greek word for revelation is *apokalupsis*.

132 Here's how Max and Molly are each going to make one of the four horses of the apocalypse at the museum. You will need these supplies: wallpaper paste (non-toxic), newspaper, scissors or a craft knife, white primer, acrylic paint, material to make your form (such as a water bottle), metal hangers with cardboard tubing at the bottom, a piece of cardboard, and clear mailing tape.

First make the body from your form. (Look at the diagram on page 119.) Next draw and cut out a horse's head from cardboard. Attach it to the water bottle with clear tape. Cut holes in the bottom of the bottle and back to stick in the cardboard tubes to make the legs and tail. Be very careful cutting the holes. You may need a grown-up to help you.

Next mix up the wallpaper paste according to the instructions. You need

Guided Instruction

132 Give students the supplies to make the four horses mentioned on pages 118-119.

Guided Instruction

Practice saying your memory verse to a friend (Teacher Guide page 126).

approximately two cups of paste in a large bowl. Let it stand for 15 minutes.

Tear newspaper into strips one inch wide and six inches long. Thoroughly wet the newspaper strips with wallpaper paste. Take the strips and place them on the form. Layer the strips in a random pattern and overlap them. When you have finished, let your horse dry completely for one to two days.

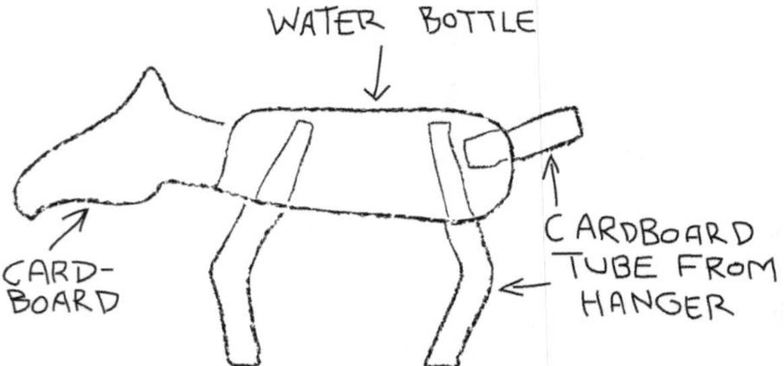

Then you can use a white primer to cover the horse as a base coat. After the primer is dry, paint your horse with acrylic paint. Be creative and have fun!

Before you head out, don't forget to practice your memory verse this week!

(page 119)

133 **THE EARTH IS SHAKEN!**

"Hey, Max! How do you like my white horse?" Molly asked as she added the finishing touches.

"It looks great." Max smiled. "I like the way you put the crown on the horse's head. Where are you going to put the bow?"

"I think I'm going to glue it on his side close to his neck. How about you? Where are you going to put the sword that goes with the red horse?"

120 WEEK FIVE

"I think I'll put it right here on his side," Max answered as he glued the sword in place.

About that time Miss Kim walked into the resource room with Uncle Jake.

"Hey, guys, you have done an awesome job on those horses. How would you like to head down the hallway to see our video presentation?" Miss Kim asked.

"That sounds like fun!" Max responded. "Let's put our horses on display on the way down there. I can't wait to see the four horses in action in the movie."

"Our video guys put in some fantastic special effects to show what these four horses represent as they gallop onto the scene, so it may be a little intense. We also have something fun that kids can do while they watch the video. They can make the special sound effects of the galloping horses as they appear on the screen."

"That sounds like fun. How do we do it?" Molly asked as they walked into the room with a huge video screen.

"Come over here to this table. We have some coconut shells like they used to use in radio and the movies to make the noise of horses galloping. You take the shells and hit the table in rhythm with them like this when you see the horses appear on-screen. Another way to make horse noises is to use plastic or paper cups."

"This is fun," Max said as he practiced his galloping techniques. "How about we each do two horses?"

"No way!" Uncle Jake joined in. "You have to let me do at least one."

"Okay, Uncle Jake, you can go first!" Max said as he handed Uncle Jake the coconut shells. Miss Kim pushed the button to start the video.

Guided Instruction

Ask God to give you clear understanding as you delve deeper into His Word.

133 Turn to page 119 and read "The Earth is Shaken!"

Guided Instruction

134 To review, answer the questions on page 121.

HOW many seals are there on the book? Seven

HOW many has the Lamb opened so far? Four

WHAT are the colors of the four horses? White, red, black, and ashen

Turn to page 156 and read Revelation 6:9–17 aloud as students follow along.

135 Copy the new key word markings on page 121 to your bookmark and wall chart and beside verses 9–17 in your Observation Worksheets.

Earthquake (draw a brown zigzag line through it)

Wrath (draw a red W through it)

Add the following key word markings to the margin.

God (draw a purple triangle and color it yellow)

Jesus (Lamb) (draw a purple cross and color the word yellow)

I looked (I saw) (color it blue)

Seals (on book) (color it orange)

White robe (color it yellow)

Throne (draw a throne and color it blue)

Those (all) who dwell on the earth (color it green)

WHERE (double-underline in green words that denote place)

WHEN (draw a green clock over each word that denotes time)

The Breaking of the Seals 121

Kids, did you make the galloping noises, too? Wasn't that fun?

Okay, let's pray and get started. Now let's take a minute to review.

134 HOW many seals are there on the book? Seven

HOW many has the Lamb opened so far? Four

Do you remember the colors of all four horses?
White, red, black, and ashen.

Let's find out what happens next!

Add the following new key words to your bookmark:

135 earthquake (draw a brown zigzag)
wrath (draw a red W)

Now turn to page 156. Read Revelation 6:9-17 and mark on your Observation Worksheets your new key words above and the ones listed below from your bookmark:

God Jesus (Lamb) I looked (I saw) seals
white robe throne those [all] who dwell on the earth

Don't forget to mark the pronouns and anything that tells you WHERE by double-underlining the WHERE in green. And don't forget to mark anything that tells you WHEN with a green clock: or green ○.

Now let's uncover the next two seals. Ask the 5 W's and an H for Revelation 6:9-17.

(page 156)

136 9 When the Lamb broke the fifth seal, I saw underneath the
altar the souls of those who had been slain because of the word of
God, and because of the testimony which they had maintained;
10 and they cried out with a loud voice, saying, "How long, O
Lord, holy and true, will You refrain from judging and avenging
our blood on those who dwell on the earth?"
11 And there was given to each of them a white robe; and they
were told that they should rest for a little while longer, until *the*
number of their fellow servants and their brethren who were to be
killed even as they had been, would be completed also.

Observation Worksheets 157

12 I looked when He broke the sixth seal, and there was a great
earthquake; and the sun became black as sackcloth *made* of hair,
and the whole moon became like blood;
13 and the stars of the sky fell to the earth, as a fig tree casts its
unripe figs when shaken by a great wind.
14 The sky was split apart like a scroll when it is rolled up, and
every mountain and island were moved out of their places.
15 Then the kings of the earth and the great men and the
commanders and the rich and the strong and every slave and
free man hid themselves in the caves and among the rocks of
the mountains;
16 and they said to the mountains and to the rocks, "Fall on us
and hide us from the presence of Him who sits on the throne,
and from the wrath of the Lamb;
17 for the great day of their wrath has come, and who is able to
stand?"

Revelation 6:9 WHAT did John see when the fifth seal was opened?

Souls under the altar, slain because of the Word of God

These souls that are under the altar are martyrs. Do you

122 WEEK FIVE

remember what it means to be a martyr? A martyr is a witness. It is someone who chooses to die rather than give up what he or she believes in. A martyr is someone who is killed for his faith. Remember Polycarp (see Week 2, Day 3)?

WHY were the people underneath the altar slain in Revelation 6:9?

Because of the word of God and the testimony they kept

[illegible] their lives for the cause of Jesus

Guided Instruction

136 Read Revelation 6:9–17 aloud using your Observation Worksheet visual aid as students follow along and call out each key word. Then mark them together as we noted on p. 41.

Read the selected verses to answer the questions on page 121-122.

Revelation 6:9 WHAT did John see when the fifth seal was opened? Souls under the altar, slain because of the Word of God

WHY were the people underneath the altar slain? Because of the word of God and the testimony they kept

Guided Instruction

Revelation 6:10 WHAT did they cry out? "How long, O Lord, holy and true, will You refrain from judging and avenging our blood on those who dwell on earth?"

Revelation 6:11 WHAT were they given? A white robe

WHAT were they told? Rest for a while longer

WHY were they told this? To patiently wait for the number of their fellow servants to be killed

Reread Revelation 6:12–17 to answer the questions on pages 123-124.

Revelation 6:12-14 WHAT did John see when the sixth seal was broken? There was a great earthquake, the sun became black, the moon became like blood, the stars of the sky fell to the earth, the sky was split apart like a scroll, and every mountain and island were moved out of their places.

Revelation 6:15 WHAT did the kings of the earth and the great men and the commanders and the rich and the strong and every slave and free man do? They hid in caves and among the rocks of the mountains.

Revelation 6:16 WHAT did they say to the mountains and to the rocks? Fall on us and hide us from the presence of Him who sits on the throne, and from the wrath of the Lamb.

Revelation 6:17 WHAT day had come? The great day of their wrath

(page 122)

These martyrs gave up their lives for the cause of Jesus Christ!

Revelation 6:10 WHAT did they cry out?

"How long, O Lord, holy and true, will You refrain from judging and avenging our blood on those who dwell on earth?"

Revelation 6:11 WHAT were they given?

A white robe

WHAT were they told?

Rest for a while longer

WHY were they told this?

To patiently wait for the number of their fellow servants to be killed

Does that sound like other people will die for their faith in Jesus before everything is finished? It sure does. Do you remember what Jesus says in Matthew 10:39? "He who has found his life will lose it, and he who has lost his life for My sake will find it."

We can deny Christ and live selfishly for a while, but in the end we will die—and by not believing in Christ, we will have lost our lives forever. But when we give our lives for the sake of Jesus, our lives aren't lost because Jesus gives us eternal life.

Jesus will avenge the blood of those who give up their lives for His sake in His perfect timing. But those who give up their lives for Him will live forever with Him.

The Breaking of the Seals 123

Revelation 6:12-14 WHAT did John see when the sixth seal was broken?

There was a great earthquake, the sun became black, the moon became like blood, the stars of the sky fell to the earth, the sky was split apart like a scroll, and every mountain and island were moved out of their places.

Revelation 6:15 WHAT did the kings of the earth and the great men and the commanders and the rich and the strong and every slave and free man do?

They hid in caves and among the rocks of the mountains.

Revelation 6:16 WHAT did they say to the mountains and to the rocks? Fall on us and hide us from the presence of Him who sits on the throne, and from the wrath of the Lamb.

Revelation 6:17 WHAT day had come?

The great day of their wrath

(page 123)

WHOSE wrath was it?

God and the Lamb's wrath

WHEN did this event take place? WHAT seal has been broken?

The sixth seal

Pretty scary isn't it? Earthquakes, the sun turning black, the moon turning like blood, stars falling, the sky being split apart, and mountains and islands being moved from their places.

Did you notice that all of the men who hid themselves know WHO is bringing this calamity about? But instead of turning to God, WHAT do they ask for? To be hid from His presence and wrath! God has brought about some pretty cataclysmic events to get their attention, but all they want to do is run away from God instead of changing their ways and running *to* Him.

HOW about you? Has there been a time when God wanted to get your attention, but instead of listening to what He wanted, you turned the other way?

Should you be scared when it looks like the world is falling apart? No. You should remember that God is the One who sits on the throne and turn to Him.

You did an incredible job today looking at some frightening events to come, at people giving up their lives for the sake of Jesus, and then watching God shake the world up with some amazing events!

Before you head out today, turn to page 155 of your

Guided Instruction

WHOSE wrath was it? **God and the Lamb's wrath**

WHEN did this event take place? WHAT seal has been broken? **The sixth seal**

Lead a discussion of the information on page 124.

Guided Instruction

137 Turn to page 155 and underline in orange the number of each one of the seals.

Write the number of each seal in the margin next to the verse that tells about it.

Practice saying the memory verse to a partner. (Teacher Guide page 126)

(page 124)

azing events!

Before you head out today, turn to page 155 of your Observation Worksheets, and underline in orange the number of each one of the seven seals you have seen so far in Revelation 6. Write the number of each seal in the margin next to the verse that tells about that seal.

All right! Way to go! As we close, don't forget to practice your memory verse. As you say it aloud, let it remind you that you do not need to fear what is coming because the Lamb is the One in the center of the throne. He will be your Shepherd. Jesus will guide you to the water of life and wipe every tear from your eyes.

them, I heard saying, "To Him who sits on the throne, and
to the Lamb, *be* blessing and honor and glory and dominion
forever and ever."
14 And the four living creatures kept saying, "Amen." And
the elders fell down and worshiped.

137

Chapter 6

#1 1 Then I saw when the Lamb broke one of the seven seals,
and I heard one of the four living creatures saying as with a
voice of thunder, "Come."
2 I looked, and behold, a white horse, and he who sat on it had a
bow; and a crown was given to him, and he went out conquering
and to conquer.
#2 3 When He broke the second seal, I heard the second living
creature saying, "Come."
4 And another, a red horse, went out; and to him who sat on it,
it was granted to take peace from the earth, and that *men* would
slay one another; and a great sword was given to him.
#3 5 When He broke the third seal, I heard the third living
creature saying, "Come." I looked, and behold, a black horse;
and he who sat on it had a pair of scales in his hand.

Guided Instruction

6 And I heard *something* like a voice in the center of the four
living creatures saying, "A quart of wheat for a denarius, and
three quarts of barley for a denarius; and do not damage the oil
and the wine."
#4 7 When the Lamb broke the fourth seal, I heard the voice of the
fourth living creature saying, "Come."
8 I looked, and behold, an ashen horse; and he who sat on
it had the name Death; and Hades was following with him.
Authority was given to them over a fourth of the earth, to kill
with sword and with famine and with pestilence and by the
wild beasts of the earth.
#5 9 When the Lamb broke the fifth seal, I saw underneath the
altar the souls of those who had been slain because of the word of
God, and because of the testimony which they had maintained;
10 and they cried out with a loud voice, saying, "How long, O
Lord, holy and true, will You refrain from judging and avenging
our blood on those who dwell on the earth?"
11 And there was given to each of them a white robe; and they
were told that they should rest for a little while longer, until *the
number of* their fellow servants and their brethren who were to be
killed even as they had been, would be completed also.

Guided Instruction

#6

12 I looked when He broke the sixth seal, and there was a great
earthquake; and the sun became black as sackcloth *made* of hair,
and the whole moon became like blood;
13 and the stars of the sky fell to the earth, as a fig tree casts its
unripe figs when shaken by a great wind.
14 The sky was split apart like a scroll when it is rolled up, and
every mountain and island were moved out of their places.
15 Then the kings of the earth and the great men and the
commanders and the rich and the strong and every slave and
free man hid themselves in the caves and among the rocks of
the mountains;
16 and they said to the mountains and to the rocks, "Fall on us
and hide us from the presence of Him who sits on the throne,
and from the wrath of the Lamb;
17 for the great day of their wrath has come, and who is able to
stand?"

138

FOUR ANGELS AT THE FOUR CORNERS OF THE EARTH

It's great to have you back at the museum! How did you like going into the room with the altar after you finished the video? Were you surprised when Max pushed the button on the wall and heard the souls crying out to the Lord?

And in the next room Sam really barked when the sixth seal was broken and the room shook because of the earthquake. Did you feel it too? Molly liked sliding the black film over the sun and the red film over the moon. And when the glittery stars fell from the sky, Uncle Jake jumped. I bet you did too! The Discovery Bible Museum is such an amazing and fun place!

Let's head back to the resource room to find out what happens after we hear the people on earth proclaim that the great day of their wrath has come. Are you ready? Great! Why don't you pray and then turn to page 157. Pull out your keyword bookmark and add the new key word:

seal, sealed (this is different from the seven seals on the book—draw a purple S)

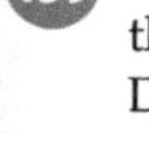
139 Now read Revelation 7:1-8 and mark your new key word and the key words listed below on your Observation Worksheets. Don't forget: If you have lost your bookmark, you can turn to page 31 for instructions or page 139.

 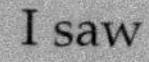 
God I saw angel

Don't forget to mark the pronouns. Anything that tells you WHERE, double-underline the WHERE in green, and mark anything that tells you WHEN by drawing a green clock or a ◯.

Guided Instruction

Ask God to give you clarity about His message today.

138 Turn to page 125 and read "Four Angels at the Four Corners of the Earth."

139 Add the new key word on page 125 to your bookmark and wall chart and above the title of Revelation 7 on page 157.

Seal, sealed (draw a purple "S" on the word)

Read Revelation 7:1-8 aloud using your Observation Worksheet visual aid as students follow along and call out each key word. Then mark them together as we noted on p. 41.

God (draw a purple triangle and color yellow)

I saw (color it blue)

Angel (draw blue wings and color them yellow)

WHERE (double-underline in green words that denote place)

WHEN (draw a green clock over words that denote time)

Guided Instruction

(page 157)

Chapter 7

140

1 After this I saw four angels standing at the four corners of
the earth, holding back the four winds of the earth, so that
no wind would blow on the earth or on the sea or on any
tree.

(page 158)

2 And I saw another angel ascending from the rising of the
sun, having the seal of the living God; and he cried out with a
loud voice to the four angels to whom it was granted to harm
the earth and the sea,
3 saying, "Do not harm the earth or the sea or the trees until
we have sealed the bond-servants of our God on their foreheads."
4 And I heard the number of those who were sealed, one
hundred and forty-four thousand sealed from every tribe of
the sons of Israel:
5 from the tribe of Judah, twelve thousand *were* sealed, from
the tribe of Reuben twelve thousand, from the tribe of Gad
twelve thousand,
6 from the tribe of Asher twelve thousand, from the tribe of
Naphtali twelve thousand, from the tribe of Manasseh twelve
thousand,
7 from the tribe of Simeon twelve thousand, from the tribe of
Levi twelve thousand, from the tribe of Issachar twelve thousand,
8 from the tribe of Zebulun twelve thousand, from the tribe

(page 159)

of Joseph twelve thousand, from the tribe of Benjamin, twelve
thousand *were* sealed.
9 [illegible] multitude

Those were some great observations! Now let's find out what these angels are up to by asking the 5 W's and an H for Revelation 7:1-8.

Revelation 7:1 WHAT did John see? Four angels standing at the four corners of the earth holding back the four winds of the earth

Look back at Revelation 6:12. WHEN is this happening? WHAT seal has been broken?

During the great day of wrath. The sixth seal

Revelation 7:2 WHAT did John see and WHAT did he have?

Another angel having the seal of the living God

HOW many angels does this make? Five

Revelation 7:3 WHAT does this angel tell the other angels?

"Do not harm the earth or the sea or the trees until we have sealed the bond-servants on their foreheads."

Revelation 7:4 HOW many people are to be sealed?

144,000 people

WHO are they?

Every tribe of the sons of Israel

Revelation 7:5-8 Name the 12 tribes of Israel.

Judah, Reuben, Gad, Asher, Naphtali, Manasseh, Simeon, Levi, Issachar, Zebulun, Joseph, and Benjamin

HOW many from each tribe were sealed?

12,000

Wow! You have discovered one of the two different groups of people that are mentioned in Revelation 7 today. This group is the 144,000 from the tribes of the sons of Israel, bond-servants of God, whom God will seal before the angels harm the earth.

Tomorrow we will find out WHO the other group of people is that John sees. Don't forget to practice your memory verse!

Guided Instruction

140 Read the selected verses to answer the questions on page 126.

Revelation 7:1 **WHAT did John see?** Four angels standing at the four corners of the earth holding back the four winds of the earth

Look back at Revelation 6:12

WHEN is this happening? During the great day of wrath.

WHAT seal has been broken? The sixth seal

Revelation 7:2 **WHAT did John see and WHAT did he have?** Another angel having the seal of the living God

HOW many angels does this make? Five

Revelation 7:3 **WHAT does this angel tell the other angels?** "Do not harm the earth or the sea or the trees until we have sealed the bond-servants on their foreheads."

Revelation 7:4 **HOW many people are to be sealed?** 144,000 people

WHO are they? Every tribe of the sons of Israel

Revelation 7:5-8 **Name the 12 tribes of Israel.** Judah, Reuben, Gad, Asher, Naphtali, Manasseh, Simeon, Levi, Issachar, Zebulun, Joseph, and Benjamin

HOW many from each tribe were sealed? 12,000

Practice saying the memory verse with a friend (Teacher Guide page 126).

Guided Instruction

Ask God to enlighten you to the truth revealed in His Word.

141 Turn to page 127 and read "A Great Multitude."

142 Add the new key word to your book mark and to the wall chart.

Tribulation (box it in black)

Add the new key word along with the following key words to the margin for Revelation 7:9–17.

God (draw a purple triangle and color it yellow)

Jesus (Lamb) (draw a purple cross and color the word yellow)

I looked (color it blue)

Angel (draw blue wings and color them yellow)

Throne (draw a throne and color it blue)

Worshiped (circle in purple and color blue)

white robe, washed their robes and made them white

WHEN (draw a green clock over words that denote time)

143 Read Revelation 7:9–17 on pages 159-169 aloud aloud using your Observation Worksheet visual aid as students follow along and call out each key word. Then mark them together as we noted on p. 41.

(page 127)

141

A GREAT MULTITUDE

It's great to have you back at the resource room. Watch out! Sam is pretty excited to see you and eager to lick your face. He is ready to solve the mystery of the second group of people mentioned in Revelation 7. How about you?

Why don't you pray, and then turn to page 159? Pull out your keyword bookmark and add this new key word:

tribulation (box it in black)

Let's solve the mystery of the people mentioned in Revelation 7. Read Revelation 7:9-17 and mark your new key word and the key words listed below on your Observation Worksheet:

142

God Jesus (Lamb) I looked angel
throne worshiped
white robe, washed their robes and made them white

Don't forget to mark the pronouns. Also mark anything that tells you WHEN by drawing a green clock or a .

143

9 After these things I looked, and behold, a great multitude
which no one could count, from every nation and *all* tribes and
peoples and tongues, standing before the throne and before the
Lamb, clothed in white robes, and palm branches *were* in their
hands;
10 and they cry out with a loud voice, saying, "Salvation to our
God who sits on the throne, and to the Lamb."
11 And all the angels were standing around the throne and
around the elders and the four living creatures; and they fell
on their faces before the throne and worshiped God,
12 saying,
"Amen, blessing and glory and wisdom and thanksgiving
and honor and power and might, *be* to our God forever and
ever. Amen."

Amen.

13 Then one of the elders answered, saying to me, "These who
are clothed in the white robes, who are they, and where have
they come from?"
14 I said to him, "My lord, you know." And he said to me,
"These are the ones who come out of the great tribulation,

and they have washed their robes and made them white in
the blood of the Lamb.
15 "For this reason, they are before the throne of God; and
they serve Him day and night in His temple; and He who
sits on the throne will spread His tabernacle over them.
16 "They will hunger no longer, nor thirst anymore; nor will
the sun beat down on them, nor any heat;
17 for the Lamb in the center of the throne will be their shepherd, and will guide them to springs of the water of life; and
God will wipe every tear from their eyes."

(page 127)

Now answer the 5 W's and an H questions.

Revelation 7:9 WHAT is the other group of people mentioned in this verse?

A great multitude

WHO are they? Are they Jews like the 144,000? WHERE do they come from?

Every nation, tribe, people, and tongue

Guided Instruction

Read the selected verses to answer the questions on pages 127-128.

Revelation 7:9 WHAT is the other group of people mentioned in this verse? A great multitude

WHO are they? WHERE do they come from? Every nation, tribe, people, and tongue

Guided Instruction

WHERE are they standing? Before the throne and before the Lamb

HOW are they clothed? In white robes

WHAT do they have in their hands? Palm branches

Revelation 7:13–14 WHERE have these people come from? The great tribulation

Are these believers? Yes

HOW do you know? They have washed their robes and made them white in the blood of the Lamb.

Will people be saved in the great tribulation? Yes

Explain your answer using verses 15–17. We know they suffered because we see that they will hunger no more, nor thirst, nor will the sun beat down on them and God will wipe every tear from their eyes.

Revelation 7:17 WHAT will the Lamb do for them? He will be their shepherd and guide them to springs of water of life.

____

____

WHERE are they standing?

Before the throne and before the Lamb

HOW are they clothed?

In white robes

WHAT do they have in their hands?

Palm branches

Revelation 7:13-14 WHERE have these people come from?

The great tribulation

Are these (the great multitude) believers? Yes

HOW do you know?

They have washed their robes and made them white in the blood of the Lamb.

Revelation 7:15-17 Have these believers in Jesus suffered during this great tribulation? Yes Explain your answer using verses 15-17.

We know they suffered because we see that they will hunger no more, nor thirst, nor will the sun beat down on them and God will wipe every tear from their eyes.

From what you have seen today, even in the great tribulation will there be people who are saved? ________

____

Revelation 7:17 WHAT will the Lamb do for them? See if you can answer this without looking, since this is your memory verse.

He will be their shepherd and guide them to springs of water of life.

144 *Wow!* You have discovered two different groups of people this week. Yesterday you saw that the first group, the 144,000, were from the tribes of the sons of Israel. Today you discovered that the other group is the great multitude made up of all tribes, tongues, and nations who have washed their robes in the Lamb's blood and will suffer in the great tribulation. But because they are saved, they will come out of their suffering and will worship and serve God in His temple. God will spread His tabernacle (sanctuary or shelter) over them, and the Lamb will lead them and wash every tear from their eyes. Isn't that awesome? God has an amazing plan. He is a God of salvation!

See if you can remember each one of the six seals you have studied so far. Draw a picture of each of the seals that you have investigated in the chart on the next page. Make sure you add all the details (for example, if you are drawing one of the horses, show what the rider of the horse is carrying). You can go back and look in your book if you aren't sure of all the details.

Guided Instruction

144 Read and discuss the information on page 129.

Guided Instruction

145 Turn to page 130 and complete the chart "The Seven Seals." Draw pictures of each seal.

First Seal Revelation 6:2
White horse
Brings peace

Second Seal Revelation 6:3-4
Red horse
Brings war

Third Seal Revelation 6:5
Black horse
Brings famine

Fourth Seal Revelation 6:7-8
Ashen horse
Death and Hades

Fifth Seal Revelation 6:9
Souls under the altar

Sixth Seal Revelation 6:12-14
Earthquake, sun, moon, stars
The great day of wrath

Seventh Seal Revelation 8:1
silence in heaven, angels given seven trumpets

145

The Seven Seals	
First Seal White horse Brings peace	**Second Seal** Red horse Brings war
Third Seal Black horse Brings famine	**Fourth Seal** Ashen horse Death and Hades
Fifth Seal Souls under the altar	**Sixth Seal** earthquake, sun, moon, stars The great day of wrath
Seventh Seal silence in heaven, angels given seven trumpets	

Great artwork! Now, HOW many seals are there on this sealed-up book? 7

 146 HOW many seals have been broken—HOW many have you uncovered so far? ________

HOW many are left? _____

That's right. You have one more seal to discover along with a lot more exciting events in Revelation 8–22 as God unfolds His plan for the future. Six seals have been broken bringing about peace, war, famine, death, martyrs, a great earthquake, the sun as black as sackcloth, the moon like blood, stars falling to earth, the sky splitting like a scroll with every mountain and island moved out of their places, and people hiding themselves in caves, rocks, and mountains crying out to be hid from the presence of God and the wrath of the Lamb!

WHAT will happen next? Will things get worse? WHEN will Jesus come with the clouds? WHO will win the war of the Lamb—the battle of good against evil?

Hang on tight! You'll find out as you continue to solve the mystery of Revelation in Max, Molly, and Sam's adventure *A Sneak Peek into the Future,* where they explore Revelation 8–22. The wrath of the Lamb has come. Join Max and Molly as they discover WHAT happens after the sixth seal.

To give you a taste of what is to come and let you finish the chart on page 130, read the first six verses of Revelation 8:

> *When the Lamb broke the seventh seal, there was silence in heaven for about half an hour. And I saw the seven angels who stand before God, and seven trumpets were given to them. Another angel came and stood at the altar, holding a golden censer; and much incense was given to him, so that he might add it to the prayers of all the saints on the golden altar which was before the throne. And the smoke of the incense, with the prayers of the saints, went up before God out of the angel's hand. Then the angel took the censer and filled it with the fire of the altar, and threw it to the earth; and there followed peals of thunder and sounds and flashes of lightning and an earthquake. And the seven angels who had the seven trumpets prepared themselves to sound them.*

Now, fill in the blanks on your chart and draw this last seal.

AWESOME! We can't wait to find out WHAT happens next! We are so proud of you!

Guided Instruction

146 Read and discuss the information on page 131.

Guided Instruction

147 Read "The Mystery Unfolds" on pages 132-133.

Good job! God sees your perseverance and is pleased.

Thank Him for the privilege of studying His Word.

If you are a classroom teacher you may want to give your students a quiz on their memory verse. There is also a quiz on Week Five on page 158 to check memory and understanding. There is also a Final Exam on page 159 to review the entire book.

You may want to act out the events in Revelation 6–7. You may also want to play a game to review all that the kids have learned in Revelation 1–7. A great game to play to review what Jesus promised the overcomers, and the events in Revelation is the *Drawing Game* on page 162.

147

Wow! You did it! You have begun to unravel the mystery of Revelation. Just look at all you have discovered in only seven chapters of Revelation. You know WHO gave the revelation, HOW it was given, and WHY it was given—so God could show us what is going to happen in the future. Absolutely amazing!

You also uncovered Jesus' messages to the seven churches in Asia and learned that these messages are also for you. You have examined your heart to see if you are living the way God wants you to. You saw that you have a choice to accept Jesus as your Savior. Jesus is patiently waiting for you to invite Him in. Isn't it awesome how much God and Jesus love you? God has an amazing plan. He is a God of salvation!

You also discovered that if you are a believer in Jesus Christ, you are an overcomer and have nothing to fear because a loving God holds you in the palm of His hand. He is in control of all your circumstances!

You got a glimpse into heaven and saw the worship before the throne with some pretty amazing creatures. You saw that Jesus is the only One worthy to break the seven seals on the book. Then you heard the gallop of the horses as Jesus breaks the first seal and God's judgments begin on those who dwell on the earth.

As we wrap up this adventure there is so much more to discover before the mystery of Revelation is solved. Don't forget to join Max, Molly, and Sam in the rest of their Revelation adventure—*A Sneak Peek into the Future!* Find out all that

132

happens when the seventh seal is broken and the seven trumpets sound. HOW many more judgments are there? WHO is the beast that comes out of the abyss? WHAT will happen to the two witnesses? And WHEN will Jesus come again?

Just remember that God is in control. He has shown you what will happen in His Word. And He is faithful. You can trust Him!

Don't forget to fill out the card in the back of this book. We have something special we want to send you for standing firm and persevering to the end. We are so very proud of you! Keep up the good work. See you back at The Discovery Bible Museum in the next book, *A Sneak Peek into the Future,* to finish our Revelation adventure in God's Word!

Molly, Max, and

(Sam)

Guided Instruction

D4Y "Bible Prophecy for Kids" Quizzes

Week 1: Unveiling a Mystery

1. What is God generally revealing to John in the third section of Revelation?
    a. Things which are
    b. Things which will take place after these things
    c. Things that won't happen
    d. Things that were

2. Who is blessed?
    a. Those who read, hear, and obey God's Word
    b. Brave people
    c. People who go to church
    d. People who share

3. Who did Jesus *first* give the mystery to?
    a. Paul
    b. Peter
    c. John
    d. The church

4. Who is John writing to?
    a. Angels
    b. Seven churches in Asia
    c. The Twelve Tribes
    d. The Apostles

5. What island was John banished to?
    a. Patmos
    b. Greece
    c. Crete
    d. Cyprus

6. What did John write to the seven churches?
    a. Thank-you notes
    b. Dreams he had
    c. What John saw
    d. Invitations

7. According to Revelation 1:12, what did John see?
    a. Many angels
    b. Adam and Eve
    c. Rivers
    d. Seven golden lampstands

8. Where was the one like the Son of Man standing?
    a. Under a tree
    b. In the middle of the lampstands
    c. In the clouds
    d. Next to John

9. What was in His right hand?
    a. Seven Swords
    b. Seven Suns
    c. Seven stars
    d. Seven Moons

10. What did these objects in His right hand represent?
    a. The choir
    b. Jesus
    c. The saints
    d. The angels of the seven churches

Memory Verse

Revelation 1:3

"Blessed is he who reads and those who hear the words of the prophecy and heed the things which are written in it; for the time is near."

Week 2: Jesus' Messages to the Churches

1. Which church left its first love?
   a. Pergamum
   b. Ephesus
   c. Sardis
   d. Smyrna

2. Which church was given *no* reproof?
   a. Smyrna
   b. Ephesus
   c. Sardis
   d. Laodicea

3. What did Jesus promise them?
   a. A party
   b. New robes
   c. No second death
   d. No trials

4. What will we receive if you remain faithful until death?
   a. The crown of life
   b. New robes
   c. Wealth
   d. Status

5. What church held the teachings of Balaam?
   a. Ephesus
   b. Sardis
   c. Pergamum
   d. Smyrna

6. What did Jesus warn Thyatira about?
   a. Tolerating immorality
   b. Not sharing
   c. Bad Worship
   d. Not praying

7. What did God choose us to be before Him?
   a. Wealthy
   b. Proud of our faith
   c. Holy and blameless
   d. Self-righteous

8. What are we to abstain from?
   a. Marriage
   b. Sexual immorality
   c. Partying
   d. Laziness

9. What are we *not* supposed to be?
   a. Too spiritual
   b. Conformed to the image of Christ
   c. Conformed to this world
   d. Too friendly

10. Who are we not to associate with?
    a. Immoral people
    b. Neighbors
    c. Classmates
    d. People in high position

Memory Verse

Revelation 2:4-5

"But I have this against you, that you have left your first love. Therefore remember from where you have fallen, and repent and do the deeds you did at first; or else I am coming to you and will remove your lampstand out of its place—unless you repent."

Week 3: Are You an Overcomer?

1. What instruction is given to the church of Sardis?
   a. Remember what you have received
   b. Return to doing good deeds
   c. Be friendly to newcomers
   d. Stay the way you are

2. What good thing did a few people do?
   a. Washed their clothes
   b. Gave up their money
   c. Didn't soil their garments
   d. Didn't wash their garments

3. What does "not soiled their garments" mean?
   a. Repent
   b. Stay pure
   c. Stay friendly
   d. Rejoice

4. What church is commended for keeping God's Word?
   a. Smyrna
   b. Sardis
   c. Philadelphia
   d. Ephesus

5. Which church is given *no* reproof?
   a. Philadelphia
   b. Sardis
   c. Smyrna
   d. Ephesus

6. What is our source of power?
   a. Working hard
   b. Wanting it
   c. The Holy Spirit
   d. Sharing

7. What church had no commendation or praise?
   a. Laodicea
   b. Pergamum
   c. Ephesus
   d. Smyrna

8. Jesus says, "Behold, I stand at the _____and knock.
   a. Window
   b. Door
   c. Curb
   d. Fireplace

9. What was the main problem of the church of Laodicea?
   a. Immorality
   b. Immature
   c. Lukewarm
   d. Apathy (didn't care)

10. What will Jesus do to them if they don't change?
    a. Ignore them
    b. Spit them out of His mouth
    c. Nothing
    d. Bless them

Memory Verse

1 John 5:5

"Who is the one who overcomes the world, but he who believes that Jesus is the Son of God?"

Week 4: The Mystery in Heaven

1. Where is John?
   a. In the Spirit, in heaven
   b. In Rome
   c. Home
   d. At Ephesus

2. What does he see?
   a. Angels
   b. A door standing open
   c. A river
   d. A large tree

3. What was before the throne?
   a. Seven angels
   b. Seven choirs
   c. Seven lamps of fire
   d. Seven seas

4. What are these seven objects (prior question)?
   a. Angels
   b. Spirits of God
   c. Singers
   d. Prayers of saints

5. What did John see in the hand of "Him who sat on the throne"?
   a. A drink
   b. A sword
   c. A book
   d. A robe

6. God's Book had seven ______.
   a. Names
   b. Seals
   c. Songs
   d. Chapters

7. What did John see between the throne and the four living creatures and elders?
   a. A goat
   b. A lion
   c. A Lamb
   d. A ram

8. What are the seven horns and seven eyes of the Lamb?
   a. Seven Lamps
   b. Seven Spirits
   c. Seven Angels
   d. Seven choirs

9. What were the Elders holding?
   a. Brass Lamps
   b. Bounded parchments
   c. Golden bowls
   d. Bronze bowls

10. What was the incense in the golden bowls?
    a. Prayers of the saints
    b. Spirits of God
    c. Acts of the saints
    d. Faith of the saints

Memory Verse

Revelation 4:11

"Worthy are You our Lord and our God, to receive glory and honor and power; for You created all things, and because of Your will they existed and were created."

Week 5: The Breaking of the Seals

1. What did John see the Lamb do?
   a. Break one of the seven seals
   b. Walk away
   c. Bless the Father
   d. Raise a sword

2. What did John see when the first seal was broken?
   a. A pale horse
   b. A white horse
   c. A red horse
   d. A black horse

3. The rider on the horse had a bow and a __________was given to him.
   a. Bowl
   b. Wings
   c. Crown
   d. Robe

4. What did John see when the second seal was broken?
   a. A large sword
   b. A white robe
   c. A red horse
   d. A black horn

5. What did the horse take from the earth?
   a. Angels
   b. Peace
   c. Fear
   d. Health

6. What did John see when the third seal was broken?
   a. Angels
   b. White horse
   c. Black horse
   d. Ashen horse

7. What did the black horse represent?
   a. Disease
   b. Famine
   c. Plague
   d. Harvest

8. What did John see when the fourth seal was opened?
   a. Red horse
   b. Ashen horse
   c. Red horse
   d. White horse

9. What did the Ashen horse represent?
   a. Famine
   b. War
   c. Death
   d. Peace

10. There was a great earthquake when the _____ seal was opened.
    a. Sixth
    b. First
    c. Third
    d. Second

Memory Verse

Revelation 7:17

"For the Lamb in the center of the throne will be their shepherd and will guide them to springs of the water of life; and God will wipe away every tear from their eyes."

D4Y "Bible Prophecy for Kids" Final Exam

1. What is God generally revealing to John in the third section of Revelation?
   a. Things which are
   b. Things which will take place after these things
   c. Things that won't happen
   d. Things that were

2. Who is blessed?
   a. Those who read, hear, and heed God's Word
   b. Brave people
   c. People who go to church
   d. People who share

3. Who did Jesus first give the mystery to?
   a. Paul
   b. Peter
   c. John
   d. The church

4. What did John write to the seven churches?
   a. Thank-you notes
   b. Dreams he had
   c. What God showed him
   d. Invitations

5. What represents the seven churches?
   a. Seven golden lampstands
   b. Seven bowls
   c. Seven trumpets
   d. Seven seals

6. What do the seven stars represent?
   a. Asia
   b. Jerusalem
   c. Angels of the seven churches
   d. The Holy Spirit

7. Which church left its first love?
   a. Philadelphia
   b. Ephesus
   c. Smyrna
   d. Sardis

8. Which two churches were given *no* reproof?
   a. Smyrna and Philadelphia
   b. Pergamum and Sardis
   c. Ephesus and Laodicea
   d. Pergamum and Ephesus

9. Which church had *no* commendation (praise)?
   a. Smyrna
   b. Sardis
   c. Laodicea
   d. Ephesus

10. Who/what is worthy to receive glory and honor?
    a. The twelve tribes of Israel
    b. Our Lord and God
    c. Believers.
    d. Priests

D4Y "Bible Prophecy for Kids" Final Exam

11. What are the seven lamps of fire?
    a. Seven Spirits of God
    b. Seven angels of the churches
    c. Seven bowls
    d. Seven choirs

12. What are those who have been bought by the blood of Jesus?
    a. Judges
    b. A kingdom and priests for God
    c. Martyrs
    d. Israelites

13. Who is worthy to break the seals?
    a. Michael the Archangel
    b. Gabriel
    c. Jesus—the Lamb standing as slain
    d. John

14. Match the seals to the correct horse.
    1. The red horse — a. death ___
    2. The white horse — b. famine ___
    3. The black horse — c. war ___
    4. The ashen horse — d. peace ___

15. Who are the martyrs under the altar?
    a. Angels watching the seals
    b. Believers who died for their testimony of Jesus
    c. Pharisees teaching righteousness
    d. James, Peter, and John

16. What happened when the sixth seal was broken?
    a. Earthquake
    b. Flood
    c. Plague
    d. Disease

17. Who are the 144,000 sealed?
    a. The Twelve Apostles
    b. Twelve kings
    c. Twelve tribes of Israel
    d. Twelve nations

18. How many were sealed from each tribe?
    a. 60,000
    b. 12,000
    c. 90,000
    d. 10,000

19. Who will stand before the throne and the Lamb after the tribulation?
    a. Believers, those who are clothed in white robes
    b. Elders
    c. Priests
    d. Singers

20. Where do these people come from?
    a. Asia
    b. Europe
    c. Every nation, tribe, people, and tongue
    d. Israel

Quiz Answer Key

Week 1	Week 2	Week 3	Week 4	Week 5
1. b	1. b	1. a	1. a	1. a
2. a	2. a	2. c	2. b	2. b
3. c	3. c	3. b	3. c	3. c
4. b	4. a	4. c	4. b	4. c
5. a	5. c	5. a	5. c	5. b
6. c	6. a	6. c	6. b	6. c
7. d	7. c	7. a	7. c	7. b
8. b	8. b	8. b	8. b	8. b
9. c	9. c	9. c	9. c	9. c
10. d	10. a	10. b	10. a	10. a

Final Answer Key

1. b
2. a
3. c
4. c
5. a
6. c
7. b
8. a
9. c
10. b
11. a
12. b
13. c
14. a. death (4) (ashen horse)
    b. famine (3) (black horse)
    c. war (1) (red horse)
    d. peace (2) (white horse)
15. b
16. a
17. c
18. b
19. a
20. c

Optional Games

Drawing Game

To play the drawing game you will need to type out what you want the kids to draw such as Jesus' Promises to the Overcomers, the six seals that are opened, and/or the events in Revelation 1–7 on a pieces of paper and cut them out individually.

Fold each slip of paper and place it in a zip-loc bag or a bowl.

Divide your class into two teams.

Have a child from Team 1 come up to the front of the class and draw out a slip of paper out of the bag. After he or she has picked a slip of paper out of the bag he or she will draw a sketch to depict what they have chosen on the whiteboard. Both teams watch as the child draws their sketch. When a child from either team thinks they know what is being drawn they may raise their hand and you call on the child whose hand you see first to answer. It can be a child from either team. If the answer is not guessed continue letting them guess until someone guesses the correct answer.

When the answer is guessed correctly, the team who answered the question receives 100 points for their team. Then, the teacher asks the student who guessed the drawing correctly a question that goes with that drawing. Such as if they were drawing "the tree of life", the teacher might ask, "WHAT church was promised if they overcame they would get to eat of the tree of life?" If the student answers the question correctly they receive another 100 points for their team for a total of 200 points. If they answer incorrectly, someone from the other team gets a chance to answer the question and receive 100 points for their team, with each team receiving 100 points.

After the points are given, it's Team 2's turn to pick a slip of paper out of the bag and draw the next promise, seal, or event. Go back and forth with each team until each paper is picked and drawn on the whiteboard. You may want to reward the winning team with a treat like a small piece of candy, or a privilege.

Optional Games

The Matching Game

You need at least ten questions and answers from the lesson you are studying.

Type the answers on a sheet of paper. Make two sets of answers and cut the answers into individual strips and place each set of answers in an envelope. For example you might want to write Jesus' Message to the churches on the slips of paper.

Divide your class into two teams. Pick a kid from each team and have them come up and stand in front of you, opposite each other (back to back) in the middle of the room. On each side of the room you have taken the answers out of each envelope and mixed them up and placed them in two piles on the floor.

You ask a question and tap the two students in front of you and say "Go." They have to run from you to their side of the room and look for the correct answer to the question you just asked in their pile. If they bring you an incorrect answer, tell them, "Wrong, try again" and they race back again to find the correct answer. The first one to race back to you and bring you the correct answer gets 100 points for their team. You continue to do this until you have answered all your questions and the team with the most points wins.

Optional Games

M&M® Draw

You will need a bag of M&M®s. Empty the bag into a container you can't see through.

Write the point values for each color of the M&M®s on a white board for all the kids to see. I choose point values depending on how many there are of each color—the more there are of a color the lower the point value with the lesser color amounts receiving the highest amount of points. Such as:

Brown: 100 points

Red: 200 points

Yellow: 300 points

Green: 400 points

Blue: 500 points

Orange: 600 points

Divide the kids into two teams and ask a question from the lesson or book you are studying. If the kid you pick from the first team answers the question correctly, he or she closes their eyes and picks an M&M® from the container. Once they have chosen a color, they get to eat the candy and you record the points they won on the board for their team. But if they miss the question, the other team gets a chance to steal the question by answering it and drawing an M&M®; then it's that team's turn to answer a question. You go back and forth with each team until you have answered all your questions. The team with the most points wins.

Reward them with a small piece of candy or a privilege.

If you are working with one student you can still play the game by asking the questions and letting the child answer and draw an M&M® if he/she answers correctly. Tell them if they get to a certain number of points they will receive a reward or privilege.

Learn how

you can be involved in "Establishing People in God's Word" at **precept.org/connect**

Use your smartphone to get connected to Precept's ministry initiatives! **Precept.org/connect**

Precept Online Community

provides support, training opportunities, and exclusive resources to help Bible study leaders and students.

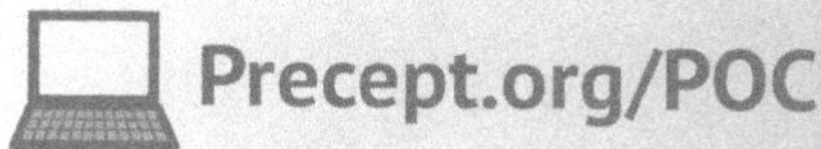

Use your smartphone to connect to Precept Online Community! **Precept.org/POC**

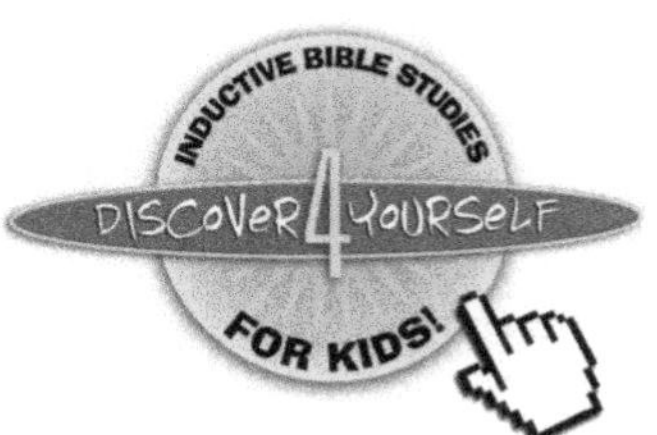

Join The Discover 4 Yourself Inductive Bible Studies for Kids! Group in Precept Online Community

CPSIA information can be obtained
at www.ICGtesting.com
Printed in the USA
FSHW021610231020
75008FS

THE MAILBOX®

Fascinating Fac

SOCIAL S UDIES

100 Comprehension-B g Activities

- Community Services
- Citizenship and National Symbols
- Time and Change
- H ic F s
- H ys and C ations

so includes ady-to-use ew game!

Managing Editor: Hope Taylor Spencer

Editorial Team: Becky S. Andrews, Kimberley Bruck, Sharon Murphy, Debra Liverman, Diane Badden, Thad H. McLaurin, Jennifer Bragg, Karen A. Brudnak, Juli Docimo Blair, Hope Rodgers, Dorothy C. McKinney, Stephanie Affinito, Juli Engel, Kim Minafo

Production Team: Lori Z. Henry, Pam Crane, Rebecca Saunders, Chris Curry, Sarah Foreman, Theresa Lewis Goode, Greg D. Rieves, Eliseo De Jesus Santos II, Barry Slate, Donna K. Teal, Zane Williard, Tazmen Carlisle, Kathy Coop, Marsha Heim, Lynette Dickerson, Mark Rainey, Amy Kirtley-Hill

www.themailbox.com

©2007 The Mailbox® Books
All rights reserved.
ISBN10 #1-56234-751-9 • ISBN13 #978-1-56234-751-2

Except as provided for herein, no part of this publication may be reproduced or transmitted in any form or by any means, electronic or mechanical, including photocopying, recording, or storing in any information storage and retrieval system or electronic online bulletin board, without prior written permission from The Education Center, Inc. Permission is given to the original purchaser to reproduce patterns and reproducibles for individual classroom use only and not for resale or distribution. Reproduction for an entire school or school system is prohibited. Please direct written inquiries to The Education Center, Inc., P.O. Box 9753, Greensboro, NC 27429-0753. The Education Center®, *The Mailbox*®, the mailbox/post/grass logo, and The Mailbox Book Company® are registered trademarks of The Education Center, Inc. All other brand or product names are trademarks or registered trademarks of their respective companies.

Printed in the United States
10 9 8 7 6 5 4 3

HPS 227868

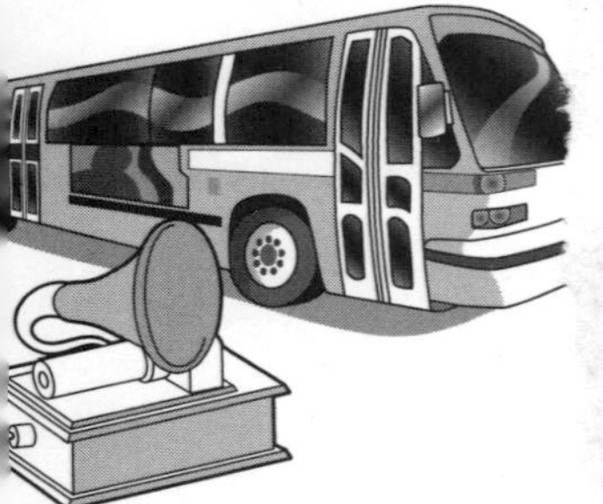

…ble of Contents

Community S…

Citizenship … nal Symbols

Time and Ch…

Historic Figures

Holidays and Celebrations

What's Inside

100 Reproducible Activities

Inside this book, you'll find activities that support 50 essential social studies topics. Each topic is reinforced with two engaging reproducible activities that can be used together or separately.

Featured Topic

Fascinating Fact

Brief Reading Passage

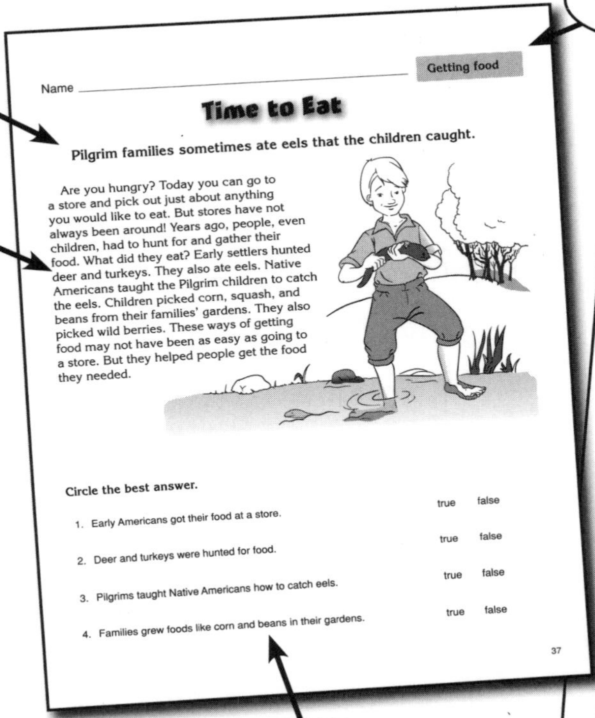

Name ______________________ Getting food

Time to Eat

Pilgrim families sometimes ate eels that the children caught.

Are you hungry? Today you can go to a store and pick out just about anything you would like to eat. But stores have not always been around! Years ago, people, even children, had to hunt for and gather their food. What did they eat? Early settlers hunted deer and turkeys. They also ate eels. Native Americans taught the Pilgrim children to catch the eels. Children picked corn, squash, and beans from their families' gardens. They also picked wild berries. These ways of getting food may not have been as easy as going to a store. But they helped people get the food they needed.

Circle the best answer.

1. Early Americans got their food at a store. true false
2. Deer and turkeys were hunted for food. true false
3. Pilgrims taught Native Americans how to catch eels. true false
4. Families grew foods like corn and beans in their gardens. true false

37

Comprehension Activity

A second fun activity further reinforces the skill.

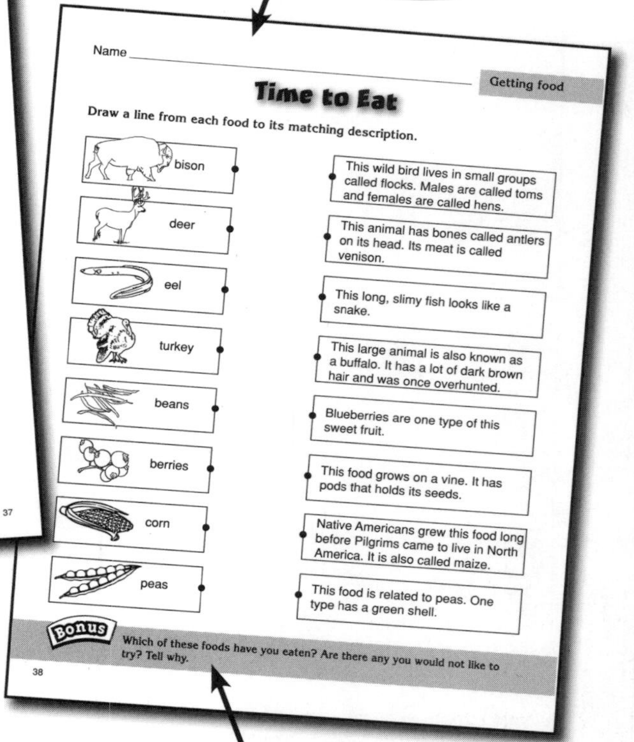

Name ______________________ Getting food

Time to Eat

Draw a line from each food to its matching description.

bison	This wild bird lives in small groups called flocks. Males are called toms and females are called hens.
deer	This animal has bones called antlers on its head. Its meat is called venison.
eel	This long, slimy fish looks like a snake.
turkey	This large animal is also known as a buffalo. It has a lot of dark brown hair and was once overhunted.
beans	Blueberries are one type of this sweet fruit.
berries	This food grows on a vine. It has pods that holds its seeds.
corn	Native Americans grew this food long before Pilgrims came to live in North America. It is also called maize.
peas	This food is related to peas. One type has a green shell.

Bonus Which of these foods have you eaten? Are there any you would not like to try? Tell why.

38

Bonus Enrichment Activity

Ready-to-Use Trivia Game

On pages 105–120, you'll find an exciting trivia game containing 150 cards that review all 50 topics covered in this book. Use the game to review just one topic or use all the cards as a fun year-end review. The game cards also make great flash cards for review.

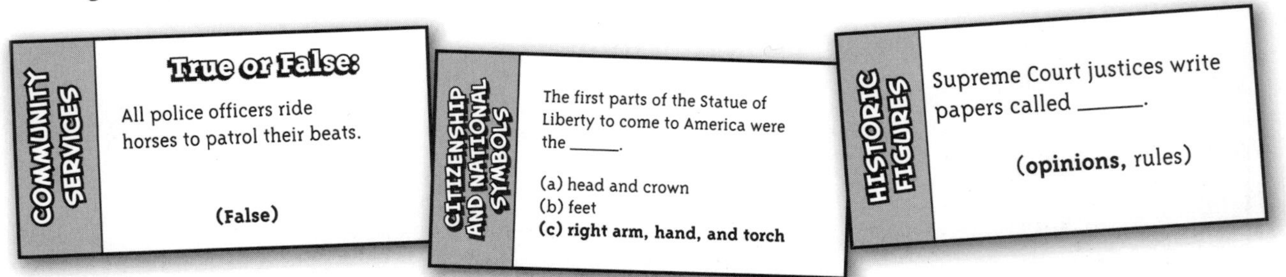

How to Use

Use *Fascinating Facts: Social Studies* as

- morning work
- a center activity
- homework
- enrichment
- remediation
- work for early finishers
- small-group practice
- independent practice

Use *Fascinating Facts: Social Studies* to

- engage students in the learning of social studies
- integrate reading with social studies
- provide independent practice of key social studies concepts
- strengthen comprehension of nonfiction texts
- provide extra practice for struggling readers
- introduce a new social studies topic
- review content before a test
- provide practice with answering questions in different formats

Name ______________________________

Work Clothes

A firefighter may wear over 75 pounds of clothing and gear.

Firefighters risk their lives each time they go to work. They save people from fires. They also help people after a flood, an earthquake, or a car wreck.

Firefighters wear special clothes and gear. These things help keep them safe while they work. Firefighters wear turnout coats. These long coats have big yellow stripes. The stripes glow in the dark and make the firefighters easier to see.

Firefighters also wear thick gloves to protect their hands from fire. Boots protect their feet. Helmets with wide brims protect them from falling objects and water. Firefighters wear air tanks to breathe clean air and carry many tools too.

Draw a line to match each word to its definition.

air tank •	• worn to protect the feet and legs from heat and fire
boots •	• has yellow stripes that make the firefighter easier to see
gloves •	• used to breathe clean air
helmet •	• worn to protect the hands and to hold on to gear
turnout coat •	• keeps the head safe from falling objects and water

Name ______________________________

Work Clothes

Unscramble the letters to form the missing words.
Use the word bank to help you.

Word Bank
boots
gloves
helmet
air tank
turnout coat

1. The __ __ __ __ __ __ __   __ __ __ __ is made of fireproof material. It is also called a bunker coat and can weigh over 20 pounds. (o o t t a r u n t c u)

2. Some __ __ __ __ __ __ are made of pigskin. They will not shrink if they get wet. They protect the firefighter's hands. (s g e l o v)

3. The __ __ __ __ __ can be made of leather or rubber. They are made to keep the firefighter's feet and legs safe. (s b o t o)

4. The __ __ __ __ __ __ protects the firefighter's head, ears, and eyes. Some are made of leather and a strong plastic. (e e t m l h)

5. The __ __ __   __ __ __ __ can weigh more than 30 pounds. It is carried on the firefighter's back. It helps the firefighter breathe clean air. (t a a i k n r)

Which piece of clothing or gear do you think is most important to a firefighter? Tell why.

©The Mailbox® • *Fascinating Facts: Social Studies* • TEC61065 • Key p. 121

Name ____________________

Getting Around Town

There are about 1,200 bicycle units across the United States.

Police officers work hard to keep their communities safe. They make sure people follow the laws. They also help people solve problems.

Some officers are assigned a beat, or a part of town to patrol. Police officers have many ways to get from place to place in their beats. Some drive patrol cars. Patrol cars can move fast and can hold lots of gear. Other officers ride motorcycles. These are good for moving around places with a lot of traffic.

If the community has bodies of water, an officer might be part of a boat patrol. Officers might even ride bikes or horses to tour their assigned beats. And some officers simply walk their beats!

Answer the questions.
Use the passage to help you.

1. What are two things police officers do to keep their communities safe? ____________________
2. What is a beat? ____________________
3. What are two ways patrol cars can help officers? ____________________
4. How are motorcycles helpful to police officers? ____________________
5. What are two other ways police officers move around their beats? ____________________

Getting Around Town

Read the clues.
Use the word bank to complete each sentence.
Write the word in the puzzle.

Across:

2. Walking, or ___ patrol, is the oldest form of patrol work.
3. ___ help officers patrol bays and rivers.
5. Police officers keep their communities ___.

Down:

1. Riding a ___ is a good way to patrol public parks.
3. There are about 1,200 ___ patrol units across the United States.
4. Patrol ___ can move fast.

Word Bank

bike	cars	boats
foot	safe	horse

If you were a police officer, how would you like to travel your beat? Tell why.

©The Mailbox® • *Fascinating Facts: Social Studies* • TEC61065 • Key p. 121

Name ____________________

Cleanup Crew

Some trash collectors make 500 stops a day!

The trash has been bagged, placed in the can, and rolled to the curb. Then what happens? A trash truck with one or two workers on board comes by to pick it up. Some trucks make 500 pickups a day!

Next, the truck goes to a transfer station. Here the driver opens the back of the truck to let out the trash. Then a bulldozer pushes the trash into a tractor trailer.

The tractor trailer takes the trash to a place called a landfill. The trash is piled into a big hole in the ground. Sometimes the trash is burned in a large pit instead.

Number the sentences to show the order in which they occur.

____ Finally, the trash is buried or burned.

____ A bulldozer pushes the trash into a tractor trailer.

____ First, workers pick up trash from the curb.

____ The workers take the truck to a transfer station.

____ The trash travels on the trailer to a landfill.

____ The trash is moved off the truck.

Name ______________________________

Cleanup Crew

Use the code below.
Write the letters on the numbered lines.

Help Wanted!
Trash Collector

Man or woman needed to ___ ___ ___ ___ trucks
7 9 1 2

with ___ ___ ___ ___ ___. Must be able to lift up
13 11 1 12 5

to 50 ___ ___ ___ ___ ___ ___ and work
10 9 14 8 2 12

___ ___ ___ ___ ___ ___. Duties also include
12 1 4 3 7 16

working ___ ___ ___ ___ ___ ___ ___ in hot and
9 14 13 12 6 2 3

cold ___ ___ ___ ___ ___ ___ ___.
15 3 1 13 5 3 11

Please call 555-0123

to apply.

Code

A	D	E	F	H	I	L	N	O	P	R	S	T	U	W	Y
1	2	3	4	5	6	7	8	9	10	11	12	13	14	15	16

What parts of being a trash collector would be fun? What parts would not be fun? Make two lists.

©The Mailbox® • *Fascinating Facts: Social Studies* • TEC61065 • Key p. 121

Name ____

Bus Stop

Bus drivers must have a special license, called a CDL, before they can drive a bus.

Bus drivers help people get from place to place. Some drivers drive small buses. Some drive large buses. Each driver has an important job. They must keep their riders safe. Drivers must pass tests before they can drive a bus. The drivers' skills are tested. When they pass the tests, they can have a CDL. Testing drivers is one way to keep riders safe.

Drivers do other things to keep riders safe. Drivers check their buses before they leave. They check the lights on the bus. They also check the brakes, steering, and tires. Other drivers have to check the safety gear on their buses. They make sure that the bus has a fire extinguisher and first aid kit. Bus drivers are busy. They have to get each rider where he wants to be. But they also have to make sure each rider is safe.

Make each sentence true.
Cross out the word that does not belong.
Write a word from the word bank above it.

Word Bank
drivers
license
safe
Some

1. All bus drivers drive large buses.
2. A driver must have a special hat before he can drive a bus.
3. Some teachers check the safety gear on their buses.
4. Drivers must keep their passengers moving.

©The Mailbox® • *Fascinating Facts: Social Studies* • TEC61065 • Key p. 121

Name ______________________________

Bus Stop

Look at the map and the map key.

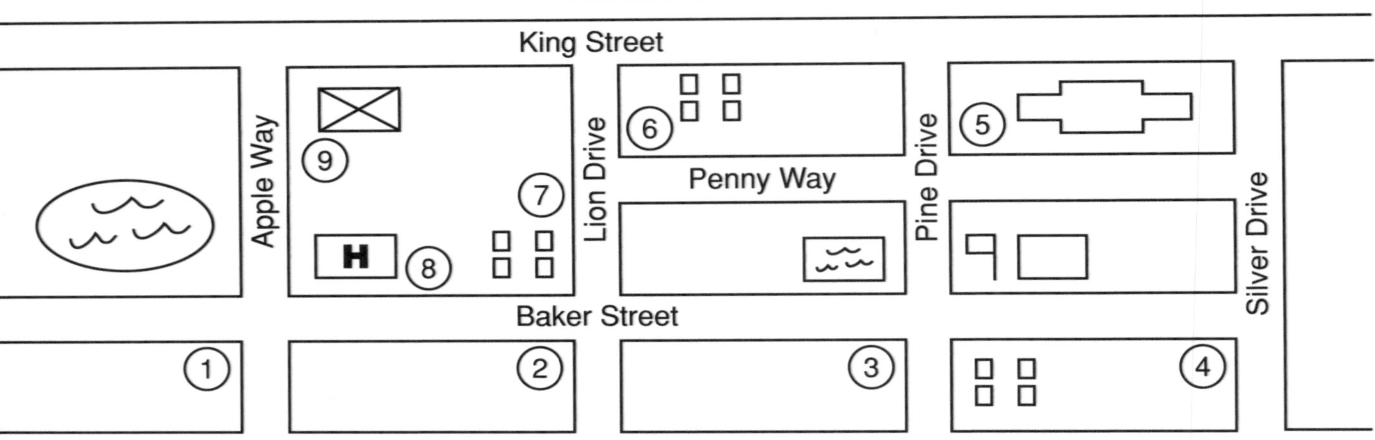

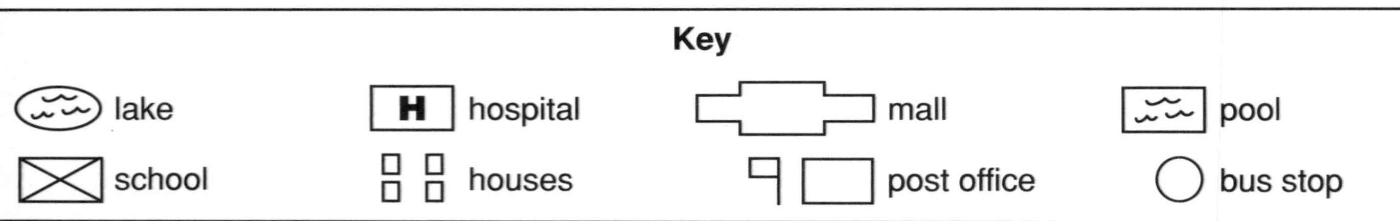

Circle the best answer for each question.

1. Which place is closest to bus stop 1?
   a. the mall
   b. the lake
   c. the pool

2. Which street is bus stop 8 on?
   a. Pine Drive
   b. Silver Drive
   c. Baker Street

3. Which of these bus stops is not by a group of houses?
   a. 5
   b. 7
   c. 3

4. Which bus stop is closest to the mall?
   a. 4
   b. 5
   c. 9

5. Which place is closest to bus stop 9?
   a. the pool
   b. the post office
   c. the school

6. Which street is bus stop 6 on?
   a. King Street
   b. Penny Way
   c. Baker Street

Why is a bus driver an important part of the community?

©The Mailbox® • *Fascinating Facts: Social Studies* • TEC61065 • Key p. 121

Name ______________________________

Check Out the Library!

There are over 117,000 libraries in the United States.

There are many types of libraries. Some are large. Some are very small. Different types of communities need different libraries. Lots of libraries have books. They also have magazines and newspapers. Some libraries even have videos and DVDs. Other libraries are more unique.

There are libraries that have special objects. Some offer equipment for people who cannot see. There is a library that carries maps and charts for explorers. There is even a library that lends tools! This library loans many types of tools, from ladders to putty knives. People borrow the tools to use in their homes.

Libraries can be found in many places. There are libraries in schools. There are libraries in prisons. There is even a library on a U.S. Navy ship! Libraries are for everyone.

Unscramble the letters to form the missing words.

1. Lots of libraries have __ __ __ __ __. (o k o b s)
2. Some libraries have __ __ __ __ __ __. (o d i v e s)
3. People can __ __ __ __ __ __ tools to use in their homes. (r b w o o r)
4. There are libraries in __ __ __ __ __ __ __. (o o s l h c s)

©The Mailbox® • *Fascinating Facts: Social Studies* • TEC61065 • Key p. 121

Name ____________________

Check Out the Library!

If the sentence is a fact, color the book red.
If the sentence is an opinion, color the book yellow.

Some libraries have books and magazines.

Kids love to go to the library!

Some libraries let people check out videos and DVDs.

Other libraries have special equipment for people who can't see well.

Big libraries are better than small libraries.

One library lets people check out tools to use in their homes.

People should visit the library once a week.

There are libraries in schools.

There is a library on a U.S. Navy ship.

There are different types of libraries.

Libraries have too many books.

Imagine that you could set up a special library in your community. What would your library offer?

©The Mailbox® • *Fascinating Facts: Social Studies* • TEC61065 • Key p. 121

Name ______________________________

He's in Charge!

The youngest mayor in America was elected when he was 18 years old.

Michael Sessions became the mayor of Hillsdale, Michigan, in 2005. He was 18 years old. Mayors are elected. Michael was too young to run for mayor when the race started. His name was not on the ballot. Michael wanted people to vote for him. He asked them to write his name on the ballot. Michael won the election!

When Michael was first elected, he was a high school student. Then, every day at 3:00, he started his job as mayor.

Michael's days are busy. He has lots of meetings. Michael leads the city council meetings. The city council is in charge of the government in Hillsdale. He also meets with the city manager. The city manager is in charge of what happens in Hillsdale. Michael spends time with city workers too. He meets with the fire chief and road workers. Although he is young, Michael does the same kind of work that many other mayors do.

Write a word that completes each sentence. Use the word bank to help you.

Word Bank		
leaders	meetings	elected

1. Some people become mayors when they are ______________.
2. A mayor is one of the city's ______________.
3. A mayor might have to go to a lot of ______________.

Name ________________________________

He's in Charge!

Read the mayor's schedule.

Wednesday	Thursday
3:00–3:30: catch up on emails	3:00–3:30: catch up on emails
3:30–4:00: meet with fire chief	3:30–4:15: meet with city manager
4:00–4:45: go downtown to store opening	4:15–5:00: meet with director of safety
4:45–5:15: meet with people from the community	5:00–5:30: meet with people from the community
5:15–6:00: lead city council meeting	5:30–6:00: ride in city parade

Circle the best answer for each question.
Use the mayor's schedule to help you.

1. Which thing does the mayor do on both days?
   a. lead the city council meeting
   b. catch up on emails
   c. meet with the fire chief

2. On which day will the mayor go to a store opening?
   a. Wednesday
   b. Thursday
   c. both days

3. How long will the mayor's meeting with the city manager last?
   a. 15 minutes
   b. 30 minutes
   c. 45 minutes

4. What will the mayor do after he meets with the director of safety?
   a. meet with people from the community
   b. lead the city council meeting
   c. meet with the fire chief

Think of a problem in your neighborhood or school. Write a letter to your mayor asking him or her to fix the problem.

©The Mailbox® • *Fascinating Facts: Social Studies* • TEC61065 • Key p. 121

Name ______________________________

The Right to Vote

In the days of early America, only white men who owned land were allowed to cast their votes.

When the country was new, only certain people could vote. White men who owned land were the only voters. Women did not get to vote until 1920. For some people, it took even longer. The 15th Amendment to the U.S. Constitution was passed in 1870. Although it said that all men had the right to vote, it wasn't true.

As time passed, some places made rules that kept black people from voting. Some charged a poll tax. A poll tax meant that people had to pay money to cast a vote. The tax was outlawed in 1964. Some places made black people take written tests to try to keep them from voting.

In 1965, a new law was passed. It was called the Voting Rights Act. Almost 200 years after the country was born, the rules were fair. Today, men and women who are at least 18 years old have the right to vote.

Write a date in each box to complete the voting timeline. Use the passage to help you.

____________ date	____________ date	____________ date	____________ date
15th Amendment All men have the right to vote.	19th Amendment Women have the right to vote.	24th Amendment Poll taxes are outlawed.	Voting Rights Act No one can be denied the right to vote.

Name ______________________________

The Right to Vote

Look at the chart.

Year of Presidential Election	Number of People That Could Sign Up to Vote	Number of People That Did Sign Up to Vote	Number of People That Signed Up and Voted
1988	182,630,000	126,381,202	91,594,693
1992	189,044,500	133,821,178	104,405,155
1996	196,511,000	146,211,960	96,456,345
2000	205,815,000	156,421,311	105,586,274
2004	221,256,931	174,800,000	122,294,978

Answer each question with a complete sentence.

1. From 1988 to 1992, did the number of people that could sign up to vote get larger or smaller? ______________________________
2. Why do you think there are four years between each of the dates on the chart?
____
____
3. In which year did the most voters sign up to vote? ______________________________
4. Do you think enough people voted in 2004? Why or why not? ______________________________
____
____

When you are old enough to vote, will you? Why or why not?

©The Mailbox® • *Fascinating Facts: Social Studies* • TEC61065 • Key p. 121

Name ______________________________

Because of Columbus

The first pledge to the flag was written to help celebrate the first Columbus Day.

A children's magazine was planning a celebration in 1892. It would soon be 400 years since Columbus found a new world across the Atlantic Ocean. It would be called Columbus Day. The magazine asked children to raise money to buy United States flags. The flags were for their schools.

Francis Bellamy was one of the people who wrote the magazine. He and other editors wanted the children to say something about the flags. Other people liked the idea too. The president said that Columbus Day would be a holiday. So Bellamy wrote a short flag pledge. His pledge was 23 words long. Some of the words were hard. Teachers helped their students learn what the words meant.

When the day came, the flags were raised. Children proudly said the pledge. Since then, the pledge has been changed three times. But the pride behind the words has stayed the same.

Write the letter for each effect statement on the line in front of its matching cause statement.

Causes

_____ 1. Schools needed flags.

_____ 2. People who wrote a magazine wanted children to have words to say about the United States flag.

_____ 3. Some words in the pledge were hard.

Effects

A. One of the editors wrote a pledge to the flag.

B. Teachers helped students understand them.

C. Children raised money to buy flags.

Name ________________________________

Because of Columbus

Read the Pledge of Allegiance.

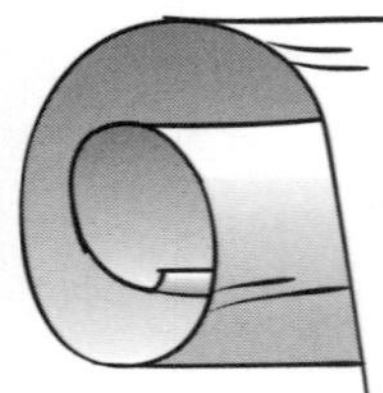

I **pledge allegiance** to the flag
of the United States of America
and to the **Republic** for which it stands,
one **Nation** under God, **indivisible,**
with **liberty** and **justice** for all.

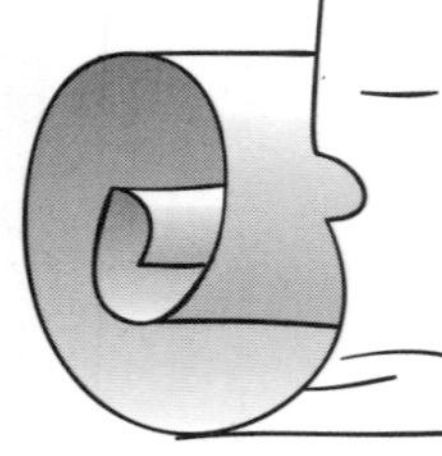

Write each bold word from above next to its definition below. Use a dictionary to help you.

1. ________________________________: fairness
2. ________________________________: country
3. ________________________________: can't be pulled apart
4. ________________________________: a government that lets people vote
5. ________________________________: to be loyal to something
6. ________________________________: a promise
7. ________________________________: freedom

Imagine that you have been asked to write a new pledge to the flag. What will you write?

©The Mailbox® • *Fascinating Facts: Social Studies* • TEC61065 • Key p. 122

Name ____________________

Flying Over Fort McHenry

"The Star-Spangled Banner" was written by Francis Scott Key while he was being held as a prisoner on a British ship.

Francis Scott Key was not a soldier. He was a lawyer. He went to Baltimore to beg for the release of a friend. British leaders heard his plea. They agreed to let his friend go. But first, they planned to attack Fort McHenry. The British did not want Key to warn those at Fort McHenry of their plans. So they held him on a ship as a prisoner. Key was helpless. All he could do was watch from the deck of his floating prison.

The bombs were bursting. The night sky was lit up. The battle roared for hours. Then morning came. In the light, Key could see it! The American flag was still flying above the fort! The British had not won the battle. Key scribbled the start of a poem on the back of a letter. At a hotel, he revised his poem. Then he shared his poem with others. Soon it became a song. Today that song is our national anthem.

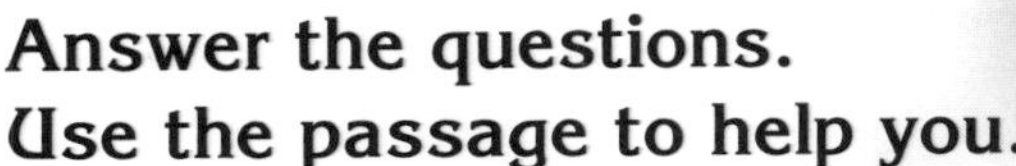

Answer the questions.
Use the passage to help you.

1. What form did Francis Scott Key use to write his thoughts? Circle your answer.

   a letter   a poem   a song

2. What would have happened to the American flag if the British had won the battle at Fort McHenry? ____________________

   ____

3. Did the British let Key go after the battle? How do you know? ____________________

   ____

   ____

Name ______________________________

Flying Over Fort McHenry

Complete "The Star-Spangled Banner."
Write a synonym for each word on the line above the word.
Use the word bank to help you.

Oh! say, can you see, by the ______________ early ______________ ,
morning's glow

What so proudly we ______________ at the ______________ last gleaming?
welcomed evening's

Whose ______________ stripes and bright stars, through the ______________ fight,
wide dangerous

O'er the ______________ we watched were so ______________ streaming?
walls nobly

And the rockets' red ______________ , the bombs bursting in air,
light

Gave proof through the ______________ that our flag was still there.
evening

Oh! say, does that star-spangled banner ______________ wave
still

O'er the land of the free and the home of the ______________ ?
bold

Word Bank

broad	ramparts	night
twilight's	brave	perilous
glare	hailed	yet
light	dawn's	gallantly

Find three words in "The Star-Spangled Banner" that rhyme. Use each of these words in a poem you write about the flag.

©The Mailbox® • *Fascinating Facts: Social Studies* • TEC61065 • Key p. 122

Name ______________________________

Stars and Stripes—and a Snake?

Before the United States adopted its official flag, Americans flew several different flags, including one with a snake on it.

In 1773, a new flag was raised at the Boston Tea Party. The flag had 13 stripes. Those stripes sent a message to England. It said that the colonies would work as one unit. But it was not the only flag flying over America. Over the years, people had made other flags. Some had pine trees on them. Others had snakes.

In 1777, Congress decided on one flag. The flag would be red, white, and blue. It would have one stripe and one star for each of the 13 colonies. But there was no rule about how the stars would be arranged. Sometimes the stars were sewn in a circle. Sometimes they were sewn in rows. In 1912, the president made a rule that the stars must be in rows.

Now there are 13 stripes on the flag, one for each of the colonies. There are 50 stars on the flag, one for each of the states.

If the sentence is true, color the flag red.
If the sentence is false, color the flag blue.

1. Some people made flags with snakes on them.
2. The first official flag was red, white, and blue.
3. The first flag had one stripe for each of the months of the year.
4. On the first flags, the stars had to be sewn in a circle.
5. There are 50 stars on the American flag.

Name ________________________________

Stars and Stripes—and a Snake?

Complete the rules for caring for the flag.
Use the word bank to help you.
Circle the words in the puzzle below.

1. The flag should be flown near the __ __ __ __ __ of every school.
2. The flag should __ __ __ __ __ touch the ground.
3. The flag should be flown only when the __ __ __ __ __ __ __ is fair.
4. The flag can only be flown at __ __ __ __ __ if it is well lit.
5. The flag should be raised __ __ __ __ __ __ __.
6. The flag should be __ __ __ __ __ __ __ slowly.

Word Bank

quickly	front	night
weather	never	lowered

							f	s	a	p	w	e	n	j
							r	l	o	w	e	r	e	d
							o	l	d	h	a	f	v	i
							n	i	g	h	t	c	e	t
q	u	i	c	k	l	y	t	o	h	w	h	m	r	g
f	l	b	n	h	e	m	b	a	n	q	e	b	u	k
g	d	l	a	k	c	j	r	z	c	v	r	y	l	x

Imagine that you have been asked to design a new flag for the United States. What would you think about before you designed the flag? Draw a picture of the new flag.

©The Mailbox® • *Fascinating Facts: Social Studies* • TEC61065 • Key p. 122

Name ______________________________

not back

Proud and Strong

Our Founding Fathers debated for six years before they chose the bald eagle as our national symbol.

The bald eagle is the national symbol of the United States. Not everybody felt that the eagle was the best choice. Ben Franklin felt that the eagle was a poor choice. He said that eagles steal food from other birds. Franklin didn't think the eagle was special enough. He said that other countries had used the eagle as their symbols.

People who wanted the eagle said that an eagle is strong. They said that an eagle is brave and flies freely. They also argued that the bald eagle can be found only in North America.

The debate went on for six years. When Congress voted, the eagle was chosen as the national symbol. Over time, it has landed in many places. An eagle can be found on money and stamps. It's on the Great Seal of the United States. It's even on U.S. mail trucks. The eagle was not a quick pick. But it has been a lasting choice.

Answer the questions.

1. List reasons why people wanted the bald eagle to be the national symbol.

____

____

____

2. Would you have voted for the bald eagle? Tell why or why not. ______________

____

____

____

Name ______________________________

Proud and Strong

Cut apart the boxes below.
Glue each one in place to label the diagram of the Great Seal of the United States.

Ben Franklin wanted the turkey to be the national symbol. He thought a turkey was a respectable bird that was native to North America. Do you think a turkey would make a good national symbol? Why or why not?

©The Mailbox® • *Fascinating Facts: Social Studies* • TEC61065 • Key p. 122

A bald eagle is in the center of the seal.	There are 13 stars above the eagle's head. The stars represent the nation of 13 states.	The eagle holds 13 arrows. The arrows stand for the first 13 states.
The shield in front of the eagle has 13 stripes on it. The stripes stand for the first 13 states.	The eagle holds an olive branch. There are 13 olives and 13 leaves. They stand for the first 13 states.	The shield is red, white, and blue. Red stands for courage. Blue stands for justice. White stands for purity.

Name ____________________

The Seat of the Nation

It took 36 years for the United States Capitol to be constructed.

In 1793, Washington, DC, was a new city. Much of the land had just been cleared. The new city was not easy to get to or live in. There were no trucks or trains to bring in people or supplies. Progress was slow. Congress kept working in Philadelphia, Pennsylvania.

After seven years, part of the Capitol was ready. Congress moved in. Then war broke out. In 1814, the British set fire to much of the city. The Capitol was badly burned.

After the war, work started up again. The dome was made bigger. The grounds were completed. Work finally ended in 1829. It had been a long road. But 36 years later, the job was done at last!

Draw a line to match each sentence starter to its ending.

1. In 1793, •	• in 1829.
2. There were no trucks or trains •	• to bring in people or supplies.
3. In 1814, •	• the British set fire to much of the city.
4. Work finally ended •	• Washington, DC, was a new city.

Name ____

The Seat of the Nation

Read the passage below.
Follow the directions.

The Statue of Freedom sits on top of the dome of the United States Capitol. The statue is 19 feet, six inches tall. It weighs about 15,000 pounds.

- The statue has a **sheathed sword** in its right hand. Color the sheathed sword blue.
- In its left hand, it has a **wreath of victory.** Color the wreath green.
- It also has the **shield** of the United States. The shield has 13 stripes on it. Color the shield red.
- The helmet has **stars** around it. Color the stars yellow.
- The helmet also has a **crest** made of an eagle's head, feathers, and talons. The crest honors Native Americans. Color the crest brown.
- The robes are secured by a **pin** that has a design that says "U.S." Color the pin orange.

Imagine that you have been asked to design a statue that represents freedom. What would your statue look like? Design your statue. Write a paragraph explaining your design.

©The Mailbox® • *Fascinating Facts: Social Studies* • TEC61065 • Key p. 122

Name ______________________________

Shades of Marble

Although the Washington Monument is made mostly of marble, the top section appears to be a different color than the bottom section.

The Washington Monument is about 555 feet tall. Its outside walls are made of white marble. But the marble at the top is not the same color as the marble at the bottom. When the tower was about 150 feet tall, work had to stop. First, the money ran out. Then the Civil War started. The project was on hold for 25 years.

Finally, the work started again. But the builders could not get marble from the same place they had gotten it before. The new marble was the same type they had been using. But after the stone had been in the weather, the colors were not a perfect match. The different colors mark the place where the two parts meet. Some people may see the line as a flaw. Others may view the ring as part of our nation's unique history.

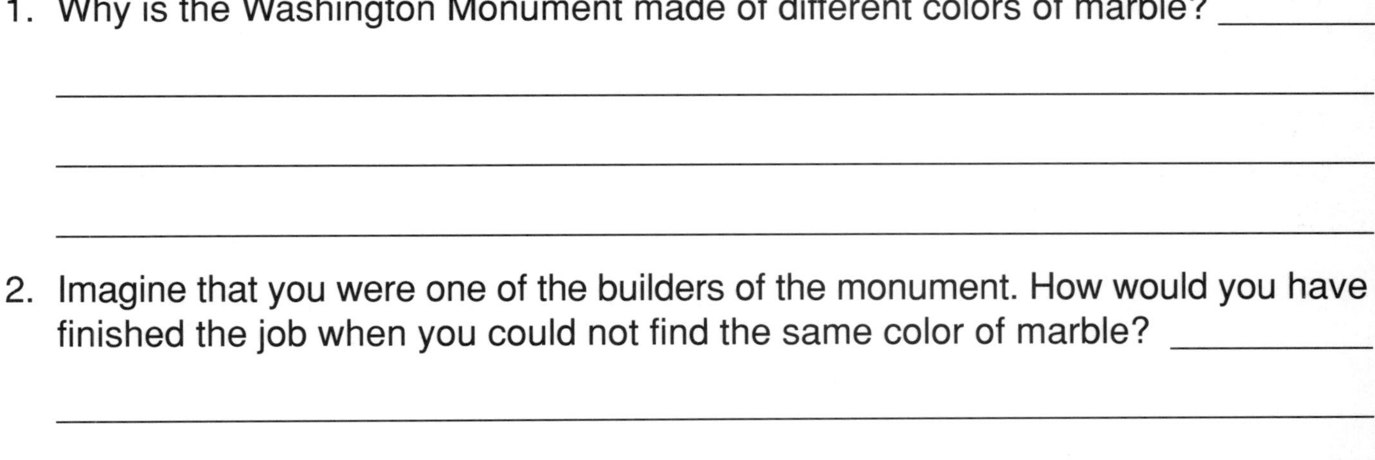

Answer the questions.

1. Why is the Washington Monument made of different colors of marble? ________

   ____

   ____

   ____

2. Imagine that you were one of the builders of the monument. How would you have finished the job when you could not find the same color of marble? ________

   ____

   ____

   ____

Name ____

Shades of Marble

Write the letter of each question next to its matching answer. Use context clues to help you.

I. How many people visit the monument each year?

L. When did work on the monument begin and end?

K. Which states did the marble come from?

S. How tall is the monument?

O. What 50 objects, one for each state, are flown around the base of the monument?

E. How much did it cost to build the monument?

B. How much does the monument weigh?

☐ 1. American flags

☐ 2. 90,854 tons

☐ 3. $1,187,710

☐ 4. 1848, 1884

☐ 5. more than one million

☐ 6. about 555 feet

☐ 7. Maryland and Massachusetts

The letters of the answers spell out a word. Explain what this word has to do with the Washington Monument.

©The Mailbox® • *Fascinating Facts: Social Studies* • TEC61065 • Key p. 122

Name ____

What a Gift!

Although the Statue of Liberty stands in New York Harbor, the statue's right arm and torch made their first appearance in Philadelphia, Pennsylvania.

The Statue of Liberty was built in France. It was started in 1875. The man who designed the statue wanted people to see it. But it wasn't finished. He sent the right arm, hand, and torch to Philadelphia, Pennsylvania. People paid 50 cents each to stand on the deck of the torch. The display was a hit! Soon, the head and crown were done too. They were put on a wagon and led through the streets of Paris. People cheered as the wagon passed.

By February 1884, the whole statue was finished. But then the builders had to take it apart! There was no way to get the gift from France to America in one piece. The pieces were packed into 214 crates. The crates were shipped across the ocean. More than a year later, the parts were put back together. In 1886, the gift was finished. And what a gift it was!

Number the events to show the order in which they occurred. The first one has been done for you.

_____ The head and crown were finished.

_____ The statue was finished.

_____ The statue was put back together in America.

_____ The gift was shipped from France.

__1__ The right arm and torch were shown in Philadelphia.

Name ____________________

What a Gift!

**Write a word from the word bank on each line.
Use the clues to help you.**

The __________ (object that gives off a flame) is 21 feet tall.

There are seven __________ (long, pointy parts) on the crown. The longest is over 11 feet long.

The right __________ (body part between the shoulder and hand) is 42 feet long.

Each __________ (part of the body that is used for sight) is two feet six inches wide.

Liberty wears __________ (open-toed shoes with straps) on her feet. They are 25 feet long.

Liberty holds a __________ (pad of paper). It is over 23 feet long.

Word Bank	
spikes	arm
torch	tablet
sandals	eye

Imagine that you are an immigrant sailing into New York Harbor. Write a paragraph describing how you feel when you see the Statue of Liberty.

©The Mailbox® • *Fascinating Facts: Social Studies* • TEC61065 • Key p. 123

Name ______________________________

A Priceless Symbol

Today the Liberty Bell is a priceless symbol of freedom, but the men who remade the original bell were paid about $225 for their work.

The Old State House Bell cracked the first time it was rung. So it was melted down. The metal was formed into a new bell. Some people thought that the sound of the new bell was not good. But the bell did the job. It was rung to call the people of Philadelphia, Pennsylvania, to meetings. The bell was rung on July 4, 1776, to tell the people that they were breaking away from British rule. It was rung in happy times. It was rung in sad times. Some people said that the bell was rung too often! Then it cracked again!

The break made people think about the bell in a new way. Some said that the crack was like the struggle that the country had gone through. Many felt that the bell stood for freedom. Before long, people began to call the bell the Liberty Bell. Now the Liberty Bell is a national symbol.

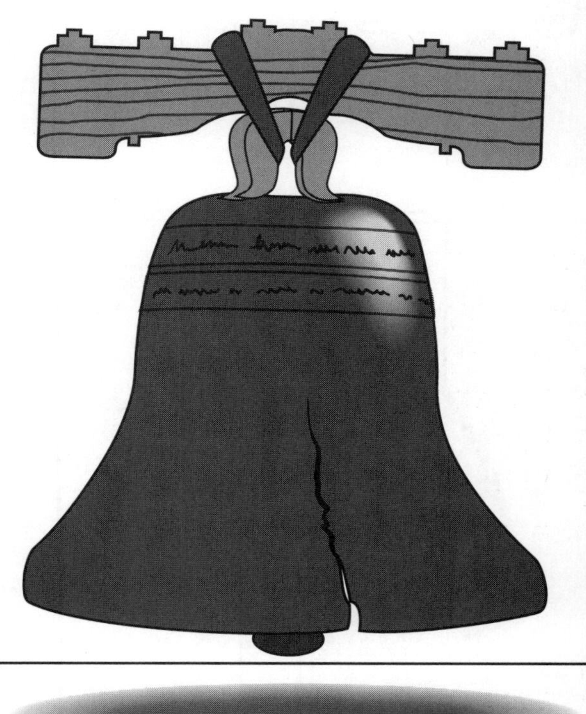

Answer the questions.

1. What do the Old State House Bell and the Liberty Bell have in common?

____

____

____

2. When the cracked bell was remade, it wasn't perfect. What didn't some people like about it? ______________________________

____

____

©The Mailbox® • *Fascinating Facts: Social Studies* • TEC61065 • Key p. 123

Name ________________________________

A Priceless Symbol

Cut out the effect statements below.
Glue each one below its matching cause statement.

The Old State House Bell cracked.

The new bell did not sound good, but it did the job.

The bell was rung in happy times and sad times.

The bell cracked again.

Many people thought the bell stood for freedom.

Imagine that you are an early settler in your home and you hear the Liberty Bell ringing. You don't know if it is ringing for good news or bad news. Write a paragraph describing how you feel.

©The Mailbox® • *Fascinating Facts: Social Studies* • TEC61065 • Key p. 123

People began to think about the bell in a new way.
They began calling it the Liberty Bell.
People decided that it would do.
Some people said that the bell was rung too often.
It was melted down.

Name ______________________________

A Mountain of a Monument

Originally, the men on Mount Rushmore were supposed to be shown from the waist up.

Mount Rushmore is a huge sculpture. It is in the mountains in South Dakota. It shows the faces of four presidents. The faces of George Washington and Abraham Lincoln are carved in Mount Rushmore. The images of Thomas Jefferson and Theodore Roosevelt are carved there too.

Crews used drills, dynamite, and other tools to clear away the rock. Then they carved each face out of the mountain with care.

The artist who planned the sculpture wanted to show the men from the waist up. But when work began on Washington's coat, the work had to stop. The workers found that the rock lower on the mountain was different. They decided to just carve the presidents' heads. The final sculpture was finished in 1941. Over two million people visit Mount Rushmore each year.

Unscramble the letters to form the missing word.

1. Mount Rushmore is in South __ __ __ __ __ __. (k t a a D o)
2. The faces of four presidents are __ __ __ __ __ __ __ in Mount Rushmore. (d a v e c r)
3. The presidents' __ __ __ __ __ are shown on the sculpture. (c f e s a)

Name ____________________

A Mountain of a Monument

Cut apart the boxes below.
Glue the presidents in the order they appear on Mount Rushmore.
Use the clues to help you.

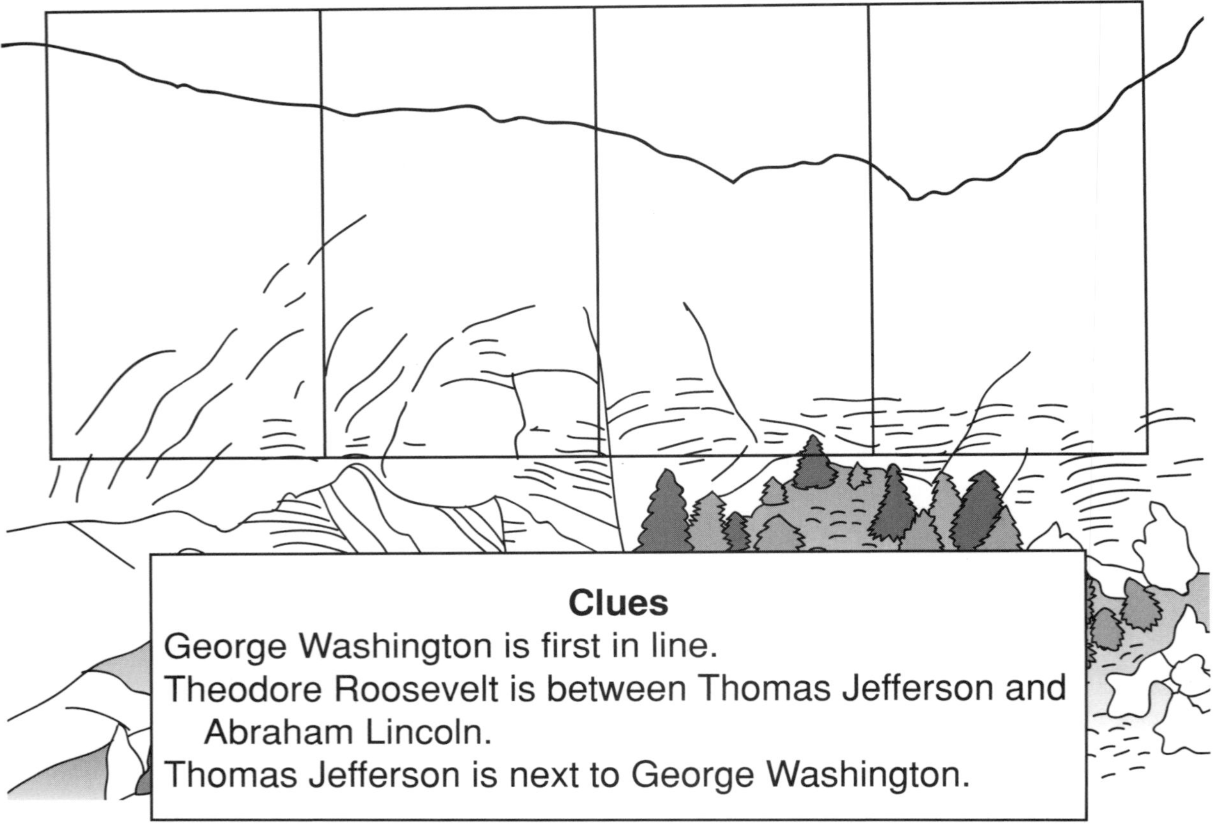

Clues

George Washington is first in line.
Theodore Roosevelt is between Thomas Jefferson and Abraham Lincoln.
Thomas Jefferson is next to George Washington.

If you were asked to choose one person to add to the memorial on Mount Rushmore, whom would you add? Why?

©The Mailbox® • *Fascinating Facts: Social Studies* • TEC61065 • Key p. 123

Name ____

Time to Eat

Pilgrim families sometimes ate eels that the children caught.

Are you hungry? Today you can go to a store and pick out just about anything you would like to eat. But stores have not always been around! Years ago, people, even children, had to hunt for and gather their food. What did they eat? Early settlers hunted deer and turkeys. They also ate eels. Native Americans taught the Pilgrim children to catch the eels. Children picked corn, squash, and beans from their families' gardens. They also picked wild berries. These ways of getting food may not have been as easy as going to a store. But they helped people get the food they needed.

Circle the best answer.

1. Early Americans got their food at a store. true false
2. Deer and turkeys were hunted for food. true false
3. Pilgrims taught Native Americans how to catch eels. true false
4. Families grew foods like corn and beans in their gardens. true false

©The Mailbox® • *Fascinating Facts: Social Studies* • TEC61065 • Key p. 123

Name ______________________________

Time to Eat

Draw a line from each food to its matching description.

 bison	This wild bird lives in small groups called flocks. Males are called toms and females are called hens.
deer	This animal has bones called antlers on its head. Its meat is called venison.
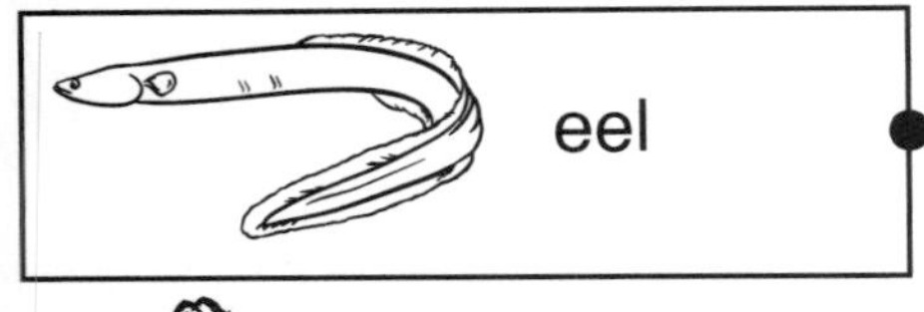 eel	This long, slimy fish looks like a snake.
 turkey	This large animal is also known as a buffalo. It has a lot of dark brown hair and was once overhunted.
 beans	Blueberries are one type of this sweet fruit.
 berries	This food grows on a vine. It has pods that hold its seeds.
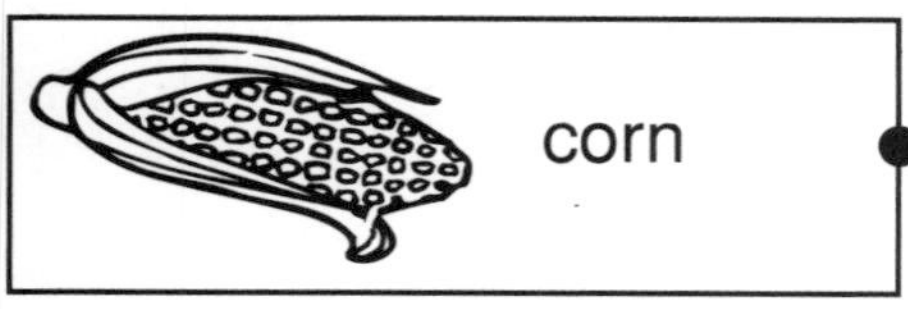 corn	Native Americans grew this food long before Pilgrims came to live in North America. It is also called maize.
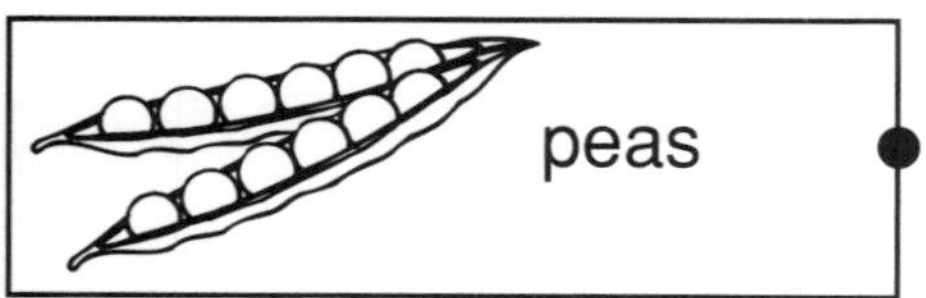 peas	This food is related to peas. One type has a green shell.

Which of these foods have you eaten? Are there any you would not like to try? Tell why.

©The Mailbox® • *Fascinating Facts: Social Studies* • TEC61065 • Key p. 123

Name ____________________

What's Cooking?

Large iron cooking pots were also used for doing laundry.

Many homes today have microwave ovens. They make cooking a meal a snap. But long ago, it was not as easy to cook a meal. Many families lived in one-room homes with a large, open fireplace in the center. The fireplace gave heat. It was also where the cooking and baking were done. Houses sometimes filled with smoke when meals were being made.

Women and girls did all the cooking. Back then they wore long skirts or dresses. Their clothes sometimes burned while they worked around the fire. The women kept a bucket of water by the fireplace to put out these small fires.

Cooking pots were made of iron, copper, or brass. They cost a lot of money. So these pots weren't used only for cooking. They also held the wash on laundry days!

Draw a line to match each sentence starter to its ending.

Long ago, fireplaces were used •	• cost a lot of money.
Women's clothes sometimes •	• for cooking and for doing laundry.
Water was kept by the fireplace •	• for heat and for cooking.
Early cooking pots •	• to put out clothing fires.
Cooking pots were used •	• burned during cooking.

What's Cooking?

Write the number of the matching sentence on the diagram.

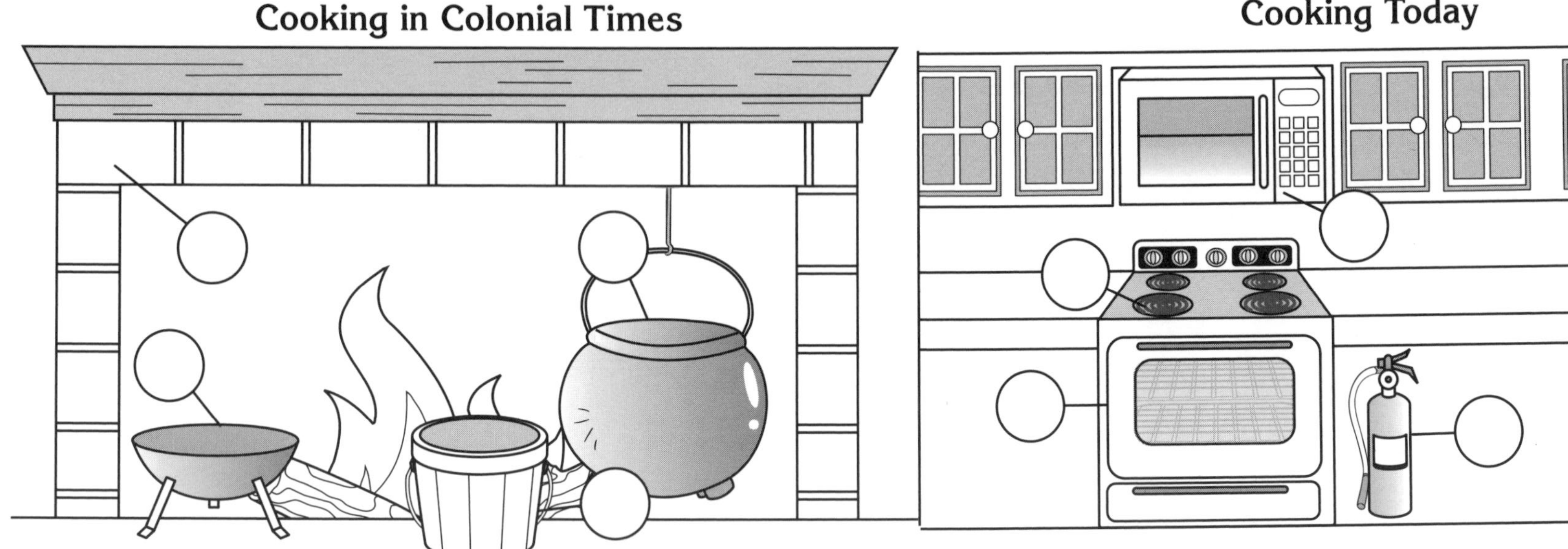

1. Iron, copper, or brass pots were used.
2. A microwave oven heats food quickly.
3. The fireplace gave heat for cooking and gave heat for the home.
4. A stove is used to boil or fry foods.
5. An oven is used to bake or broil foods.
6. A water bucket put out fires.
7. A fire extinguisher puts out fires.
8. A *spider* was a frying pan with three legs.

Women sometimes burned their clothes while cooking in the fireplace. What other problems do you think women faced while cooking in colonial times?

Name ______________________________

Settling In

Early American homes were often made of wood, including the chimneys.

Early settlers set up towns and cities along the East Coast. Our country began to grow and change. The houses the settlers built changed too. At first, houses were small. They had only one or two rooms. They were made of mud and wood. The roofs were made of thatched grass.

The houses got a little bigger as time passed. But they were still made of wood. They even had a few windows. Windows were covered with things like oiled fabric because glass cost a lot of money.

Many years later, some settlers had made a lot of money. These wealthy settlers built even bigger houses. Their houses were made of brick. They had many rooms on each floor. There were many windows. The windows were made of glass. Some of these houses are still standing today.

Circle the best answer to complete each sentence.

1. At first, houses were _______.	small	large
2. Early houses were made of _______ and wood.	metal	mud
3. Windows were covered with _______ instead of glass.	plastic	fabric
4. Wealthy settlers built homes of _______.	brick	mud
5. Wealthy settlers had homes with many _______.	rooms	rugs

Settling In

Cut out the pictures below.
Glue each picture next to its matching description.

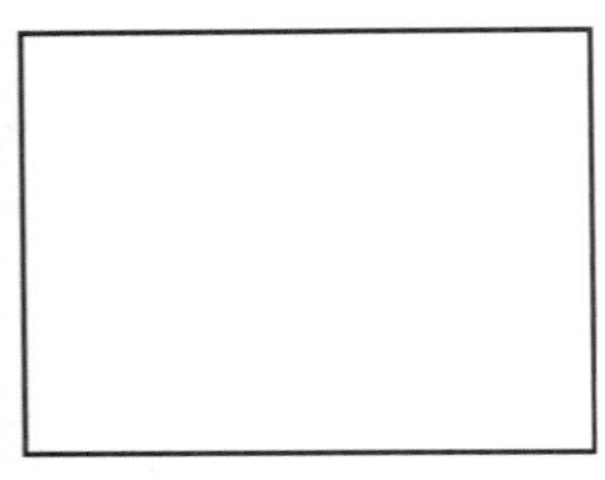

People moved west in the 1800s. At first, these settlers built **sod houses.** Sod is grass with its roots and dirt. Since there was a lot of grassland around, sod was a cheap way to build. But there were many bugs. Muddy water dripped from the ceiling when it rained.

A **dugout** was a place some settlers lived in while they got their land and crops ready. It was made by digging out the land on the side of a hill. It looked something like a cave. Only a front wall was built.

In the dry Southwest, settlers used clay to make their **adobe houses.** They made bricks from the clay and water. The bricks were stacked to make thick walls. More clay was used on the walls and floors.

Frame houses were another kind of house found in the West. These homes were made from wood planks. The inside walls and floors were made of smooth wood. The flat wood made these homes easier to paint and keep clean.

If you were a settler in the 1800s, which of these houses would you like to live in? Tell why.

©The Mailbox® • *Fascinating Facts: Social Studies* • TEC61065 • Key p. 123

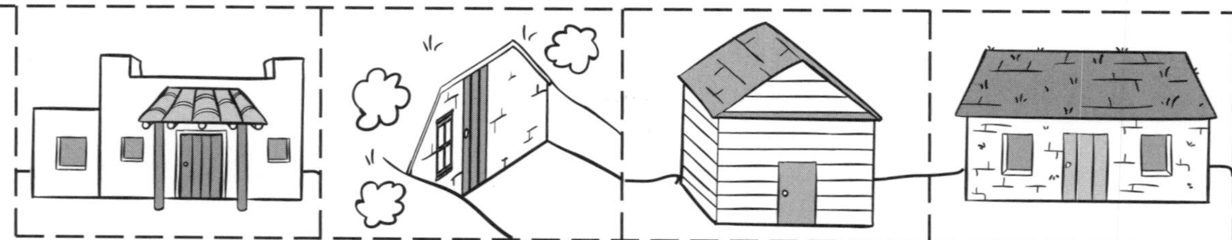

Name ____________________

Heavy-Duty Pants

The first jeans were brown and made of tent fabric.

During the gold rush of the 1850s, lots of people hoped to get rich by finding gold. They needed strong pants that would not rip while they searched. So a man named Levi Strauss used a brown tent fabric called canvas to make pants. These canvas pants were strong enough for the gold miners. He made the canvas pants for a short time.

Then Levi Strauss started using blue denim to make his pants. These pants were still strong. They were called jeans. For a long time after that, only people who worked outdoors, like farmers and cowboys, wore jeans. It wasn't until the 1940s that jeans were worn to places other than work. Today, almost all Americans own a pair of jeans.

Answer the questions.
Use the passage to help you.

1. Who needed strong work pants during the 1850s? ____________________

2. At first, what did Levi Strauss use to make pants? ____________________

3. For a long time, who were the only people to wear jeans? ____________________

4. When did it become more common to wear jeans? ____________________

©The Mailbox® • *Fascinating Facts: Social Studies* • TEC61065 • Key p. 123

Name ____________________

Heavy-Duty Pants

Use the clues to complete the puzzle.
Use the word bank to help you.

1. Today, almost ____________ Americans own a pair of jeans.
2. Today's jeans are made of ____________.
3. The first jeans were made of ____________.
4. Gold ____________ wore the first jeans.
5. They wanted ____________ pants to wear to work.
6. ____________ fabric was strong enough.
7. It wasn't blue. It was ____________.
8. The first ____________ were brown, but now they are often blue.
9. For a long time, only people who worked ____________ wore jeans.
10. Now, almost everyone ____________ them.

Word Bank

all brown canvas
denim jeans miners
outdoors strong tent wears

Who made the first jeans in the United States?

To find out, copy the letters in the bold boxes in order from top to bottom.

__ __ __ __   __ __ __ __ __ __ s

Why do you think so many people today like to wear jeans? Make a list of as many reasons as you can name.

©The Mailbox® • *Fascinating Facts: Social Studies* • TEC61065 • Key p. 123

Name ______________________________

Paving the Way

Early steam cars were so loud that they scared horses.

People long ago used boats, horses, or mules to go from place to place. Then, in the late 1700s, automobiles, or cars, were invented.

At first the cars moved by steam. These cars did not have a steering wheel. Drivers used a bar called a tiller instead. These cars were loud. They were so loud that they scared horses.

By the late 1800s, there were cars that were powered by batteries. These cars were quieter than the steam cars. But the batteries had to be charged often.

Cars that ran on gasoline were being built around that same time. Most cars on the road today still use gas. Who knows what kinds of changes the future will bring to our cars!

Fill in the blanks.
Use the passage to help you.

1. Before cars, people traveled by boat, horse, and ______________.
2. Cars were invented in the late ______________.
3. Drivers steered early cars with ______________.
4. Cars run by batteries had to be ______________ often.
5. For the past 100 years, cars have used ______________ to run.

Paving the Way

Late 1700s: The automobile was invented. It ran on steam. It was loud.

Late 1800s: The electric car was built. It ran on battery power. It could not travel far.

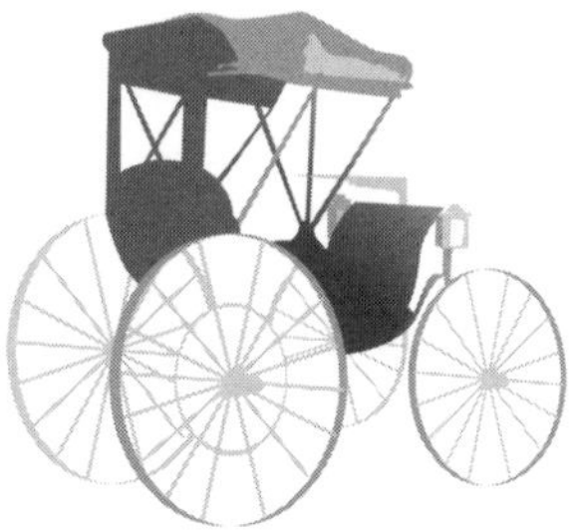

Late 1800s: The gasoline-powered car was built. Better tires were being made too.

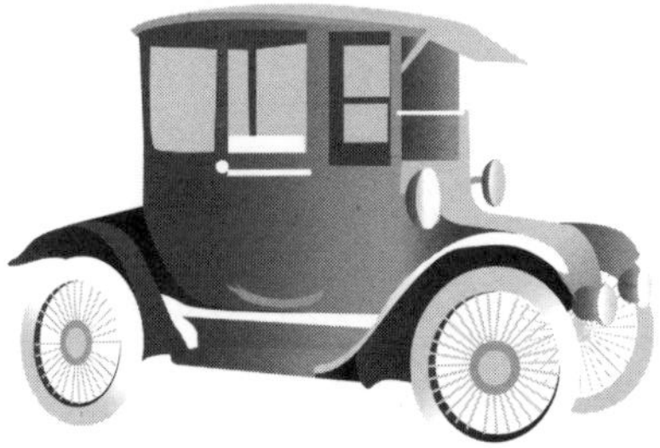

Today: Most cars still run on gasoline. New fuels made from corn and plant sugars are being tested.

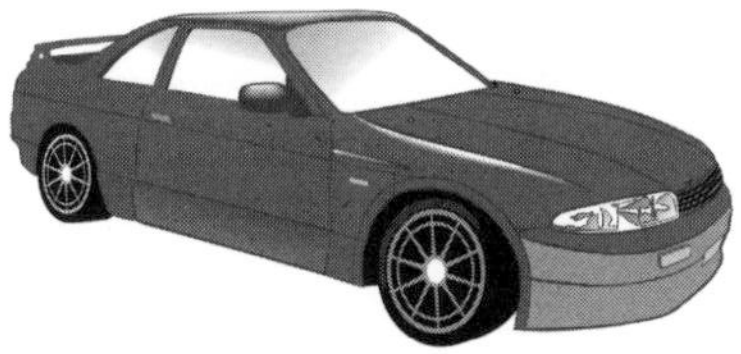

Complete the chart.
Use the timeline to help you.

How Cars Have Changed	How Cars Have Stayed the Same
1. ____________	1. ____________
2. ____________	2. ____________

What do you think cars will be like in the future?

Name ______________________________

Try for the Sky

One early flying machine had 200 wings.

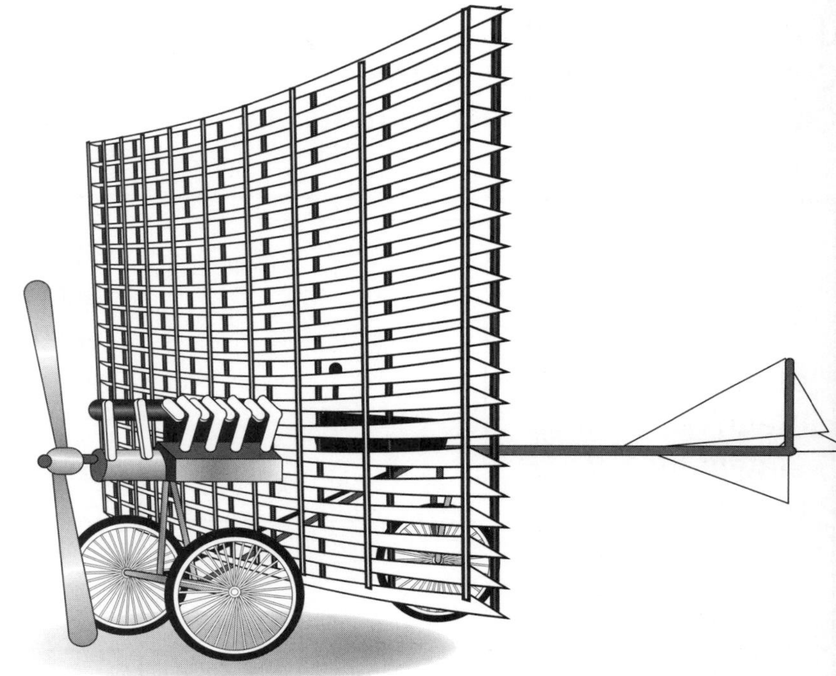

Flying in the sky was a dream for many. People made all kinds of machines to try to make that dream come true. Hot-air balloons worked. But they were hard to steer.

Other flying machines were built. One even had 200 wings! But these machines did not stay in the air. Some were too heavy to fly. Others did not have enough power.

It was Wilbur and Orville Wright who put a gas engine in a plane and made it fly for a half hour. New planes were built using their model. These planes had more speed. They could be flown for fun, or they could be used in battle. The work of the Wright brothers and all of the inventors before them made flying possible for us today.

Answer each question with a complete sentence.

1. What kind of flying machine was hard to steer? ______________________

   ____

2. What was another problem with early flying machines? ______________________

   ____

3. Who used a gas engine to help a plane fly? ______________________

   ____

4. How were newer planes different from the Wright brothers' plane? __________

   ____

©The Mailbox® • *Fascinating Facts: Social Studies* • TEC61065 • Key p. 124

Name ______________________________

Try for the Sky

Fill in each blank with the best word.
Use the word bank.
Cut apart the picture cards.
Glue each one next to its matching description.

Word Bank

air	balloon	engine	hours
steer	wings	world	Wright

The hot-air ___________ was one kind of early flying machine. It could stay in the air, but it was hard to ___________.	Other kinds of flying machines were tested. One even had 200 ___________! They were hard to keep in the ___________.
In 1905, the ___________ brothers made their plan work. They put a gas ___________ in a plane and flew for more than 30 minutes!	Today, planes can stay in the air for ___________. They can take people all over the ___________.

Bonus If you could travel on a plane to anywhere in the world, where would you go? Tell why.

©The Mailbox® • *Fascinating Facts: Social Studies* • TEC61065 • Key p. 124

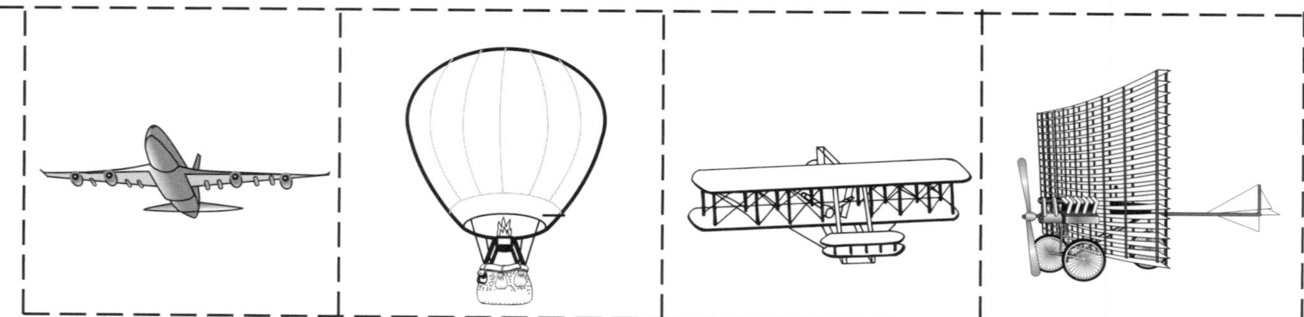

Name ______________________________________

On the Line

The first coast-to-coast phone call was made in 1915.

The telephone was invented in 1876. At first, people could only use the phone to talk to a person a few miles away. Iron wires linked their phones together. Then, as more people used phones, more wires were linked. Callers started to talk to people who were farther away.

In 1891, a telephone call was made between people in the two countries of England and France. Then, in 1915, a call was made between New York and California. It was the first call across the United States.

Today, people can make phone calls all over the world. And phones aren't used for just talking. People use their phones to read the news, take pictures, and play games.

Complete the timeline.

1876 ______________________________________

______ A phone call is made between people in different countries.

1915 ______________________________________

Today ______________________________________

Name ____

On the Line

Write the words that complete the paragraph. Use the word bank to help you.

The __ __ __ __ __ __ __ __ __ changed a lot in its early years. At first, iron __ __ __ __ __ linked phones together. Then more people were using phones. So __ __ __ __ __ __ __ __ __ __ __ __ helped with connections. The first switchboard was used in __ __ __ __ __ __ in 1877. In 1892, callers turned a __ __ __ __ __ to make a call. In 1896, the first __ __ __ __ phones were used.

Word Bank
dial
crank
wires
Boston
telephone
switchboards

Circle each word in the puzzle.

S	A	C	A	R	H	O	D	T	P	F	G
W	O	S	R	U	J	B	E	M	X	T	A
I	T	M	P	L	I	V	R	S	D	K	H
T	E	L	E	P	H	O	N	E	C	A	L
C	N	F	S	A	X	M	O	P	R	B	U
H	R	S	T	D	T	Q	U	C	A	F	L
B	G	E	W	I	R	E	S	E	N	O	D
O	H	W	I	A	U	S	J	P	K	C	P
A	T	O	X	L	M	E	F	U	W	N	N
R	P	Z	A	T	O	S	N	G	D	I	R
D	V	C	A	B	B	O	S	T	O	N	E
S	U	N	P	J	E	N	D	E	G	Z	A

Bonus Describe what life would be like without the telephone.

©The Mailbox® • *Fascinating Facts: Social Studies* • TEC61065 • Key p. 124

Name ____________________

Across the Airwaves

The years from about 1925 to the early 1950s are known as the Golden Age of Broadcasting.

As early as the 1920s, people spent their free time sitting in front of a radio. That's right! A radio! Women tuned in to stories known as soap operas. These programs were paid for by soap makers and were on during the day. Kids rushed home after school to hear their favorite adventure shows. These shows sometimes gave away fun prizes like rings and badges. Families spent their nights sitting by their radios. They listened to music, dramas, and newscasts. Radio was a favorite way to pass the time until the early 1950s. That was when people started watching television instead.

Complete the chart.
Use the passage to help you.

	Women	Kids	Families
What did they listen to?			
When did they tune in?			

Name ____

Across the Airwaves

Draw a line to match each sentence starter to its ending.

1. People used to spend their free time •	• during the day.
2. Women often tuned in to programs called •	• by their radios.
3. Soap operas were on •	• soap operas.
4. Kids liked to hear adventure shows •	• dramas, newscasts, and music.
5. Adventure shows often •	• watching television instead.
6. Families spent time by their radios •	• after school.
7. They listened to •	• gave away prizes.
8. In the early 1950s, people started •	• at night.

Could you live without radio? Tell why or why not.

©The Mailbox® • *Fascinating Facts: Social Studies* • TEC61065 • Key p. 124

Name ____

Home Entertainment

Lazy Bones was the name of the first TV remote control.

Televisions, often called TVs, were first shown to Americans at the 1939 World's Fair. Back then, TVs were very different from those today. The first TVs only could show programs in black and white. The TV screen sizes were only seven to ten inches. Color TVs were not sold until the early 1950s.

Remote controls were first made around the same time. The first remote control was named Lazy Bones. But remote controls were known as clickers. They made a clicking sound when channels were changed. They also had a cord that linked the clicker to the TV. If the TV did not have a clicker, a viewer turned a knob on the set to change the channel. By the early 1980s, wireless remote controls were common. By 2000, almost all TVs sold in the United States came with a remote control.

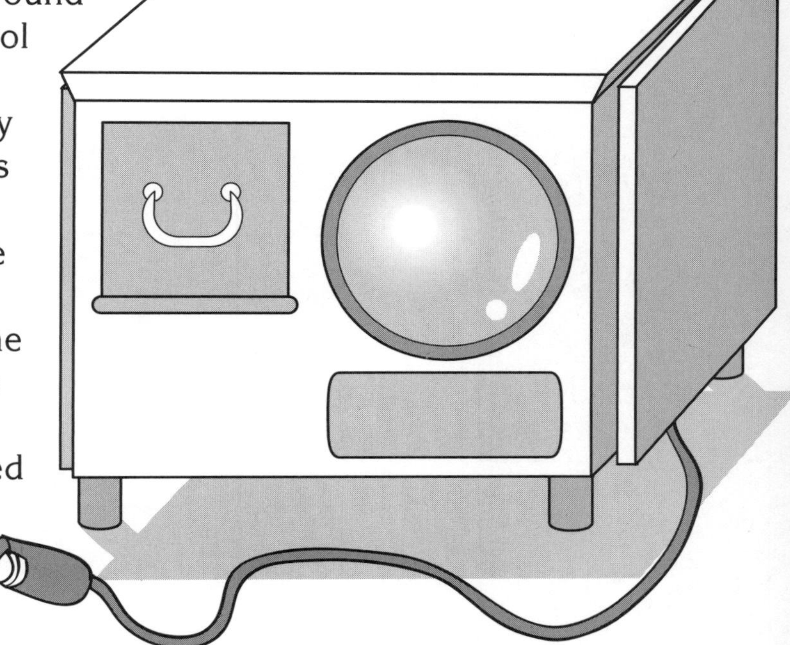

Fill in the blank to complete each sentence.
Use the passage to help you.

1. Americans first saw televisions at the 1939 ________________________.
2. Early TVs showed programs in ________________________.
3. Color TVs were first sold in the early ______________.
4. ________________________ were called clickers because of the sound they made when used.
5. Each clicker had a cord that connected it to the ______________.

Name ____________________

Home Entertainment

Cut apart the picture cards.
Glue each one next to the matching clue.

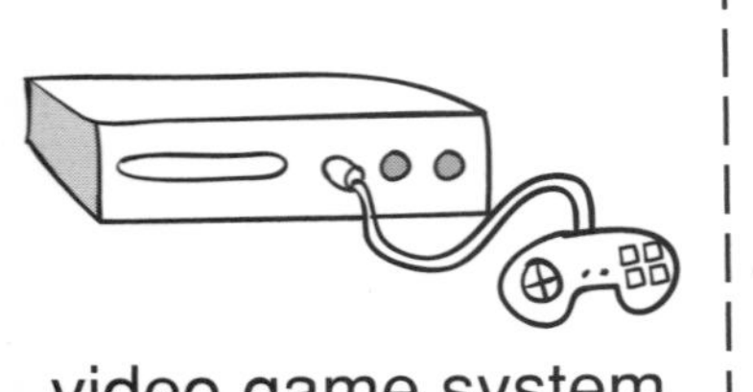
video game system

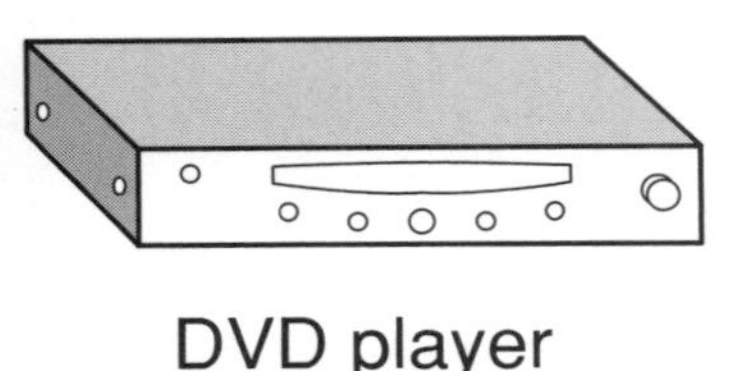
DVD player

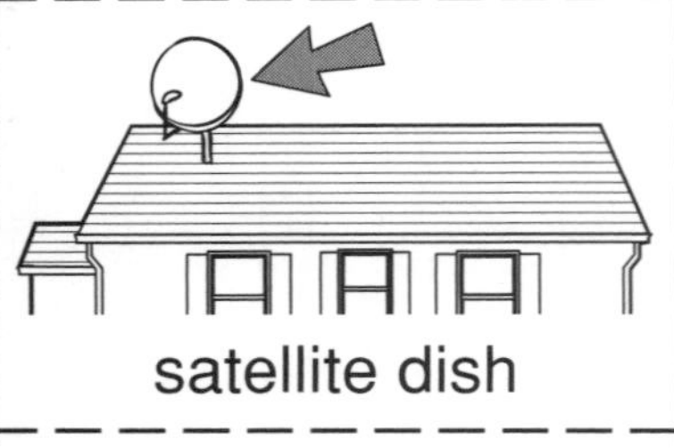
satellite dish

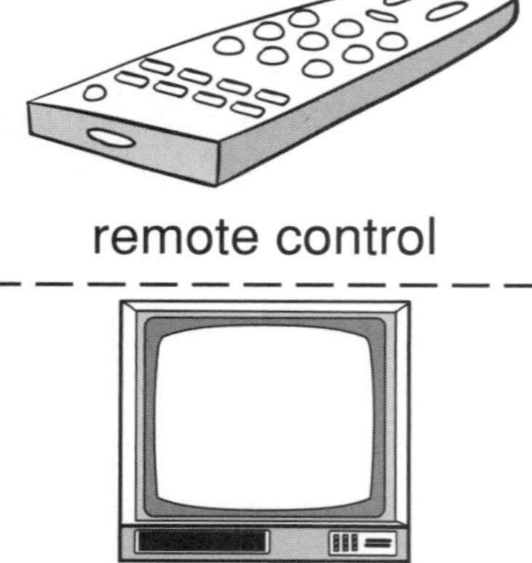
remote control

television

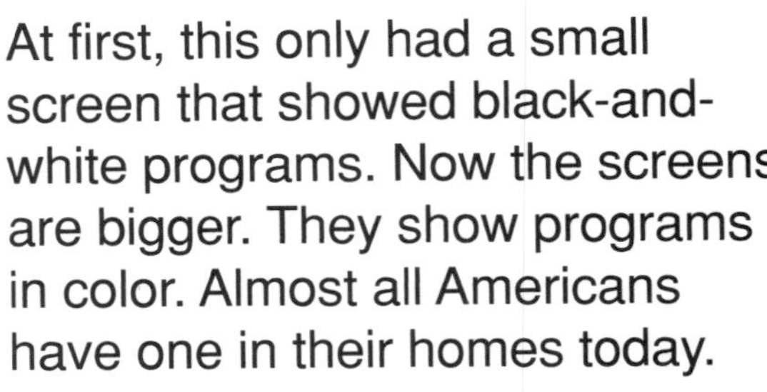
At first, this only had a small screen that showed black-and-white programs. Now the screens are bigger. They show programs in color. Almost all Americans have one in their homes today.

This was first sold in 1996. A disk is put into this machine. It often plays movies on the TV.

This handheld unit was first made in the 1950s. Back then it had a cord. Newer models use batteries. It lets the viewer stay seated while changing channels.

This first came into American homes in the late 1970s. It lets people play computerized games on their TVs.

This service has been around since the early 1980s. It did not become widespread until the 1990s. It lets the viewer choose from many different channels.

Make a list of the inventions named above. Order the list from the oldest invention to the newest.

©The Mailbox® • *Fascinating Facts: Social Studies* • TEC61065 • Key p. 125

Name ____________________

Chipping Away

The first computers were so large that they filled up entire rooms.

Today there are computers that are small enough to be held in a person's hands. But just 50 years ago that could not happen. Early computers were so big that they filled a whole room. And even though they were big, they were often programmed for just one job.

These big machines cost a lot of money. They were found at some workplaces but not in homes. Soon the big parts were replaced with smaller ones called microchips. Using microchips made computers smaller. Now people have computers at home and just about any place they go!

Make each sentence true.
Cross out the word that does not belong.
Write a word from the word bank above it.

Word Bank
workplaces big small
cost microchips

1. Early computers were small.

2. Early computers spent a lot of money.

3. Early computers were found in homes.

4. Big parts were replaced with mini-parts.

5. Some computers today are big enough to hold in a person's hands.

Name ____

Chipping Away

Use the code below.
Write the letters on the numbered lines.

The first computers were used by companies to work with ___ ___ ___ ___ ___ ___ ___. Today computers are used
10 15 9 2 4 12 13

at work, home, and school to do many things. People send messages from one computer to another when they use ___ ___ ___ ___ ___. They also use computers to store
4 9 1 7 8

___ ___ ___ ___ ___ ___ ___ ___ from their digital cameras.
11 7 3 14 15 12 4 13

Kids play ___ ___ ___ ___ ___ on their computers. They also
6 1 9 4 13

look up ___ ___ ___ ___ ___ for school reports. Then they
5 1 3 14 13

might ___ ___ ___ ___ ___ those reports on the computer.
16 12 7 14 4

These are just a few ways that computers are used today.

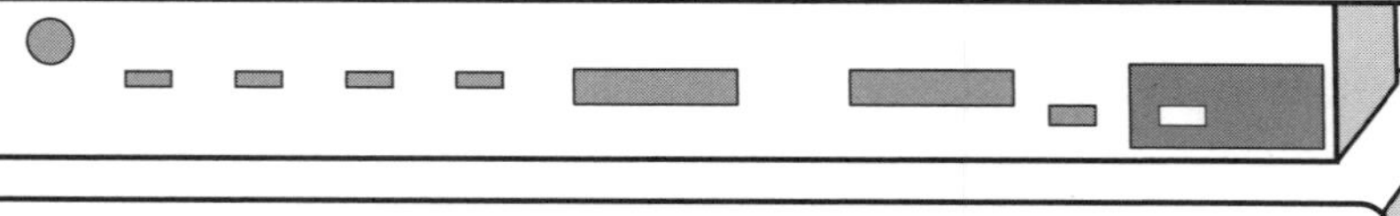

A	B	C	E	F	G	I	L	M	N	P	R	S	T	U	W
1	2	3	4	5	6	7	8	9	10	11	12	13	14	15	16

How else do people use computers? Make a list of at least five ways.

©The Mailbox® • *Fascinating Facts: Social Studies* • TEC61065 • Key p. 125

Name ______________________________

He Was the First

George Washington is the only president who has a state named after him.

George Washington was our first president. He helped our country grow. He made such a mark that we honor him in many ways. One of our states is named after him. His picture is on the dollar bill. It is also on the quarter. Many roads, lakes, and parks are named for him.

Washington helped our country by leading an army. His troops won a war against England. Winning the war meant that the United States could make its own laws. Washington was also the leader of a meeting in 1787. The meeting lasted for four months. When it was over, the men had written the U.S. Constitution. The Constitution set up our country's government. Washington's leadership helped our country become what it is.

Make each sentence true.
Cross out the word or phrase that does not belong.
Write a word from the word bank above it.

Word Bank
Constitution
army
quarter
first
England

1. Washington was the leader of an opera.
2. He helped America win a war against Germany.
3. Washington led the men who wrote the Pledge of Allegiance.
4. Washington was the fourth president of the United States.
5. Washington's picture is on the nickel.

Name ________________________________

He Was the First

Read the clues.
Solve the puzzle.

Across

1. George Washington was the ______________ president.
4. His leadership helped our ______________ grow.
5. Washington's help meant that our country could make its own ______________.
6. Many things, such as ______________, are named after Washington.

Down

1. Washington was born in the month of ______________.
2. Americans ______________ Washington in many ways.
3. Washington was a brave ______________ during a war.
5. He was a great ______________ when he was in charge of his troops.

Washington's picture is on the dollar bill and the quarter. If you were planning to honor him, where else would you want to put his picture? Why?

©The Mailbox® • *Fascinating Facts: Social Studies* • TEC61065 • Key p. 125

Name ______________________________

In a Stovepipe Hat

Although he had only about one year of schooling, Abraham Lincoln is thought to be one of the world's greatest writers.

Abraham Lincoln's father was a farmer. He taught Abe to work hard. Abe didn't want to be a farmer. Abe wanted to learn. He went to school when he could. He read many books. He learned how to write by reading.

In Lincoln's time, there was no TV or radio. He could not speak to many people at the same time. Lincoln thought he could talk to many people by writing to them. He began by writing poetry.

Later, Lincoln became a lawyer. Lincoln had to write for the job. He learned to write short pages that made his point. As a politician, Lincoln had to write speeches. He was careful about what he said. He knew that his words were powerful. Lincoln hoped that people would read his writing for years to come. And people do. No other president is quoted as often as Abraham Lincoln.

If the sentence is true, color the hat black.
If the sentence is false, color the hat yellow.

1 Lincoln's father was a lawyer.

2 Lincoln read a lot.

3 Lincoln went to school for years.

4 Lincoln wrote some poetry.

5 Many people read what Lincoln wrote.

Name ______________________________

Write the word that best completes each sentence.
Use the word bank to help you.

1. Abraham Lincoln was born in the month of
__ __ __ __ __ __ __ __.
(10 under the 1st blank, 11 under the 5th)

2. He liked to __ __ __ __ books.
(14 under the 1st blank, 7 under the 2nd)

3. He also liked to tell __ __ __ __ __ __ __ and jokes.
(4 under the 2nd blank, 6 under the 3rd, 5 under the 7th)

4. Lincoln's picture is on a __ __ __ __ that we use every day, the penny.
(16 under the 1st blank, 15 under the 3rd)

5. Lincoln was a talented __ __ __ __ __ __ __ who gave many speeches.
(8 under the 1st blank, 9 under the 3rd, 13 under the 6th)

6. Lincoln was our __ __ __ __ __ __ __ __ __ president.
(12 under the 2nd blank, 1 under the 3rd, 2 under the 7th, 3 under the 9th)

Abraham Lincoln was our tallest president. To find out how tall he was, write the letters from above on the numbered lines below.

__ __ __   __ __ __ __   __ __ __ __   __ __ __ __ __ __
5 12 1   10 7 13 4   10 6 11 14   15 2 16 3 9 8

Why do you think it's important for a president to be a good writer?

©The Mailbox® • *Fascinating Facts: Social Studies* • TEC61065 • Key p. 125

Name ________________________________

Book Smarts

Benjamin Franklin had only two years of formal schooling.

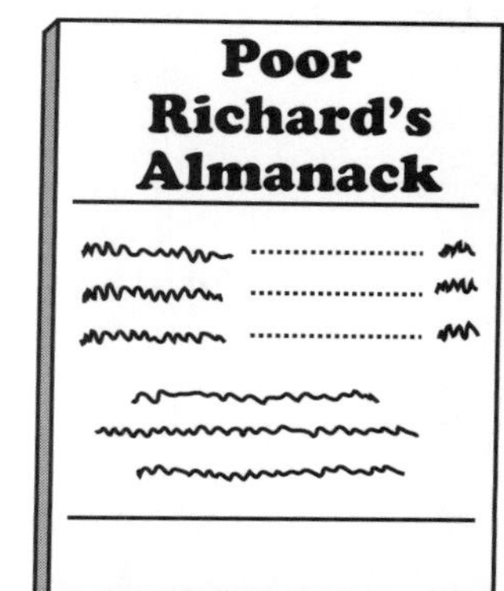

Benjamin Franklin was part of a big family. They needed him to work at his dad's candle and soap shop. So Ben went to school for only two years. But did he stop learning after he left school? No way! In fact, young Ben read anything he could. Reading helped him learn math, science, and writing.

Ben grew up to do many important things for our country. Ben was an inventor. He made things like swim fins, better street lights, and special reading glasses.

Ben was a writer. He worked on a newspaper. He also wrote a book called an almanac. He started a fire station and library where he lived. He even helped the post office work better.

Ben died in 1790. But the results of his hard work still help people today.

Write two examples for each heading.
Use the passage to help you.

Inventor	Writer	Community Helper
1. ____________	1. ____________	1. ____________
2. ____________	2. ____________	2. ____________

Name ______________________________

Book Smarts

If the sentence is a fact, color the book blue.
If the sentence is an opinion, color the book red.

1. Benjamin Franklin was smart.
2. Reading helped Benjamin Franklin learn.
3. Benjamin Franklin was an inventor.
4. His best idea was for special reading glasses.
5. Benjamin Franklin was a great writer.
6. Benjamin Franklin wrote a newspaper.
7. Benjamin Franklin started a fire station.
8. Benjamin Franklin was one of the greatest men in U.S. history.

What do you think was the most important thing Benjamin Franklin did in his lifetime? Explain why.

©The Mailbox® • *Fascinating Facts: Social Studies* • TEC61065 • Key p. 125

Name ____

Studying the Stars

Benjamin Banneker was the first African American to publish an almanac.

Benjamin Banneker was born in 1731. Benjamin liked to wonder. He wondered why the stars moved. He wondered how the sun came up at the right time. He wondered why the moon changed. But Benjamin didn't have a lot of time to study these things. He worked all day on his farm. He had to study at night. He borrowed a telescope. He used it to watch the stars.

Benjamin also read the Bible and an almanac every day. The almanac was important to farmers. It told them when the sun would rise and set each day. It told about the weather and moon patterns. Benjamin thought he could write an even better almanac. Benjamin wrote an almanac for 1792. When it was published, Benjamin became famous. He was the first African American to publish an almanac.

Circle the best answer.

1. Benjamin Banneker used a ___ to watch the night skies.
   a. microscope
   b. magnifying glass
   c. telescope

2. Benjamin Banneker read an ___ every day.
   a. newspaper
   b. almanac
   c. library book

3. Benjamin Banneker wrote an ___.
   a. article
   b. almanac
   c. essay

©The Mailbox® • *Fascinating Facts: Social Studies* • TEC61065 • Key p. 126

Name ________________________________

Studying the Stars

Study the almanac page.

August has 31 days.			
	Comments	Rises	Sets
1	windy	6:26	8:25
2	rainy	6:27	8:24
3	stormy	6:27	8:23
4	windy	6:28	8:22
5	wind and rain	6:29	8:21
6	stormy	6:30	8:20
7	warm weather	6:31	8:19
8	warm weather	6:31	8:18
9	high winds	6:32	8:17

Answer the questions.

1. Which month is shown on this page?
   a. May
   b. December
   c. August

2. How many days are in the month of August?
   a. 31
   b. 30
   c. 29

3. What time will the sun rise on August 4?
   a. 6:26
   b. 6:28
   c. 6:18

4. What time will the sun set on August 7?
   a. 8:23
   b. 8:20
   c. 8:19

5. What is shown in the comments column?
   a. weather predictions
   b. star patterns
   c. moon patterns

6. How many days are shown on this almanac page?
   a. six
   b. nine
   c. 12

Why do you think an almanac would be important to farmers?

©The Mailbox® • *Fascinating Facts: Social Studies* • TEC61065 • Key p. 126

Name ____________________________________

Green Thumb

George Washington Carver got the nickname Plant Doctor for helping his neighbors heal their sick plants.

George Washington Carver loved learning about plants. When he was a young boy, he spent hours looking at flowers and trees. He also helped his neighbors make their sick plants better. They called him the Plant Doctor.

George wanted to learn as much as he could. He studied hard in school and put himself through college. Then he got an offer to teach at the Tuskegee Institute. There he worked with southern farmers.

The southern land was worn out from constant cotton crops. George showed the farmers how to plant peanuts to make the soil richer. George also shared with the farmers many ways to use the peanut crops. He had discovered over 300 uses! Dr. Carver helped the farmers and their land. His lessons even help farmers today.

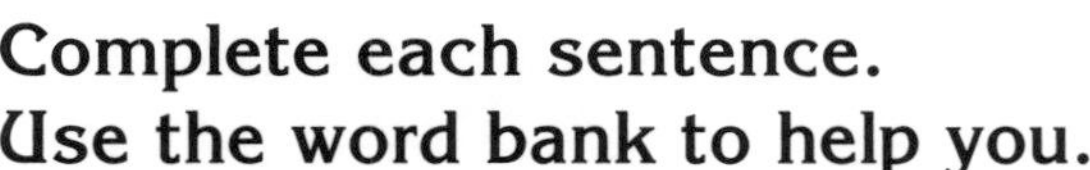

Complete each sentence.
Use the word bank to help you.

Word Bank
Plant Doctor
farmers
plants
peanuts
neighbors

1. George Washington Carver loved to study ____________________.
2. He helped his ____________________ make their sick plants better.
3. George was called the ____________________.
4. After college, George helped ____________________ improve their land.
5. George shared over 300 uses for ____________________.

©The Mailbox® • *Fascinating Facts: Social Studies* • TEC61065 • Key p. 126

Name ____________________

Green Thumb

Make each sentence true.
Cross out the underlined word.
Write an antonym from the word bank above it.

Word Bank			
young	use	loved	better
much	helped	richer	work

1. George Washington Carver hated learning about plants.
2. He helped his neighbors make their sick plants worse.
3. They called him the Plant Doctor, even though he was too old to be one.
4. George worked hard in school to learn as little as he could.
5. After college, George went to play at the Tuskegee Institute.
6. He taught farmers how to make their soil poorer.
7. He also taught the farmers how to waste peanuts.
8. Dr. Carver hurt the farmers and their land.

Dr. Carver knew over 300 ways to use peanuts. How many do you know? Make a list of at least five ways.

©The Mailbox® • *Fascinating Facts: Social Studies* • TEC61065 • Key p. 126

Name ______________________________

Trying to Fly

The Wright brothers owned a bicycle-repair shop before they began working on their airplane.

Orville and Wilbur Wright worked as printers in Dayton, Ohio. But the brothers were good with machines. People brought their broken bicycles to Orville and Wilbur. The brothers fixed them. They opened their own bike shop. The shop kept them busy. But soon Wilbur and Orville started learning about flying. Other men had tried to fly. The brothers studied what these men had learned.

They started by building a kite. But they needed more wind to test their work. They moved their tests to Kitty Hawk, North Carolina. The brothers tested many gliders. They kept trying to fly. In 1903, Orville took the first successful plane flight! The brothers' dream of a flying machine wasn't a dream anymore.

Make each sentence true.
Cross out each incorrect word.
Write a homophone above it.

1. The Right brothers lived in Dayton, Ohio.
2. They wanted to make a plain.
3. They traveled to North Carolina because they kneaded more wind.
4. It took them a long thyme to get their idea to work.
5. Their first flight was 120 feat.

©The Mailbox® • *Fascinating Facts: Social Studies* • TEC61065 • Key p. 126

Name ____________________

Trying to Fly

Cut apart the strips below.
Put the strips in the order in which they happened.
Glue the strips on the blocks.

Orville and Wilbur kept trying to fly, even though they failed many times. Have you ever tried to do something and failed many times? Tell about that time. Did you keep trying? Why or why not?

©The Mailbox® • *Fascinating Facts: Social Studies* • TEC61065 • Key p. 126

In Kitty Hawk, the brothers tested many gliders. They finally built a plane that would fly on its own power.

Orville and Wilbur started a bicycle business. Later, they sold the printing business.

After they sold the printing business, they made a kite to test a flying idea. They were still in Dayton, Ohio.

They needed a windier place than Dayton, Ohio. They tested their first glider in Kitty Hawk, North Carolina.

The Wright brothers lived in Dayton, Ohio. Orville's first business was a printing business.

Name ____

Full of Questions

Thomas Edison was once voted "America's Most Useful Man."

Young Thomas Edison loved to ask questions. He asked questions about the things that he saw. Adults couldn't answer all of his questions. Thomas began to find the answers by himself. Thomas's search for answers led him to create many inventions. His inventions would change people's lives. People even voted him "America's Most Useful Man."

One of Thomas's first inventions improved the telegraph. People used a telegraph to send messages to each other. He received a large check for his idea. He used the money to start his own company. Then he was able to spend all of his time making inventions. His company invented the first phonograph. The phonograph recorded a voice. Then the recording could be played back. They also improved the telephone. But one of Thomas's most important inventions was the lightbulb. Because of Thomas Edison, the age of electric light and power began in 1882.

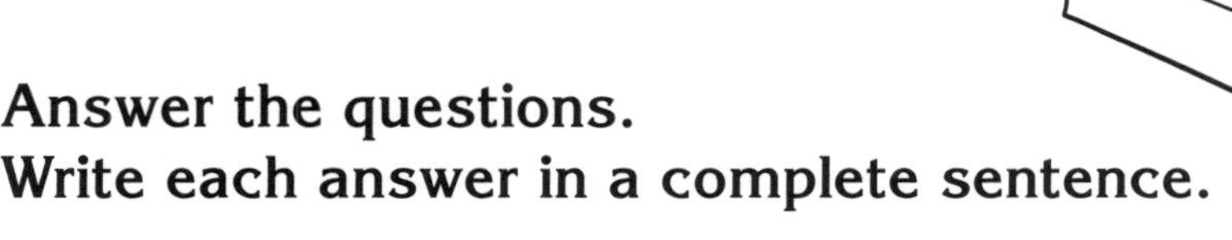

Answer the questions.
Write each answer in a complete sentence.

1. Why do you think people called Thomas Edison "America's Most Useful Man"?

____

____

____

2. The phonograph was an important invention. What invention do you use today that is like a phonograph? ____

3. How would the world be different if the lightbulb had not been invented?

____

____

____

Name ______________________________

Full of Questions

Cut apart the invention pictures below.
Glue each one next to its description.

1. At first, this invention could only be used in homes with electric wiring. It lets people see where it used to be dark. It took thousands of tries before this invention was right.

2. This invention was used to record and play back messages. The machine has a needle that lies against a moving, tinfoil-covered cylinder. Thomas Edison was asked to show it to President Rutherford B. Hayes.

3. This invention improved the telephone. With this invention, the speaker's voice was easier to hear.

4. This invention was better than the telegraph that people already used. It could send two messages at the same time. It sent messages with printed words instead of messages that were in Morse code. This was one of Thomas Edison's first inventions.

Which of Edison's inventions do you think was the most important? Why?

©The Mailbox® • *Fascinating Facts: Social Studies* • TEC61065 • Key p. 126

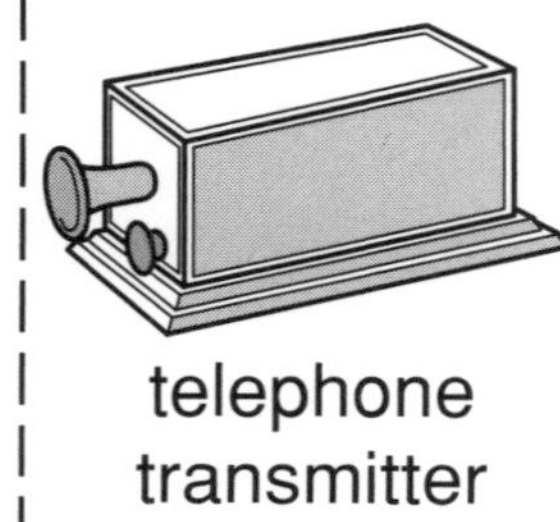

telephone transmitter

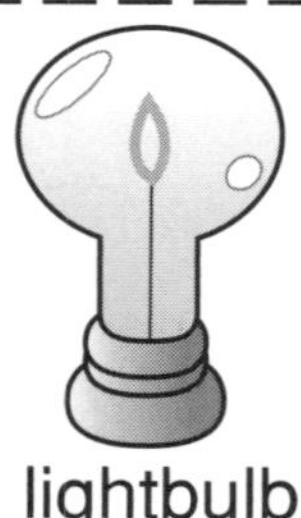

lightbulb

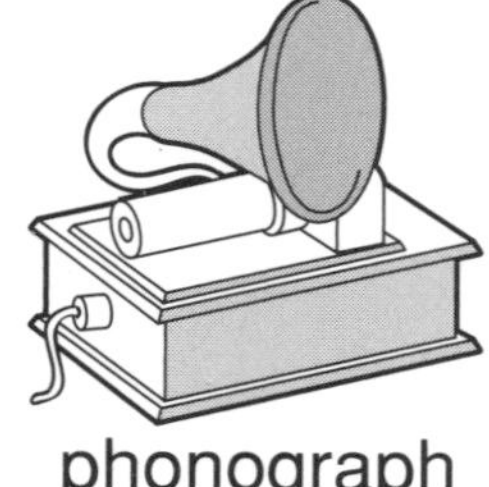

phonograph

telegraph

Name ______________________________

A Talking Machine and More

Alexander Graham Bell worked as a teacher for the deaf.

Alexander Graham Bell was born in Scotland. His father worked with people who were deaf and mute. He helped them learn how to communicate. His mother lost most of her hearing. Bell wanted to help deaf people. He became a teacher. Many people wanted Bell to teach their deaf children.

Bell had been thinking about an invention. He wanted to make a talking telegraph. He had a student whose father wanted to put money into Bell's invention. Bell began working on the invention. In 1876, he made the first telephone. Bell's telephone was very successful. But he wanted to make other things that would help people. He invented a machine that doctors could use. The machine found bullets in wounded soldiers. He also tried to make a machine that would help babies with weak lungs. Alexander Graham Bell always wanted to help others.

Unscramble the letters to form each missing word.

1. Alexander Graham Bell was a __ __ __ __ __ __ __. (e c t r h a e)

2. He was also an __ __ __ __ __ __ __ __. (v n o t r i e n)

3. Bell invented the __ __ __ __ __ __ __ __ __. (p o t e h l e n e)

4. He wanted to invent things that would help __ __ __ __ __ __. (h o e r t s)

Name ____________________

A Talking Machine and More

Alexander Graham Bell had a famous friend.
To find out about their friendship, use the code below.
Write the letters on the numbered lines.

__ __ __ __ __ __ __ __ __   __ __ __   __ __ __ __ __
1 11 5 21 1 13 4 5 16   12 5 18   8 5 11 5 13

__ __ __ __ __ __   __ __ __ __   __ __ __   __ __ __
10 5 11 11 5 16   20 8 5 13   17 8 5   20 1 17

__ __ __   __ __ __ __ __   __ __ __.   __ __ __ __ __   __ __ __
17 9 21   22 5 1 16 17   14 11 4   8 5 11 5 13   1 13 4

__ __ __ __ __ __ __ __ __   __ __ __ __   __ __ __
1 11 5 21 1 13 4 5 16   19 17 5 4   18 8 5

__ __ __ __ __ __   __ __ __ __ __ __ __ __   __ __
12 1 13 19 1 11   1 11 15 8 1 2 5 18   18 14

__ __ __ __   __ __   __ __ __ __   __ __ __ __ __.
18 1 11 10   18 14   5 1 3 8   14 18 8 5 16

__ __ __ __   __ __ __ __   __ __ __ __
18 8 5 22   20 5 16 5   7 14 14 4

__ __ __ __ __ __ __.
6 16 9 5 13 4 17

Code

A	B	C	D	E	F	G	H	I	K	L
1	2	3	4	5	6	7	8	9	10	11

M	N	O	P	R	S	T	U	W	X	Y
12	13	14	15	16	17	18	19	20	21	22

Alexander Graham Bell wanted to invent things that would help others. What kind of invention would you like to make to help others?

©The Mailbox® • *Fascinating Facts: Social Studies* • TEC61065 • Key p. 126

Name ______________________

A Hard Worker

Martin Luther King Jr. skipped two grades in school.

Martin Luther King Jr. worked hard all of his life. He studied hard in school. He was able to skip both ninth and 12th grades. He went to college when he was 15.

In college, Martin knew that he wanted to be a minister. He kept working toward this goal, earning several degrees along the way.

Once out of school, he focused his hard-working ways on the civil rights movement. He wanted all people to be treated the same way. He led marches and made speeches for his cause.

Some people joined in to help him. They looked up to him and his goal. But not everyone agreed with Dr. King's beliefs. They made his work more difficult. He kept working toward his goal until his death in 1968.

Read each cause statement.
Write its effect.
Use the passage to help you.

Cause	Effect
Martin studied hard in school.	
Dr. King wanted everyone to be treated the same.	
Some people agreed with Dr. King.	
Some people did not agree with Dr. King.	

©The Mailbox® • *Fascinating Facts: Social Studies* • TEC61065 • Key p. 126

 Name ______________________

A Hard Worker

Use the word bank to complete each sentence.
Circle each word in the puzzle.

Martin Luther King Jr. skipped two _ _ _ _ _ _ in school. In college, he wanted to become a _ _ _ _ _ _ _ _. After college, Dr. King worked hard so all people would be treated _ _ _ _ _ _ _. He led _ _ _ _ _ _ _ and gave _ _ _ _ _ _ _ _ to work toward his goal.

Word Bank

equally, grades, marches, minister, speeches

T	G	B	W	G	Z	N	P	R	M
S	O	N	G	R	U	D	F	H	A
J	E	Q	U	A	L	L	Y	S	R
Y	A	R	C	D	S	T	E	R	C
S	P	E	C	E	Q	U	A	L	H
M	I	N	I	S	T	E	R	H	E
H	J	S	P	E	E	C	H	E	S
K	I	N	M	O	N	E	E	M	F

Bonus

Imagine that you could have met Dr. King. What are two questions you would have asked him?

Name ____

Equal Rights

Rosa Parks became known as the Mother of the Civil Rights Movement.

For much of Rosa Parks's life, African Americans did not have the same rights as white people. For instance, Rosa went to a school just for African American children. There was a different school for white children.

Also at that time, African Americans could not sit with white people on the bus. They had to sit in the back. After work one day, an adult Rosa sat in the middle of the bus. When a white man wanted her seat, she would not move. Rosa was sent to jail.

After that, many African Americans stopped riding the bus. They thought what happened to Rosa was unfair. In 1956, a law was changed. African Americans could sit anywhere they chose on a bus. Rosa had helped make things better for African Americans. People began to call her the Mother of the Civil Rights Movement.

Draw a line to match each sentence starter to the rest of its sentence.

Rosa Parks went to school •	• African Americans could sit where they wanted on a bus.
African Americans had to sit •	• change seats on the bus.
Rosa would not •	• with other African American children.
In 1956, a law was changed so •	• Mother of the Civil Rights Movement.
Rosa's efforts earned her the nickname •	• in the back of the bus.

©The Mailbox® • *Fascinating Facts: Social Studies* • TEC61065 • Key p. 126

Name ____________________

Equal Rights

If the sentence is a fact, color the bus yellow.
If the sentence is an opinion, color the bus orange.

 1. Rosa Parks went to a school for African American children.

 2. Rosa's school was not fun.

 3. Rosa would not move to the back of the bus.

 4. Rosa was sent to jail.

 5. Rosa should have moved to the back of the bus.

 6. Rosa should not have been sent to jail.

 7. Rosa's arrest helped get a law changed.

 8. Rosa became known as the Mother of the Civil Rights Movement.

Think about a time when you were treated unfairly. How was it like the time Rosa was treated unfairly? How was it different?

©The Mailbox® • *Fascinating Facts: Social Studies* • TEC61065 • Key p. 126

Name ____

Upholding the Law

Sandra Day O'Connor was the first woman to serve on the United States Supreme Court.

Sandra Day O'Connor is a retired Supreme Court justice. She was the first female justice in the United States. A justice makes sure the law is followed. The Supreme Court is called the highest court in the land.

O'Connor's days were busy when she was an active justice. She started three mornings a week with exercise. There is a gym on the top floor of the Supreme Court building.

Next, O'Connor would go down to her chambers. A justice's office is called her chambers. In her chambers, O'Connor read many letters. She did research too. Then she wrote papers called opinions. Opinions tell the results of the Supreme Court's decisions. On some days O'Connor also gave speeches. A Supreme Court justice has a lot to do!

Make each sentence true.
Cross out the word that does not belong.
Write a word from the word bank above it.

Word Bank	
laws	justice
opinions	chambers

1. Sandra Day O'Connor was the first female president.

2. A justice's job is to make sure recipes are followed.

3. A justice's office is called her library.

4. The papers justices write are called letters.

©The Mailbox® • *Fascinating Facts: Social Studies* • TEC61065 • Key p. 126

Name ______________________________

Upholding the Law

If the sentence is a fact, color the seal red.
If the sentence is an opinion, color the seal blue.

 1. Sandra Day O'Connor is a retired Supreme Court justice.

 2. She worked in Washington, DC.

 3. She is very wise.

 4. She worked hard.

 5. The Supreme Court works to uphold the law.

 6. It would be fun to be a Supreme Court justice!

 7. Supreme Court justices spend a lot of time reading.

 8. Justices also spend time writing papers.

 9. Sandra Day O'Connor gave speeches.

 10. It would be exciting to meet her!

If you could meet Sandra Day O'Connor, what questions would you ask her about the law?

©The Mailbox® • *Fascinating Facts: Social Studies* • TEC61065 • Key p. 126

Name ______________________________

Feast and Friendship

The first Thanksgiving celebration lasted three days.

The first Thanksgiving in New England took place in 1621. It lasted three days! The Pilgrims held the feast. They had been through hard times. Many Pilgrims died during the first winter. It was cold. They did not have enough food. The ones who lived were grateful. The Native Americans helped them grow food. They also taught them how to hunt. The Pilgrims were happy to have lots of food. They were glad that the next winter would be better. This is why they held the feast.

Today, Thanksgiving lasts one day. It is on the fourth Thursday in November. Some people like to decorate their homes. They want their houses to look like harvesttime. It reminds them of the first Thanksgiving. People eat good food. They spend time with family and friends. They are grateful for good times.

Write the word or words that complete each sentence. Use the passage to help you.

1. The first Thanksgiving lasted ________________ days.
2. The ____________________ held the first Thanksgiving.
3. The ____________________ helped the Pilgrims.
4. Thanksgiving is on the fourth Thursday in ____________________.

©The Mailbox® • *Fascinating Facts: Social Studies* • TEC61065 • Key p. 127

Name ____

Feast and Friendship

If the sentence is a fact, color the drumstick brown.
If the sentence is an opinion, color the drumstick orange.

1 Thanksgiving is the best holiday.

2 The first Thanksgiving lasted three days.

3 The Pilgrims held the feast because they were happy.

4 The Pilgrims' food was great!

5 The Native Americans helped the Pilgrims.

6 The Native Americans were good hunters.

7 Thanksgiving is a lot of fun.

8 My mom makes the best turkey.

9 Some people decorate for Thanksgiving.

10 People eat a lot of food on Thanksgiving.

Imagine that you are in charge of Thanksgiving at your house. Write a paragraph describing what you will serve for dinner and what you will plan for the day.

©The Mailbox® • *Fascinating Facts: Social Studies* • TEC61065 • Key p. 127

Name ______________________________

An Eight-Day Celebration

Hanukkah is also called the Feast of Lights.

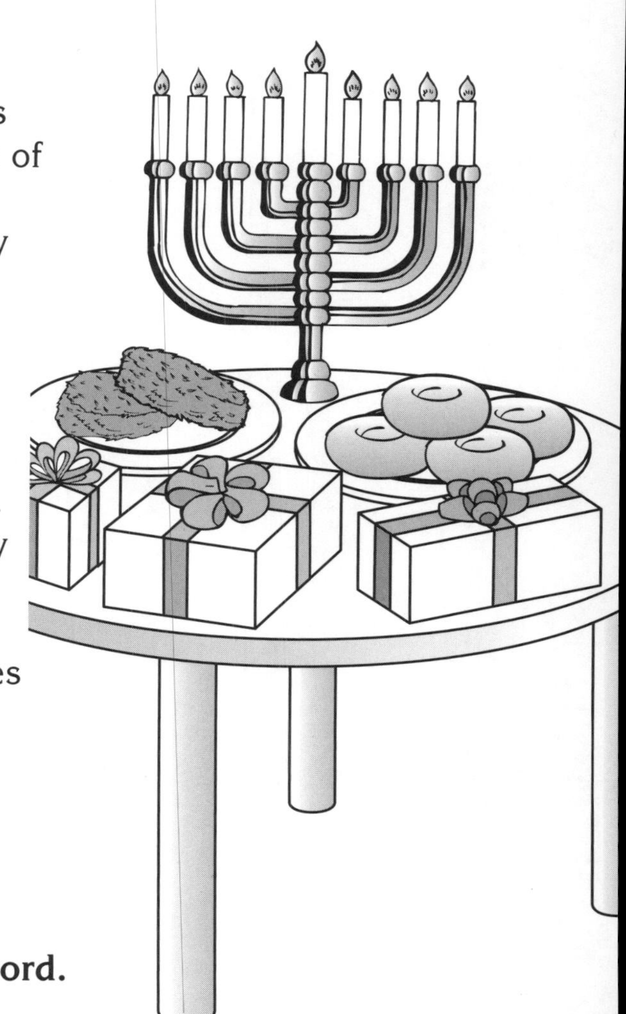

Hanukkah is a Jewish holiday. It takes place in winter. It lasts eight days. People light candles each day. Some people call Hanukkah the Feast of Lights.

Often families spend Hanukkah together. They play games. They also sing songs. Families eat special foods during Hanukkah. They eat potato pancakes. The pancakes are called latkes. They also eat doughnuts. People eat foods made with cheese during Hanukkah too.

Some people may give gifts during Hanukkah. People may give money to children. Or they may give chocolate coins to children! Some families give a small present to their children on each day of Hanukkah. Some families may help families in need. They give time or money to charity.

Hanukkah is a special time for families. It is a time for important customs. It is also a time to enjoy each other.

Unscramble the letters to form the missing word.

1. Hanukkah is a ____________________ holiday. (n r i e w t)

2. Hanukkah is also called the ____________________ of Lights. (t s a F e)

3. Families may eat ____________________, or potato pancakes. (s k l a t e)

4. People may give chocolate ____________________ to children. (n i s c o)

5. Some families give time or money to ____________________. (y c r i t a h)

©The Mailbox® • *Fascinating Facts: Social Studies* • TEC61065 • Key p. 127

Name ____

An Eight-Day Celebration

Cut apart the strips below.
Glue the strips on the plate to show the correct order.

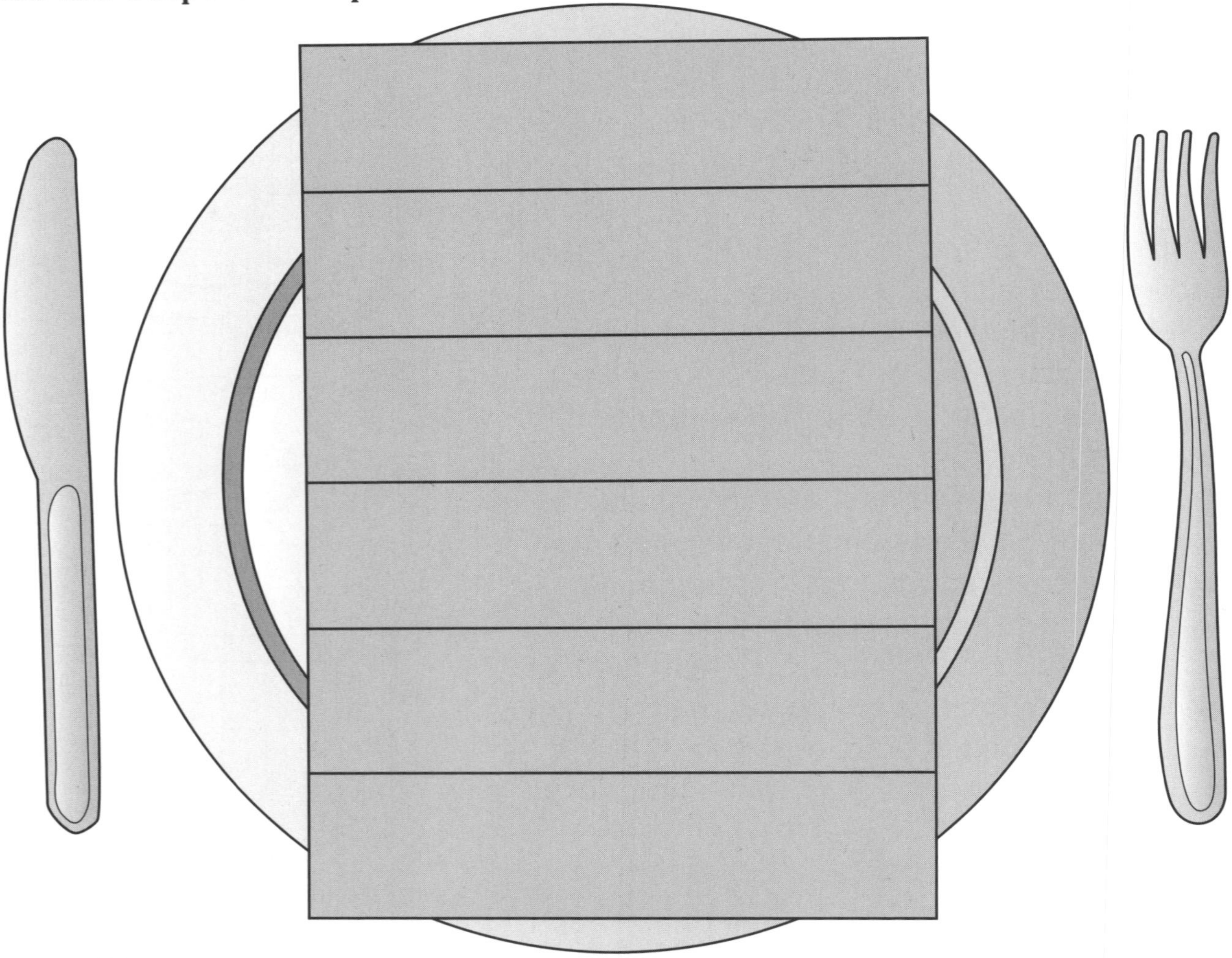

Latkes are a food that families serve at Hanukkah. Do you and your family have a favorite holiday food? Write about it.

©The Mailbox® • *Fascinating Facts: Social Studies* • TEC61065 • Key p. 127

Remove the fried latkes from the oil. Place them on a baking sheet lined with paper towels.	After the ingredients are gathered, wash the potatoes. Grate them and drain them. Peel and grate the onion.
Heat some oil in a frying pan. Scoop some of the mixed batter into the oil. Fry the latkes on both sides.	Finally, serve the warm latkes with applesauce or sour cream.
Next, mix together the eggs, flour, salt, and baking powder. Add the grated potatoes and onions to the mixture. Stir.	First, gather potatoes, an onion, eggs, flour, salt, baking powder, and oil.

Name ____________________

Oh Christmas Tree!

Christmas trees are grown in all 50 states.

In the 1840s, many Americans knew about Christmas trees. Their trees were small. People put them on tables. Later, people had more ornaments. They needed bigger trees. They moved the trees to the floor. They decorated their trees with treats. They used treats like cookies, fruits, candies, and popcorn. They also trimmed the trees with gifts. Some gifts that hung on the trees were dolls, books, shoes, and mittens. After 1880, some gifts were bigger. They were too big to hang on the trees. People began putting gifts under the trees.

A man named Mark Carr had the first Christmas tree lot in the United States. He had his lot in 1851. He sold trees to people who lived in New York City. Today, Christmas trees are grown in all 50 states. Christmas trees can be found in many homes. There is even a Christmas tree in the White House!

Circle the best answer.

1. Early American Christmas trees were displayed on ______.
   a. tables
   b. dinner plates
   c. fireplace mantles

2. Early Americans decorated their trees with ______.
   a. plants and flowers
   b. drawings and photographs
   c. gifts and treats

3. Christmas trees are grown in _____.
   a. Michigan and California
   b. the Midwest
   c. all 50 states

Name ______________________________

Oh Christmas Tree!

**Write the word that completes each sentence.
Circle the words in the puzzle.**

C
S H C
K R H
F C I F G
E I S C L
M I T T E N S
P S J Y M A I D H
L T M B G A W H I T E
S W G I F T S C O O K I E S
W

1. ______________ trees are grown in all 50 states.

2. People decorated trees with treats like ______________, fruits, and candies.

3. They also decorated trees with gifts like dolls, books, and ______________.

4. After 1880, people began putting ______________ under the tree.

5. The first Christmas tree lot was in New York ______________.

6. There is a Christmas tree in the ______________ House.

Decorating a Christmas tree is a favorite holiday tradition for some families. What are some of your family's favorite traditions? Write about them.

©The Mailbox® • *Fascinating Facts: Social Studies* • TEC61065 • Key p. 127

Name ______________________________

A Celebration of Culture

Kwanzaa lasts seven days.

The number seven is important to Kwanzaa. Kwanzaa is spelled with seven letters. Kwanzaa lasts for seven days. It starts on the day after Christmas. The last day of Kwanzaa is New Year's Day.

There are seven values of Kwanzaa. Each day, people focus on one value. Each value teaches something. One value teaches people to work together. Another one teaches people to be themselves. Two other values teach people to be creative and to have faith.

There are seven symbols of Kwanzaa. One symbol is a mat. People put the mat in their homes. Fruits and vegetables are Kwanzaa symbols. People put them on the mat. Another symbol is a unity cup. People display their cup on the mat.

A special candleholder is a Kwanzaa symbol. The holder holds seven candles. Three of the candles are red. One candle is black. Three of the candles are green. Red, black, and green are the colors of Kwanzaa.

Make each sentence true.
Cross out the word that does not belong.
Write a word from the word bank above it.

1. Kwanzaa lasts for nine days.
2. Values may help animals get along.
3. One Kwanzaa symbol is a tablecloth.
4. Red, green, and blue are the Kwanzaa colors.

Word Bank
people
black
mat
seven

Name ____________________

A Celebration of Culture

Cut apart the symbol cards below.
Glue each symbol next to its description.

1. fruits and vegetables of the harvest

2. mat on which the rest of the symbols are placed

3. unity cup

4. candleholder

5. seven candles

6. dry ears of corn

7. gifts

During Kwanzaa, people learn about values like unity, creativity, and purpose. Imagine that you are asked to teach your friends about an important value. What value will you teach about? Why?

©The Mailbox® • *Fascinating Facts: Social Studies* • TEC61065 • Key p. 126

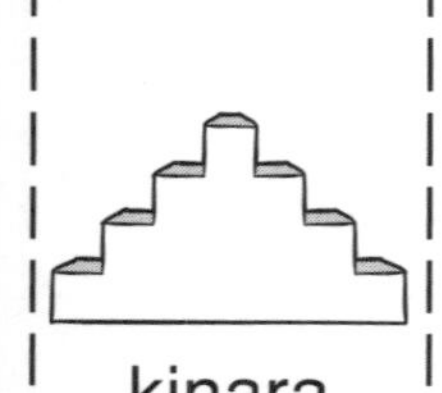

kinara

zawadi

mazao

mishumaa saba

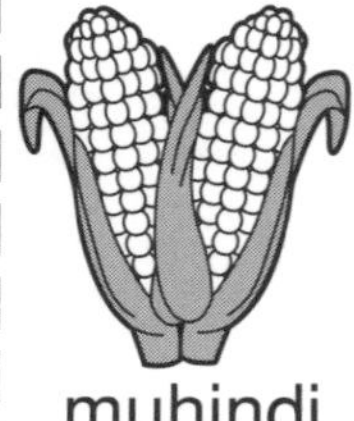

muhindi

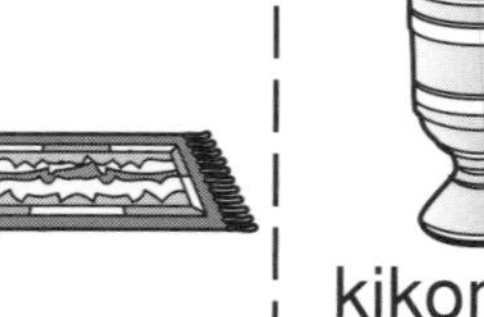

mkeka

kikombe cha umoja

Name ______________________________

Hail to the Chiefs

Presidents' Day is officially called Washington's Birthday.

George Washington was born on February 22, 1732. He was our first president. In 1885, his birthday became a national holiday. He was the first president to have his birthday named a national holiday.

In 1968, Congress changed the date of the holiday called Washington's Birthday. They moved the holiday to the third Monday in February. President Richard Nixon wanted to change the name of the holiday. He wanted to honor all presidents. He called the day Presidents' Day. Congress did not support the name change. The holiday is still officially called Washington's Birthday. Some states call it Presidents' Day.

People honor Washington on Presidents' Day. Some people also honor Abraham Lincoln on Presidents' Day. Some people honor other presidents too.

Circle the word that completes each sentence. Write the word on the line.

1. George Washington was the first ____________________.
   (soldier, president)

2. Washington was born in ____________________.
   (February, August)

3. Presidents' Day is officially called ____________________ Birthday.
   (Lincoln's, Washington's)

4. People may honor ____________________ on Presidents' Day.
   (Congress, Lincoln)

©The Mailbox® • *Fascinating Facts: Social Studies* • TEC61065 • Key p. 127

Name ____

Hail to the Chiefs

Read the clues.
Solve the puzzle.
Use the word bank to help you.

Word Bank
Washington
Harrison
Tyler
Lincoln
Taft
Wilson
Roosevelt

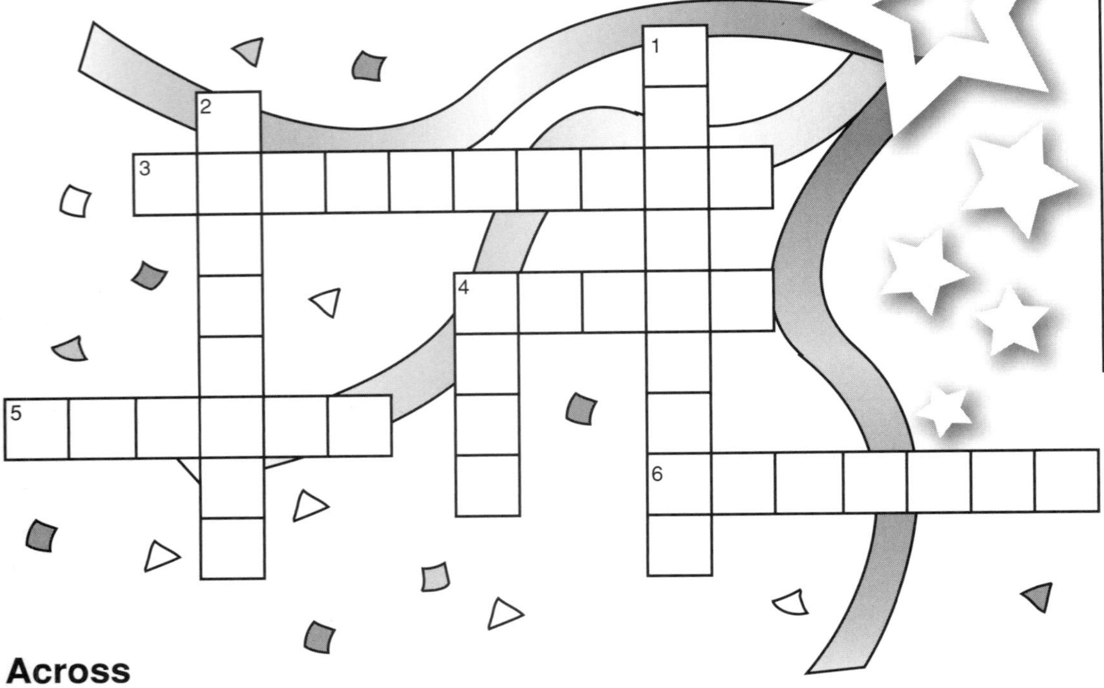

Across

3. George ___________ was the first president of the United States.
4. John _____ had 15 children. No other president had more children than he did.
5. Woodrow _______ is the only president who is buried in Washington, DC.
6. Abraham ________ was the tallest president. He was six feet four inches tall.

Down

1. Franklin D. __________ was the only president to serve four terms.
2. William Henry _________ was only president for a month. He was president for a shorter time than any other president.
4. William H. ____ was the 27th president. He was the first president to own a car.

People honor presidents on Presidents' Day. What would you do to honor a president?

©The Mailbox® • *Fascinating Facts: Social Studies* • TEC61065 • Key p. 127

Name ____________________

Planet Pride

About 20 million people took part in the first Earth Day.

Many years ago, dirty air and trash on the ground were hurting the earth. So a U.S. senator named Gaylord Nelson had an idea. His idea led to the first Earth Day on April 22, 1970. About 20 million Americans took part. They learned about ways to help keep the earth clean. They picked up trash and took nature walks. In New York City, the mayor even shut down a busy street. He wanted to show how clean and quiet it could be without the cars.

People tried hard to take care of the earth for a while. But soon there were problems again. So another Earth Day was held in 1990. This time about 200 million people all over the world took part. People again learned about ways to take care of the earth. Now Earth Day is held each year in April.

Answer the questions.
Use the passage to help you.

1. Who thought of having the first Earth Day?
   a. Senator Green
   b. Senator Nelson
   c. New York City's mayor

2. What did people do on the first Earth Day?
   a. They picked up trash.
   b. They went swimming.
   c. They played games.

3. When was the second Earth Day held?
   a. 1970
   b. 1980
   c. 1990

4. Why is Earth Day important?
   a. It is a day off from school.
   b. It reminds us to take care of the earth.
   c. It honors Senator Nelson.

Name ____

Planet Pride

Help the Earth!

Scraps

At Home   At School

Write the number of the matching sentence on the diagram.

1. Pack your lunch in a lunchbox instead of a paper bag.
2. Turn off the water while you brush your teeth.
3. Keep paper scraps to use for another project.
4. Use a cloth towel or napkin, not a paper one.
5. Collect and recycle plastic bottles and jugs, as well as cans and newspapers.
6. Save paper and money by getting books at your library.
7. Plant a tree and lay mulch around it.
8. Turn off the lights when you leave a room.

How do you help the earth? Make a list of as many ways as you can think of.

©The Mailbox® • *Fascinating Facts: Social Studies* • TEC61065 • Key p. 127

Name ____________________

Gone but Not Forgotten

About 24 towns believe they started the Memorial Day holiday.

Memorial Day is held each year on the last Monday in May. It honors those Americans who died fighting in wars. It started in 1866 after the Civil War. At that time, it was called Decoration Day. Women covered, or decorated, soldiers' graves with flowers. Soon whole towns took a day to honor those who died in the Civil War.

Many of these towns claim to be the first to have such a day. In 1868, this day became known as Memorial Day. It was held on May 30. But it wasn't until 1971 that it became a U.S. holiday.

Today, soldiers are honored in many ways. There are parades. Flags are flown at half-mast. Services are held and special music is played. Flowers and flags are placed on soldiers' graves.

Make each sentence true.
Cross out the word that does not belong.
Write a word from the word bank above it.

Word Bank		
1868	Services	Decoration
half-mast	graves	

1. Decorating Day was a day to honor those who died in the Civil War.
2. Women put flowers on soldiers' houses.
3. This day became known as Memorial Day in 1968.
4. Today there are parades, and flags are flown at halftime.
5. Hands are held and special music is played.

Name ______________________________

Gone but Not Forgotten

Many towns say they were the first to honor soldiers who died in war. Which town does the U.S. government say was the first to do this?

Use the code below.
Write the letters above the numbered boxes.

			1	9	6	6	,									,
8	12							18	1	17	5	15	10	13	13	

								,							
12	5	18		19	13	15	9		2	5	3	1	11	5	

9	12	13	18	12		1	16		17	7	5	

2	8	15	17	7	14	10	1	3	5		13	6	

												.
11	5	11	13	15	8	1	10		4	1	19	

Code

A	B	C	D	E	F	H	I	K	L	M	N	O	P	R	S	T	W	Y
1	2	3	4	5	6	7	8	9	10	11	12	13	14	15	16	17	18	19

How does your town observe Memorial Day?

©The Mailbox® • *Fascinating Facts: Social Studies* • TEC61065 • Key p. 128

Name ____________________

Freedom Foods

About 150 million hot dogs are eaten on the Fourth of July.

What comes to mind when you think of the Fourth of July? Do you hear bands playing American songs? Do you see fireworks lighting up the night sky? Or do you think about family picnics with lots of food? Many Americans celebrate their freedom on the Fourth of July with a picnic.

People enjoyed food on the Fourth of July in the early days of this country too. They ate things like clam soup and deviled eggs. They also ate beans, ham sandwiches, and ice cream. Today, many Americans eat foods like potato chips and hot dogs. In fact, about 150 million hot dogs are eaten on the Fourth of July. What is one of the foods from early days that is still on today's menu? Ice cream! Americans still like to eat this cold treat on this holiday.

Complete the chart.
Use the passage to help you.

What do people do on the Fourth of July?	What do people eat at Fourth of July picnics today?	What did people eat on the Fourth of July in the past?
1. ________ ________	1. ________	1. ________
2. ________ ________	2. ________	2. ________
3. ________ ________	3. ________	3. ________

Name ______________________________

Freedom Foods

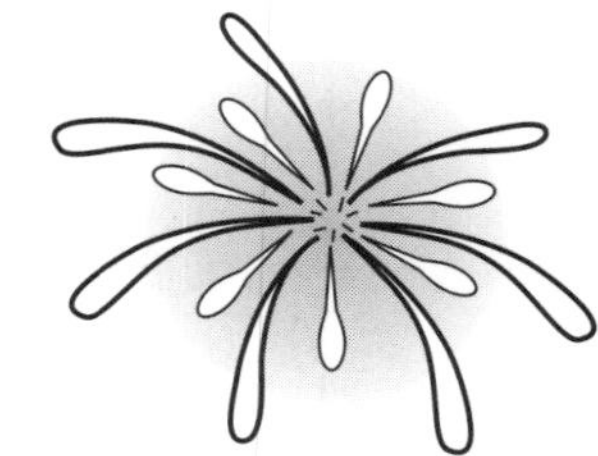

If the sentence is a fact, color the firecracker red.
If the sentence is an opinion, color the firecracker blue.

1. The Fourth of July is a fun holiday!

2. Some people go on picnics on the Fourth of July.

3. Ice cream is the best dessert.

4. Hot dogs are better than hamburgers.

5. In the past, people ate clam soup at picnics.

6. About 150 million hot dogs are eaten on the Fourth of July.

7. Some people eat potato chips at picnics.

8. Some Americans eat ice cream on the Fourth of July.

9. Fireworks are the best part of the Fourth of July.

10. Parades are too noisy.

What do you like to eat on the Fourth of July? Make a menu of your favorite picnic foods.

©The Mailbox® • *Fascinating Facts: Social Studies* • TEC61065 • Key p. 128

Name ____________________

For the Working People

Labor Day was first held on September 5, 1882.

A labor union is a group of people who do the same kind of job. The union tries to make the workplace safer. It also tries to keep the workers' hours and pay fair. A union in New York held the first Labor Day in 1882. There was a picnic and a parade. The union wanted to thank its members for all of their hard work. As more unions popped up around the country, Labor Day was celebrated in more places. In 1894, it became a national holiday. Today Labor Day is held on the first Monday in September. People take a break from their jobs. Many have picnics, just as they did in 1882.

Answer the questions.
Use the passage to help you.

1. What is a labor union? ____________________

____

2. When was the first Labor Day held? ____________________

3. How was it celebrated? ____________________

____

4. When did Labor Day become a national holiday? ____________________

5. Now when is Labor Day celebrated? ____________________

____

Name ____________________

For the Working People

Read each paragraph.
Write its main idea on the lines above it.
Use the main idea sentences to help you.

Main Ideas
Do you think you could be a mechanic?
Many skills are needed to be a doctor.
Labor Day honors people who work hard.
How is a baker different from a chef?

____
____

It is celebrated on the first Monday in September. Many workers get the day off from work. They have picnics and parades.

____
____

A baker might work in a supermarket or small shop. A baker makes baked foods, such as cakes and breads. A chef also makes food. But a chef makes many kinds of foods, such as soups, salads, side dishes, and desserts. A chef might work in a restaurant.

____
____

A person doing this job needs to like working with people. She needs to know what makes people sick. She also needs to know how to make them feel better.

____
____

You need to know a lot about fixing cars to do this job. You also need to be a good problem solver. You could get dirty doing this job. You might also need to lift heavy parts.

Which of the jobs above would you like to have? Tell why.

©The Mailbox® • *Fascinating Facts: Social Studies* • TEC61065 • Key p. 128

Name ____________________

We the People

The U.S. Constitution has lasted longer than any other nation's written constitution.

A constitution is a set of laws used to guide a group of people. Many nations around the world have their own constitutions. The U.S. Constitution was written during the summer of 1787. Men known as delegates worked hard during their meetings to get the words just right. They wanted to be sure that Americans were treated fairly and were free.

James Madison agreed to write down everything discussed at the meetings. He became known as the Father of the Constitution. George Washington was the first to sign it. The Constitution was approved in 1788.

The first part of the U.S. Constitution is called the preamble. Later, the Bill of Rights was added to the Constitution. The Bill of Rights is the first ten amendments, or changes, to the Constitution. We honor the U.S. Constitution on September 17.

Draw a line to match each term to its description. Use the passage to help you.

1. constitution •	• the first part of the U.S. Constitution
2. James Madison •	• a set of laws for a group of people
3. preamble •	• the first ten changes to the U.S. Constitution
4. Bill of Rights •	• September 17
5. Constitution Day •	• the Father of the Constitution

We the People

1788 ____	September 17 ____	Bill of Rights ____
George Washington ____	Constitution ____	delegates ____
amendments ____	James Madison ____	preamble ____

Read the clues.
Write the number of each clue in the square with the matching item.

1. first part of the Constitution
2. first person to sign the Constitution
3. date of Constitution Day
4. set of laws that guide U.S. citizens
5. first ten amendments to the Constitution
6. changes to the Constitution
7. year the Constitution was approved
8. person called the Father of the Constitution
9. men who wrote the Constitution and are known as the founding fathers

Would you have wanted to help write the Constitution in 1787? Tell why or why not.

Name ____

Gift Swap

Christopher Columbus helped to bring horses to the Americas.

Christopher Columbus was an explorer. Columbus Day is on the second Monday in October. It honors him. So what did he find? Columbus thought he found a short new route from Europe to Asia in 1492. But what he found was an island in the Atlantic Ocean. Columbus explored the region. Then he went back to Europe with gifts for the king and queen of Spain. He gave them spices and tobacco. He also brought back a new food called corn.

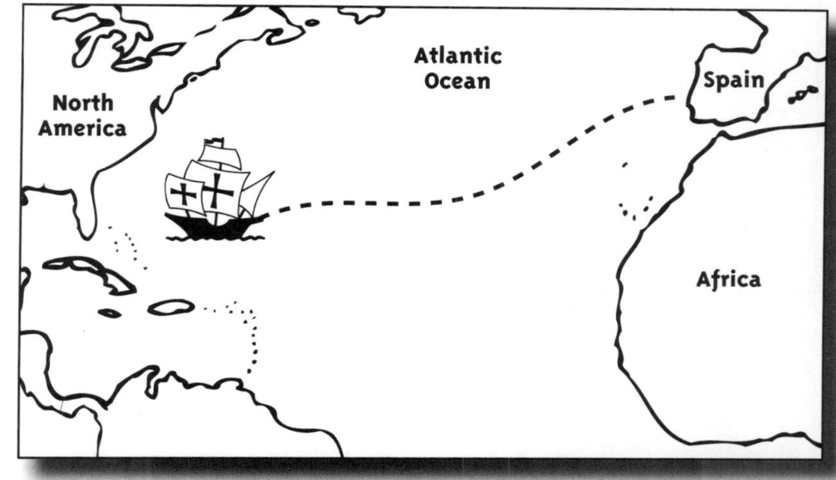

Soon people began sailing from Europe to this new place. They took along gifts from their homelands. Horses, pigs, and sheep were brought to the Americas. So were honeybees and certain kinds of trees. People on both sides of the ocean got to know new foods and animals. Christopher Columbus's discovery changed the way people all over the world lived.

Unscramble the letters to form the missing word. Use the passage to help you.

1. Christopher Columbus was an __ __ __ __ __ __ __ __. p e r e l x o r

2. He thought he found a new route from Europe to __ __ __ __. s A a i

3. He took spices and __ __ __ __ __ __ __ back to Spain. t a c c b o o

4. People brought __ __ __ __ __ __, pigs, and honeybees to the place Columbus found. e o s r h s

5. Columbus Day is held on the second Monday in __ __ __ __ __ __ __. O r c e t b o

Name ______________________

Read the clues.
Complete the puzzle.
Use the word bank to help you.

Word Bank

honeybees, corn, gifts, world, route, horses, Atlantic

1. Christopher Columbus wanted to find a new ___ to Asia.
2. He found an island in the ___ Ocean instead.
3. After he explored this new place, he took ___ back to the king and queen of Spain.
4. He brought them a new food called ___.
5. Then people began to visit this new land. They brought ___ and sheep to America.
6. They also brought pigs and ___.
7. Because of Columbus, new foods and animals were exchanged all over the ___.

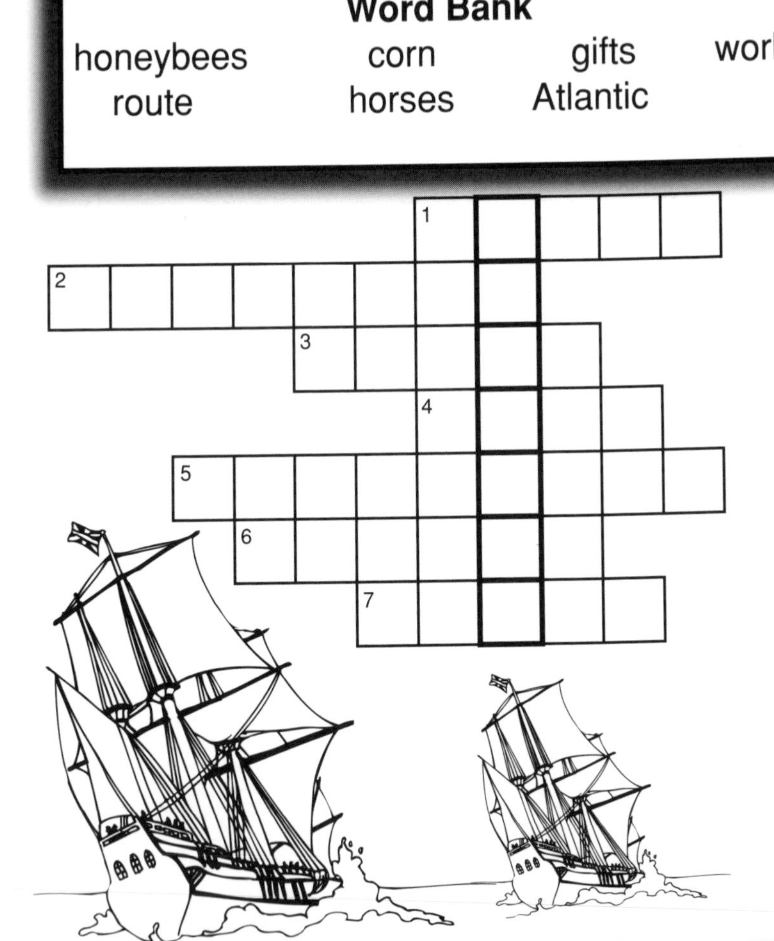

In what month is Columbus Day celebrated?

To find the answer, write the letters in the bold boxes in order from top to bottom.

Start your answer with a capital letter.

___ ___ ___ ___ ___ ___ ___

Would you like to travel to a new place? Tell why or why not.

©The Mailbox® • *Fascinating Facts: Social Studies* • TEC61065 • Key p. 128

Name ________________________________

Time to Vote

Holding Election Day in November helped early American farmers.

Election Day is a day for voting. It is held on the Tuesday after the first Monday in November. Do you know why? When the United States was just starting out, most of the voters were farmers. So voting day was set up to help them out.

By November, all of the farmers' crops had been picked. Since this work was done, the farmers had time to vote. The weather was still nice at this time of year too. Good weather made it easier for the farmers to travel to the voting sites. Tuesday was the day chosen for voting. Some farmers had to travel a long way to get to their voting site. Many early Americans did not travel on Sundays. They used Monday to get to their voting site. Then they were ready to vote on Tuesday.

Read each cause statement.
Write its effect.
Use the passage to help you.

Cause	Effect
1. By November, farmers' crops had been picked.	1. ________________________
2. The weather was still nice in November.	2. ________________________
3. People did not travel on Sundays.	3. ________________________
4. Farmers got to their voting site on Monday.	4. ________________________

Name ____________________

Time to Vote

Cut apart the statement cards.
Glue each one under the question that it answers.

Voting in November helped early American farmers.

1. **Who** voted?

2. **When** did they vote?

3. **Where** did they vote?

4. **Why** was this time chosen for voting?

5. **How** else did this help farmers?

If you were in charge, what month and day would you choose for Election Day? Tell why.

©The Mailbox® • *Fascinating Facts: Social Studies* • TEC61065 • Key p. 128

Early on, most American voters were farmers.	This also meant that the weather was still nice for traveling.
By November, farmers had picked their crops. They had time to vote.	The Tuesday after the first Monday in November was chosen as the day to vote.
Some farmers had to travel far from home to vote.	

Name ____

A Salute to Service

There are over 24 million veterans in the United States.

Do you know a veteran? A veteran is a man or woman who served in the U.S. Army, Navy, Air Force, Marines, or Coast Guard. Veterans kept the United States safe in times of war and peace. There are over 24 million veterans in the United States. We take time out on November 11 to think about all the veterans and their efforts. This day is called Veterans Day. Some towns honor veterans with a parade or a special program.

So what is the story behind this holiday? World War I ended on November 11, 1918. The next year, President Wilson called this day Armistice Day. He wanted to remind Americans about the hardships of war. Armistice Day became a national holiday in 1938. Then, in 1954, the name was changed to Veterans Day. The name change honored those who served in the armed forces.

Answer the questions.

1. What is someone who served as a member of the armed forces called?
   a. the president b. the Coast Guard c. a veteran

2. When is Veterans Day?
   a. November 11 b. November 24 c. November 30

3. About how many U.S. veterans are there?
   a. 24 b. 11 million c. 24 million

4. What was November 11 called before it got the name Veterans Day?
   a. Presidents' Day b. Armistice Day c. Service Day

Name ____________________

A Salute to Service

**If the sentence is true, color the star in the "true" column.
If the sentence is false, color the star in the "false" column.**

True False

1. Veterans Day is always on November 11.
2. Veterans Day honors only men who served in the armed forces.
3. Soldiers who were in the U.S. Army would be honored on Veterans Day.
4. Parades are held on Veterans Day.
5. Veterans Day was first called Armistice Day.
6. President Bush started Armistice Day in 1919.
7. Armistice Day became a national holiday in 1938.
8. Armistice Day became known as Veterans Day in 1954.

What are the members of the U.S. Army, Navy, Air Force, Marines, and Coast Guard called?

To find the answer, write the colored letters from above on the numbered lines below.

THE __ __ M __ __   __ __ __ __ __ __
1 6 2 8 7 5 6 3 2 4

How would you honor a veteran? Make a list of at least five things you could do.

©The Mailbox® • *Fascinating Facts: Social Studies* • TEC61065 • Key p. 128

The Fascinating Facts About Social Studies Game

Getting Ready to Play

1. Make a copy of the game cards on pages 106–120. Laminate the cards for durability.
2. Divide students into teams of two to four players each.
3. Sort the cards into three stacks: true/false, multiple choice, and fill in the blank.
4. Explain the point system to students:
   true/false = 5 points
   multiple choice = 10 points
   fill in the blank = 10 points

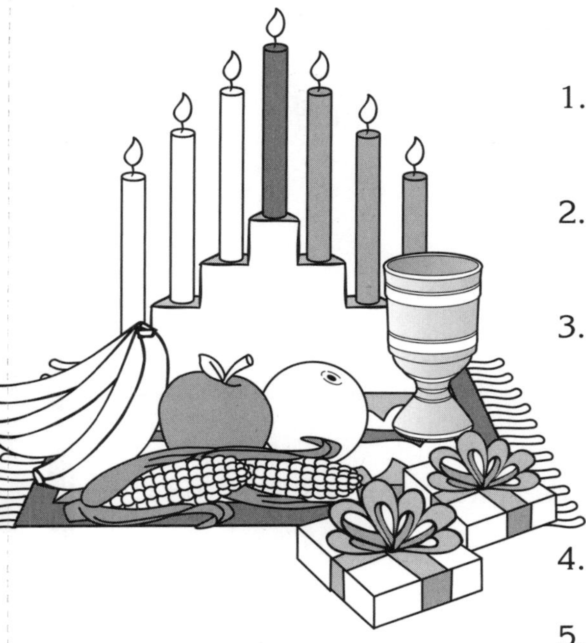

How to Play

1. Player 1 on Team 1 chooses the type of question he wants to answer: true/false, multiple choice, or fill in the blank.
2. The teacher reads aloud the question on the top card of the appropriate stack. If the player answers correctly, his team receives the appropriate number of points.
3. If that player answers incorrectly, Player 1 on Team 2 gets an opportunity to answer the question correctly and earn points for his team. (If the question was a true/false question, the opponent will automatically get it correct if he was listening.) If he answers incorrectly, no team earns the points and the teacher gives the correct answer.
4. The game continues with a player from Team 3 choosing the type of question he wants to answer.
5. The first team to earn 50 points wins. To extend the game, play until one team earns 100 points.

Variation

Use the game cards as flash cards with the whole class. Shuffle all of the cards into one stack and ask one question at a time from the top of the deck. Award one point for each correct answer. Use the game to review just the topic(s) you've recently covered or use all the cards as a fun year-end review.

Game Cards

COMMUNITY SERVICES

True or False:

An air tank helps a firefighter breathe clean air.

(True)

TEC61065

COMMUNITY SERVICES

The area a police officer patrols is called the ______.

(**beat**, block)

TEC61065

COMMUNITY SERVICES

Firefighters wear special clothes to ______.

(a) look good
(b) stay warm
(c) stay safe

TEC61065

COMMUNITY SERVICES

True or False:

Trash is sometimes burned at a landfill.

(True)

TEC61065

COMMUNITY SERVICES

A firefighter may wear over ______ pounds of clothing and gear.

(7, **75**)

TEC61065

COMMUNITY SERVICES

Trash at a landfill gets ______.

(a) cleaned
(b) buried
(c) sent away

TEC61065

COMMUNITY SERVICES

True or False:

All police officers ride horses to patrol their beats.

(False)

TEC61065

COMMUNITY SERVICES

Some trash trucks make up to ______ stops a day.

(**500**, 5,000)

TEC61065

COMMUNITY SERVICES

Police officers might patrol areas with heavy traffic on ______.

(a) motorcycles
(b) boats
(c) roller skates

TEC61065

COMMUNITY SERVICES

True or False:

Bus drivers must keep their passengers safe.

(True)

TEC61065

COMMUNITY SERVICES	Bus drivers must have a special ______ before they can drive a bus. (a) kit (b) tool **(c) license** TEC61065
COMMUNITY SERVICES	**True or False:** Mayors are elected. **(True)** TEC61065
COMMUNITY SERVICES	Drivers check the ______ gear on their buses before they pick up their riders. (**safety,** metal) TEC61065
COMMUNITY SERVICES	A mayor is one of the leaders in a ______. (a) room (b) time **(c) community** TEC61065
COMMUNITY SERVICES	**True or False:** There are many types of libraries. **(True)** TEC61065
COMMUNITY SERVICES	A mayor may have a lot of ______. (books, **meetings**) TEC61065
COMMUNITY SERVICES	Libraries can be found in many ______. **(a) places** (b) colors (c) rooms TEC61065
CITIZENSHIP AND NATIONAL SYMBOLS	**True or False:** Women gained the right to vote before men did. **(False)** TEC61065
COMMUNITY SERVICES	At one library, people can borrow ______ to use in their homes. (**tools,** flowers) TEC61065
CITIZENSHIP AND NATIONAL SYMBOLS	Some people tried to keep other people from voting by making them pay a ______. **(a) poll tax** (b) fine (c) ticket fee TEC61065

Game Cards

CITIZENSHIP AND NATIONAL SYMBOLS

Some people had to pass a ______ before they could vote.

(paper, **test**)

TEC61065

CITIZENSHIP AND NATIONAL SYMBOLS

Francis Scott Key was being held prisoner by the ______ when he wrote "The Star-Spangled Banner."

(a) Americans
(b) French
(c) British

TEC61065

CITIZENSHIP AND NATIONAL SYMBOLS

True or False:

The first Pledge of Allegiance was 23 words long.

(True)

TEC61065

CITIZENSHIP AND NATIONAL SYMBOLS

"The Star-Spangled Banner" was a ______ before it was a song.

(letter, **poem**)

TEC61065

CITIZENSHIP AND NATIONAL SYMBOLS

The Pledge of Allegiance was written for a celebration that would take place on the first ______.

(a) Flag Day
(b) Columbus Day
(c) Memorial Day

TEC61065

CITIZENSHIP AND NATIONAL SYMBOLS

True or False:

The first American flag had a snake on it.

(False)

TEC61065

CITIZENSHIP AND NATIONAL SYMBOLS

In 1892, schoolchildren raised money to buy ______.

(**flags,** bricks)

TEC61065

CITIZENSHIP AND NATIONAL SYMBOLS

The American flag has 50 stars on it, one for each ______.

(a) state
(b) president
(c) colony

TEC61065

CITIZENSHIP AND NATIONAL SYMBOLS

True or False:

The flag that inspired Francis Scott Key to write "The Star-Spangled Banner" was flying over Fort McHenry.

(True)

TEC61065

CITIZENSHIP AND NATIONAL SYMBOLS

There are ______ stripes on the American flag.

(50, **13**)

TEC61065

©The Mailbox® • *Fascinating Facts: Social Studies* • TEC61065

CITIZENSHIP AND NATIONAL SYMBOLS

True or False:

The pigeon is the national symbol of the United States.

(False)

TEC61065

CITIZENSHIP AND NATIONAL SYMBOLS

In 1814, the ______ set fire to much of the United States capital.

(**British,** French)

TEC61065

CITIZENSHIP AND NATIONAL SYMBOLS

A bald eagle can be found on money, on stamps, and on the ______.

(a) doors of hospitals
(b) Great Seal of the United States
(c) penny

TEC61065

CITIZENSHIP AND NATIONAL SYMBOLS

True or False:

The top section of the Washington Monument is a different color than the bottom section.

(True)

TEC61065

CITIZENSHIP AND NATIONAL SYMBOLS

The ______ was chosen as the national symbol of the United States.

(snake, **bald eagle**)

TEC61065

CITIZENSHIP AND NATIONAL SYMBOLS

The Washington Monument is about ______ feet tall.

(a) 555
(b) 150
(c) 25

TEC61065

CITIZENSHIP AND NATIONAL SYMBOLS

True or False:

The United States Capitol was built in less than one year.

(False)

TEC61065

CITIZENSHIP AND NATIONAL SYMBOLS

The outside of the Washington Monument is made of ______.

(**marble,** steel)

TEC61065

CITIZENSHIP AND NATIONAL SYMBOLS

While waiting for the United States Capitol to be built, Congress met in ______.

(a) New York City, New York
(b) Philadelphia, Pennsylvania
(c) Boston, Massachusetts

TEC61065

CITIZENSHIP AND NATIONAL SYMBOLS

True or False:

The Statue of Liberty was made in France.

(True)

TEC61065

CITIZENSHIP AND NATIONAL SYMBOLS

The first parts of the Statue of Liberty to come to America were the ______.

(a) head and crown
(b) feet
(c) right arm, hand, and torch

TEC61065

CITIZENSHIP AND NATIONAL SYMBOLS

True or False:

Mount Rushmore is in Washington, DC.

(False)

TEC61065

CITIZENSHIP AND NATIONAL SYMBOLS

The ______ was a gift from France.

(Washington Monument, **Statue of Liberty**)

TEC61065

CITIZENSHIP AND NATIONAL SYMBOLS

There are ______ faces carved in Mount Rushmore.

(a) four
(b) five
(c) six

TEC61065

CITIZENSHIP AND NATIONAL SYMBOLS

True or False:

The Liberty Bell was always called the Liberty Bell.

(False)

TEC61065

CITIZENSHIP AND NATIONAL SYMBOLS

______'s image is on Mount Rushmore.

(**George Washington,** John F. Kennedy)

TEC61065

CITIZENSHIP AND NATIONAL SYMBOLS

The Liberty Bell was rung in ______.

(a) New York City, New York
(b) Philadelphia, Pennsylvania
(c) Washington, DC

TEC61065

TIME AND CHANGE

True or False:

Long ago, women made meals in a fireplace.

(True)

TEC61065

CITIZENSHIP AND NATIONAL SYMBOLS

The ______ is a national symbol.

(trumpet, **Liberty Bell**)

TEC61065

TIME AND CHANGE

Cooking pots were used for both cooking and doing laundry because they ______.

(a) kept the water hot
(b) were easy to use
(c) cost a lot of money

TEC61065

©The Mailbox® • *Fascinating Facts: Social Studies* • TEC61065

TIME AND CHANGE

Long ago, women kept a ______ by the fireplace to put out clothing fires.

(**bucket of water,** fire extinguisher)

TEC61065

TIME AND CHANGE

Wealthy settlers used ______ to build their houses.

(a) mud
(b) bricks
(c) adobe

TEC61065

TIME AND CHANGE

True or False:

Americans have always been able to shop for food at stores.

(False)

TEC61065

TIME AND CHANGE

Early houses were often made of wood, even their ______.

(windows, **chimneys**)

TEC61065

TIME AND CHANGE

Native Americans taught Pilgrims how to catch ______.

(a) eels
(b) turkeys
(c) deer

TEC61065

TIME AND CHANGE

True or False:

The first jeans were made of blue canvas.

(False)

TEC61065

TIME AND CHANGE

Early Americans grew foods like corn and ______ in their gardens.

(flowers, **beans**)

TEC61065

TIME AND CHANGE

Levi Strauss used tent fabric to make pants for gold miners because it was ______.

(a) soft
(b) strong
(c) pretty

TEC61065

TIME AND CHANGE

True or False:

All early houses were big.

(False)

TEC61065

TIME AND CHANGE

For many years, only people who worked ______ wore jeans.

(**outdoors,** indoors)

TEC61065

Game Cards

TIME AND CHANGE

True or False:

One of the first kinds of cars was loud enough to scare horses.

(True)

TEC61065

TIME AND CHANGE

The inventors who used a gas engine to keep a plane flying for over 30 minutes were the ______.

(French, **Wright Brothers**)

TEC61065

TIME AND CHANGE

Cars run by batteries were better than cars run by steam because they ______.

(a) were quieter
(b) were faster
(c) could go farther

TEC61065

TIME AND CHANGE

True or False:

When the telephone was first invented, calls could only be made to people nearby.

(True)

TEC61065

TIME AND CHANGE

Most cars today are powered by ______.

(**gasoline,** steam)

TEC61065

TIME AND CHANGE

The ______ was invented in 1876.

(a) radio
(b) telephone
(c) computer

TEC61065

TIME AND CHANGE

True or False:

All early flying machines had two wings.

(False)

TEC61065

TIME AND CHANGE

Telephones used to be linked by iron ______.

(nails, **wires**)

TEC61065

TIME AND CHANGE

______ were early flying machines that stayed in the air but were hard to steer.

(a) planes
(b) helicopters
(c) hot-air balloons

TEC61065

TIME AND CHANGE

True or False:

During the Golden Age of Broadcasting, people did not like to listen to the radio.

(False)

TEC61065

©The Mailbox® • *Fascinating Facts: Social Studies* • TEC61065

TIME AND CHANGE

Women listened to soap operas on the radio ______.

(a) first thing in the morning
(b) during the day
(c) late at night

TEC61065

TIME AND CHANGE

True or False:

The first computers were very small.

(False)

TEC61065

TIME AND CHANGE

Some kids' shows on the radio gave away ______.

(**prizes,** radios)

TEC61065

TIME AND CHANGE

______ helped make computers smaller.

(a) Monitors
(b) Robots
(c) Microchips

TEC61065

TIME AND CHANGE

True or False:

Early remote controls were known as clickers.

(True)

TEC61065

TIME AND CHANGE

An early computer was as big as a ______.

(**room,** house)

TEC61065

TIME AND CHANGE

Before remote controls, TV viewers changed the channel by ______.

(a) turning a knob on the TV
(b) spinning a wheel on the TV
(c) pushing a button on the TV

TEC61065

HISTORIC FIGURES

True or False:

George Washington was the first president.

(True)

TEC61065

TIME AND CHANGE

The first TV remote control was called ______.

(R.C., **Lazy Bones**)

TEC61065

HISTORIC FIGURES

George Washington led the men who wrote ______.

(a) the U.S. Constitution
(b) "The Star-Spangled Banner"
(c) the Declaration of Independence

TEC61065

Game Cards

HISTORIC FIGURES

George Washington's picture is on the dollar bill and the ______.

(**quarter,** penny)

TEC61065

HISTORIC FIGURES

Benjamin Franklin invented ______.

(a) the television
(b) books
(c) special reading glasses

TEC61065

HISTORIC FIGURES

True or False:

Abraham Lincoln went to school for many years.

(False)

TEC61065

HISTORIC FIGURES

One way Benjamin Franklin helped his community was by starting a ______.

(**fire station,** fire)

TEC61065

HISTORIC FIGURES

Abraham Lincoln wanted to ______.

(a) teach
(b) learn
(c) swim

TEC61065

HISTORIC FIGURES

True or False:

Benjamin Banneker wrote an almanac.

(True)

TEC61065

HISTORIC FIGURES

Abraham Lincoln is known as a great ______.

(**writer,** farmer)

TEC61065

HISTORIC FIGURES

Benjamin Banneker liked to ______ things.

(a) wonder about
(b) teach
(c) color

TEC61065

HISTORIC FIGURES

True or False:

Benjamin Franklin taught school for two years.

(False)

TEC61065

HISTORIC FIGURES

Benjamin Banneker ______ every day.

(**read,** drew)

TEC61065

©The Mailbox® • *Fascinating Facts: Social Studies* • TEC61065

HISTORIC FIGURES

True or False:

George Washington Carver did not like to study plants.

(False)

TEC61065

HISTORIC FIGURES

Orville and Wilbur Wright made a ______ to test ideas about how to fly.

(helicopter, **kite**)

TEC61065

HISTORIC FIGURES

George Washington Carver found more than 300 uses for ______.

(a) pecans
(b) peanuts
(c) sweet potatoes

TEC61065

HISTORIC FIGURES

True or False:

Thomas Edison was a president of the United States.

(False)

TEC61065

HISTORIC FIGURES

George Washington Carver's nickname as a child was ______.

(Plant Man, **Plant Doctor**)

TEC61065

HISTORIC FIGURES

Thomas Edison invented the ______.

(a) glass windowpane
(b) computer chip
(c) lightbulb

TEC61065

HISTORIC FIGURES

True or False:

Orville and Wilbur Wright built automobiles before they built airplanes.

(False)

TEC61065

HISTORIC FIGURES

As a boy, Thomas Edison had lots of ______.

(books to read, **questions**)

TEC61065

HISTORIC FIGURES

The first airplane flight took place in ______.

(a) Dayton, Ohio
(b) Kitty Hawk, North Carolina
(c) Augusta, Maine

TEC61065

HISTORIC FIGURES

True or False:

Alexander Graham Bell was a teacher.

(True)

TEC61065

Game Cards

HISTORIC FIGURES

Alexander Graham Bell wanted to ______.

(a) discover new places
(b) invent a talking telegraph
(c) visit presidents

TEC61065

HISTORIC FIGURES

True or False:

Rosa Parks was sent to jail.

(True)

TEC61065

HISTORIC FIGURES

Alexander Graham Bell invented the ______.

(radio, **telephone**)

TEC61065

HISTORIC FIGURES

Rosa Parks was ______ when she was arrested.

(a) on a bus
(b) on a plane
(c) at school

TEC61065

HISTORIC FIGURES

True or False:

Martin Luther King Jr. skipped two grades in school.

(True)

TEC61065

HISTORIC FIGURES

Rosa Parks helped ______ get equal treatment.

(bus drivers, **African Americans**)

TEC61065

HISTORIC FIGURES

Martin Luther King Jr. studied to be a ______ in college.

(a) teacher
(b) writer
(c) minister

TEC61065

HISTORIC FIGURES

True or False:

The Supreme Court writes new laws for each state.

(False)

TEC61065

HISTORIC FIGURES

Martin Luther King Jr. wanted everyone to be treated ______.

(differently, **equally**)

TEC61065

HISTORIC FIGURES

Sandra Day O'Connor was the first woman to ______.

(a) serve as a Supreme Court justice
(b) run for president
(c) fly an airplane

TEC61065

©The Mailbox® • *Fascinating Facts: Social Studies* • TEC61065

HISTORIC FIGURES

Supreme Court justices write papers called ______.

(**opinions,** rules)

TEC61065

HOLIDAYS AND CELEBRATIONS

Families eat ______ pancakes called latkes during Hanukkah.

(a) blueberry
(b) potato
(c) oatmeal

TEC61065

HOLIDAYS AND CELEBRATIONS

True or False:

The pioneers held the first Thanksgiving.

(False)

TEC61065

HOLIDAYS AND CELEBRATIONS

Some families give children chocolate ______ during Hanukkah.

(**coins,** stamps)

TEC61065

HOLIDAYS AND CELEBRATIONS

The Pilgrims held the feast because they were ______.

(a) bored
(b) hungry
(c) grateful

TEC61065

HOLIDAYS AND CELEBRATIONS

True or False:

Early American Christmas trees were small enough to be displayed on tables.

(True)

TEC61065

HOLIDAYS AND CELEBRATIONS

Thanksgiving is on the ______ Thursday in November.

(**fourth,** third)

TEC61065

HOLIDAYS AND CELEBRATIONS

Early Americans decorated their Christmas trees with gifts and ______.

(a) tinsel
(b) electric lights
(c) treats

TEC61065

HOLIDAYS AND CELEBRATIONS

True or False:

Hanukkah is a summer holiday.

(False)

TEC61065

HOLIDAYS AND CELEBRATIONS

Christmas trees are grown in ______ states.

(12, **50**)

TEC61065

HOLIDAYS AND CELEBRATIONS

True or False:

There are seven symbols of Kwanzaa.

(True)

TEC61065

HOLIDAYS AND CELEBRATIONS

Presidents' Day is officially called ______.

(**Washington's Birthday,** Nixon's Birthday)

TEC61065

HOLIDAYS AND CELEBRATIONS

Kwanzaa lasts ______ days.

(a) eight
(b) seven
(c) six

TEC61065

HOLIDAYS AND CELEBRATIONS

True or False:

There has been only one Earth Day.

(False)

TEC61065

HOLIDAYS AND CELEBRATIONS

______, black, and green are the colors of Kwanzaa.

(**Red,** Blue)

TEC61065

HOLIDAYS AND CELEBRATIONS

Earth Day is celebrated in ______.

(a) March
(b) April
(c) May

TEC61065

HOLIDAYS AND CELEBRATIONS

True or False:

Abraham Lincoln was the first president whose birthday was named a national holiday.

(False)

TEC61065

HOLIDAYS AND CELEBRATIONS

We celebrate Earth Day to ______.

(**take care of the earth,** make a mess of the earth)

TEC61065

HOLIDAYS AND CELEBRATIONS

Presidents' Day is the third Monday in ______.

(a) January
(b) February
(c) March

TEC61065

HOLIDAYS AND CELEBRATIONS

True or False:

Only one town claims to have started Memorial Day.

(False)

TEC61065

HOLIDAYS AND CELEBRATIONS

______ are honored on Memorial Day.

(a) All Americans
(b) All American soldiers
(c) All American soldiers who died fighting in a war

TEC61065

HOLIDAYS AND CELEBRATIONS

True or False:

Labor Day honors people who work.

(True)

TEC61065

HOLIDAYS AND CELEBRATIONS

Memorial Day is observed on ______.

(the first Monday in March, **the last Monday in May**)

TEC61065

HOLIDAYS AND CELEBRATIONS

______ held the first Labor Day in 1882.

(a) A labor union
(b) The government
(c) Families

TEC61065

HOLIDAYS AND CELEBRATIONS

True or False:

Millions of hot dogs are eaten on the Fourth of July.

(True)

TEC61065

HOLIDAYS AND CELEBRATIONS

Labor Day is celebrated on the first Monday in ______.

(**September,** May)

TEC61065

HOLIDAYS AND CELEBRATIONS

______ has been served at Fourth of July picnics for many years.

(a) Ice cream
(b) Salad
(c) Spaghetti

TEC61065

HOLIDAYS AND CELEBRATIONS

True or False:

The United States is the only country with a constitution.

(False)

TEC61065

HOLIDAYS AND CELEBRATIONS

Americans celebrate their ______ on the Fourth of July.

(hot dogs, **freedom**)

TEC61065

HOLIDAYS AND CELEBRATIONS

______ is known as the Father of the Constitution.

(a) James Madison
(b) George Washington
(c) Bill Right

TEC61065

Game Cards

HOLIDAYS AND CELEBRATIONS

Constitution Day is observed on ______.

(August 17, **September 17**)

TEC61065

HOLIDAYS AND CELEBRATIONS

Voting in November helped early American ______.

(a) millers
(b) farmers
(c) bakers

TEC61065

HOLIDAYS AND CELEBRATIONS

True or False:

Christopher Columbus was looking for a new route to Asia when he found the Americas.

(True)

TEC61065

HOLIDAYS AND CELEBRATIONS

Election Day is held in ______.

(**November,** December)

TEC61065

HOLIDAYS AND CELEBRATIONS

Christopher Columbus took ______ to the king and queen of Spain.

(a) horses
(b) pigs
(c) corn

TEC61065

HOLIDAYS AND CELEBRATIONS

True or False:

Veterans Day was once called Armistice Day.

(True)

TEC61065

HOLIDAYS AND CELEBRATIONS

Columbus Day is held on the second ______ in October.

(Sunday, **Monday**)

TEC61065

HOLIDAYS AND CELEBRATIONS

Veterans Day honors ______.

(a) men who sailed in ships
(b) men and women who served in the armed forces
(c) men who flew in planes

TEC61065

HOLIDAYS AND CELEBRATIONS

True or False:

Election Day is a day for farmers.

(False)

TEC61065

HOLIDAYS AND CELEBRATIONS

Veterans Day is in ______.

(**November,** December)

TEC61065